684040736363

D1338597

The New Politics of Class

The New Politics of Class

The Political Exclusion of the British
Working Class

Geoffrey Evans and James Tilley

OXFORD
UNIVERSITY PRESS

OXFORD
UNIVERSITY PRESS

Great Clarendon Street, Oxford, OX2 6DP,
United Kingdom

Oxford University Press is a department of the University of Oxford.
It furthers the University's objective of excellence in research, scholarship,
and education by publishing worldwide. Oxford is a registered trade mark of
Oxford University Press in the UK and in certain other countries

First Edition published in 2017
Impression: 4

Published in the United States of America by Oxford University Press
198 Madison Avenue, New York, NY 10016, United States of America

British Library Cataloguing in Publication Data
Data available

Library of Congress Control Number: 2016949255

ISBN 978–0–19–875575–3

Printed in Great Britain by
CPI Group (UK) Ltd, Croydon, CR0 4YY

Acknowledgements

Over the course of this project, we have received many valuable suggestions from colleagues that have helped us improve the analysis and the arguments presented in the different chapters of this book. We would like to extend a special thanks to Rob Ford and Oliver Heath who gave us very helpful comments on several chapters, as well as John Goldthorpe for his warm support and encouragement.

The key to a project of this sort is being able to examine an unusually wide range of themes in British politics and society using high-quality data. For this purpose many people have shared data with us and we would like to thank them for their generosity. In Chapter 2 we examine social inequalities in detail and are very grateful to: Mark Williams for sharing with us the New Earning Survey data on inequalities in pay; Felix Busch for supplying us with data from the Labour Force Survey on unemployment; and Erzsebet Bukodi for the social mobility data from the cohort studies. For Chapter 5, extracts from *The Guardian* have been reproduced courtesy of Guardian News & Media Ltd, extracts from *The Times* courtesy of News Corp UK & Ireland Ltd, and extracts from the *Daily Mirror* courtesy of Trinity Mirror PLC. In Chapter 6 we use a variety of data that other very helpfully gave to us. Alan Finlayson and Judi Atkins kindly sent us Churchill's conference speeches, which are not publically available. Mads Thau supplied us with data on class appeals coded directly from party manifestos. Ian Budge and Judith Bara very swiftly supplied us with the latest 2015 manifesto data to include in our overtime analysis. And Jennifer van Heerde-Hudson and Rosie Campbell generously gave us their data on MPs' biographical information (these data were collected with the support of the Leverhulme Trust (RPG-2013-175)).

We gratefully acknowledge financial support from the Jesus College Major Research Grants Fund and the Danish Research Council (grant number 1327-00113) for helping to fund the 2015 British Social Attitudes module on social class used in Chapter 3. We would also like to thank Rune Stubager for his excellent collaboration in designing and helping to find funding for this module. And Geoff would like to thank his colleagues in the 2015 BES team for their patience while this book was completed, as well as support for the inclusion of relevant questions in the face-to-face survey that are used in Chapters 3 and 6.

We were also fortunate to have a wide range of research assistance from many colleagues and students. Chris Prosser undertook word score coding of both the party manifestos and party leaders' speeches in Chapter 6. Sarah Coombes coded the media data used in Chapter 5, and gave us many useful suggestions for the qualitative analysis. William van Taack coded MPs' biographical information in Chapter 6, the occupational class codes for the 2015 BES face-to-face survey and undertook some of the analysis for Chapters 2 and 3. Zack Grant and Stuart Perrett coded the open-ended class responses used in Chapter 3. Jon Mellon provided us with figures from the BES surveys in Chapter 6 and some tables in Chapter 3. Noah Carl proofread and indexed the book as well as providing more general assistance. Many thanks to all of them for their invaluable help.

Finally, we would like to thank Allen and Irene Evans for providing part of the motivation for wanting to tell this story, and Claire Vickers, Elizabeth Tilley, and Roger Tilley for proofreading the whole manuscript and listening to James' grumbling.

Contents

List of Figures

List of Tables

1

Introduction

There was a time when, odd though it may seem today, British politics was focused on the needs and desires of the working class. Post-war Britain saw the emergence of not just the welfare state but also a determination by politicians of all parties never to return to the mass unemployment of the 1930s. Both these developments were implemented in the name of the working class. A form of corporatism was adopted by both Conservative and Labour governments so that working class interests were represented politically and the 'forward march of labour' was consolidated as part of the 'long revolution' (Williams 1961; Westergaard 1995). It was the working class 'whose claims could henceforth never be ignored by governments' (Marwick 1980, p.229). This emphasis was so engrained that *The Middle Class Vote*, published in the 1950s, actually labelled the middle class 'the not working class' and argued that the middle class were 'the class without a party' (Bonham 1954, p.30).

This seems a long time ago now. The economic structure of Britain today is quite different to that of the 1950s. There has been radical deregulation of the economy, the trade union movement has become a shadow of its former self, and, most importantly, there are simply many more people with middle class jobs. The rise of the middle class has often been seen as indicating the end of both class division and of the political importance of class. Shrinking divisions between social classes are seen as a natural consequence of deindustrialization, increased affluence, greater welfare provision and the breakdown of traditional class communities. At the extreme, it is claimed that 'the dynamism of the labour market backed up by the welfare state has dissolved the social classes' (Beck and Beck-Gernsheim 2002, p.203). We are thus left with an amorphous social structure devoid of class difference: a society in which everyone is middle class or has no class at all.

While the social science literature of the 1950s, 1960s, and 1970s talks of little else but the working class (Willmott and Young 1960; Dennis et al. 1956;

Hoggart 1957; Roberts 1971),[1] this is no longer the case. By the turn of the millennium, British sociologists appeared to have turned their backs on the very idea of class: 'The study of class is no longer central to British sociological analysis, and the debate on class is largely about whether this should be celebrated or lamented' (Savage 2000, p.7).[2] But has the class structure dissolved? We argue that it has not. In support of this argument, we examine class in Britain over the last fifty years and how it has both shaped and been shaped by social and political change. We focus on the working class, not as the left's traditional harbingers of revolution and social transformation, but as an increasingly marginalized political group. We show while the size of class groups has changed, there are remarkably stable class divisions in values and policy preferences. Class division thus remains a key element of Britain's political picture, but in a new way. Whereas working class people once formed the heart of the class structure and the focal point of political competition, they now lack political representation. This is because the political environment has changed. Parties have reacted to changing class structures by changing their ideology, policy programmes, rhetoric, and elite recruitment strategies. Vote-seeking parties now focus on the middle class, not the working class, and it is the working class, not the middle class, that has become Bonham's 'class without a party'. That, in essence, is the argument of this book. In this introductory chapter, we lay out precisely these mechanisms of change and the evidence that we use to show these processes at work. First, however, we explain what we mean by class.

What Is Class?

Social class is one of the most widely discussed, and disputed, concepts in social science. Characterizations of class position have included numerous occupational classifications, including distinctions between manual versus non-manual workers and owners versus employees, status rankings, income levels, educational levels, subjective class identifications and lifestyles. Sometimes two or more of these have been combined.[3] Much ink has been spilled over whether class positions are best thought of as 'relational' or 'gradational' (Ossowski 1963) and even more on whether a given measure of class position truly reflects the ideas of Marx or Weber.[4] We have no desire to immerse the reader in disputes about which idea of class is 'best'. In part, this is because different measures of class position are often closely correlated, but also because this debate is fundamentally unresolvable. As Calvert (1982, p.214) observed, class is an 'essentially contested concept', due in no small part to its great political and social significance.

This means that no one characterization of class is definitive. Measures of class position are useful to the degree that they allow us to demonstrate important relationships between social position and outcomes. We do not therefore spend time comparing different class characterizations or measures.[5] We focus on occupation, and to a lesser extent education, as key measures of where people are positioned in the class structure. Occupation matters because it determines people's current and future earnings, and the security of that employment. Writing shortly after the Second World War, at the very start of the period we are examining, Ferdynand Zweig argued that:

> Security is one of the basic differences between the working class and the middle class, but the working man not only lacks security of employment but also of earnings. His earnings depend not only on hours of work but also on overtime, shifts, changing conditions of work, piecework, individual and collective bonuses, the materials and machines he handles. (Zweig 1952, pp.203–4)

These same themes of insecurity in both job tenure and earnings remain the key aspects of occupation that concern social scientists today (Goldthorpe 2004, 2007; Rose and Pevalin 2003). It is less important to know how much someone earns at any given point in time than how they earn that money, and the security, promotion prospects, and job uncertainty that characterize their conditions of employment.[6] The measure of occupational class that informs our approach is one that not only focuses on divisions between occupations but is also an established and widely used measure of class position. The Goldthorpe schema (Erikson and Goldthorpe 1992; Goldthorpe 2004, 2007) has been carefully developed with respect to what it *is* about occupations that enables them to be clustered into class positions. It has been shown to be associated with many important aspects of people's lives, and has been extensively validated as a way of characterizing occupational divisions and understanding social and political change.[7]

We use a slightly modified version of this schema to allow us to track the social and political impact of changing occupational class sizes most accurately. Table 1.1 shows the key groups that we focus on and how we translate the nineteen-category socio-economic group (SEG) classification into meaningful social classes.[8] Table 1.1 also provides illustrative examples of both more traditional and newer types of jobs included in the classes. Although almost all the traditional jobs are still to be found, new occupations within those classes have obviously emerged. For people not currently working, due, for example, to unemployment or retirement, we use their last occupation, and for those who have never had a job, or who were unable to be assigned to a SEG, we use their husband's or wife's occupation. We separate people into three different middle class occupational groups and one working class group. The working class in our analyses is composed of skilled, semi-skilled, and unskilled workers in manual occupations. It also includes agricultural workers (but not farmers). On average, these working class jobs offer lower and more

Table 1.1. Occupational class groups

	SEG categories	Traditional jobs	Newer jobs
Old Middle Class	Managers large, managers small, self-employed with employees, self-employed professionals, farmers	Manager, small business owner with employees, shopkeeper, barrister, farmer	Self-employed website designer, HR manager
New Middle Class	Employed professionals, intermediate non-manual	Architect, teacher, university lecturer, nurse, social worker	Occupational therapist, dietician, paramedic, dental hygienist
Junior Middle Class	Junior non-manual	Bank cashier, clerk, secretary, typist	Legal assistant, dispatch technician
Own Account	Self-employed without employees	Shop owner with no employees, self-employed own account plumber	
Personal Service	Personal service workers	Nursery assistant, assistant, chauffeur	Personal care assistant, tour guide
Foreman	Foremen and supervisors	Lead hand, production supervisor, construction foreman	Packing manager
Working Class	Skilled manual, semi-skilled manual, unskilled manual, farm worker	Machine operator, seamstress, warehouseman, quarry worker, miner, farm labourer	Packer, order picker, HGV driver, gardener, waste treatment officer

Note: People in the armed forces are assigned to the old middle class if they have management responsibilities (i.e. are officers), and the working class if not. People with no current occupation are assigned to a class by their previous occupation, or if no previous occupation their spouse's occupation.

insecure incomes than middle class jobs. They also tend not to offer guaranteed sick pay, generous pensions, or clearly-defined promotion opportunities, while also involving more supervised monitoring, less autonomy, less hourly flexibility, and more unpleasant working conditions. These jobs may no longer be heavily concentrated in traditional heavy manufacturing, but they have many similar constraints and disadvantages. As we shall see in Chapter 2, the differences in resources, prospects and security between people in different classes have not changed (Felstead et al. 2015). The people who would once have been found on a factory shop floor are now more likely to be found in service jobs, but are still struggling to get by on erratic and insecure incomes. Indeed class differences in pay may have actually increased (Gallie 2015) as labour markets have become polarized with fewer jobs in the middle and more at the top and bottom (Autor and Dorn 2013; Oesch 2013).

Compared with the working class, middle class workers occupy relatively secure salaried positions, often with occupational pensions and other benefits. These are generally regarded as the most desirable positions in the labour market, although there will be considerable variation between those in senior and junior posts. We distinguish between three main middle class occupational groups, which we term the old middle class, the new middle class, and the junior middle class. This is a slight departure from the initial formulation of the Goldthorpe scheme.[9] We do this to capture changes in the middle class occupational structure. Importantly, we therefore separate professionals from managers (see Hout et al. 1995).[10] The old middle class was the dominant group within the middle class immediately after the war. This group includes managers, but also small employers, farmers, and self-employed professionals. The new middle class is the dominant group within the middle class today: professional employees, ancillary non-manual workers, and non-manual supervisors. Finally, we have the junior middle class: this comprises junior non-manual employees, or what are typically referred to as 'routine white collar workers'.

Finally, there are also three other smaller groups, which we include in our statistical models, but rarely show in any tables. These are the people who fall into the SEG categories of own account workers, foremen and supervisors, or personal service workers. These are quite small (each around 5 per cent of population) and very heterogeneous categories. The changing composition in the sorts of people who are own account workers makes over-time comparisons particularly problematic.[11] This heterogeneity is also true for personal service workers and, to a lesser extent, foreman and technicians. For these reasons, we pay less attention to these relatively small groups, although as a rule of thumb personal service workers and foremen are most similar in attitudes and behaviour to our working class group.

Occupation is important, but we are also interested in education. Educational qualifications are an increasingly differentiated source of information about people's capacities, transferable skills, and potential attainment. This is especially the case among young people, whose occupational class position is likely to be less firmly established. Education has also been shown to shape values and political preferences differently to occupational class (Evans et al. 1996; Tilley and Heath 2007; Chan and Goldthorpe 2007). Significantly, like the class structure, the distribution of educational qualifications has also changed radically in a relatively short period of time. In analyses reported in later chapters we measure education mainly through the level of qualifications someone has obtained. Some distinctions are quite easy to make. We can identify people with degree-level qualifications straightforwardly in our data and can also fairly easily distinguish people who either left school at the minimum age (fourteen until 1947, fifteen until 1972, and sixteen afterwards), or gained no qualifications. These groups form the top and bottom of our education categories. For the longest time span, we use a combination of school leaving age (compared to when someone went through the educational system) and higher education level qualifications to form a five category measure. This is the second column in Table 1.2. For all our data from 1979 onwards, we can use a better measure of highest qualification. This is shown in the third column of Table 1.2. Generally, the key distinctions we make are

Table 1.2. Educational groups

	Education (5 groups)	Education (7 groups)
High	*Degree or above* Some higher education	*Degree or above* Some higher education
Medium	*Left school at 17/18* Left school above minimum leaving age, but before 17/18	*A Level or equivalent* O Level or equivalent CSE or equivalent Apprenticeship
Low	*Left school at minimum leaving age*	*No qualifications*

between people with what we call high, medium, and low levels of education. High relates to degree level education, medium to A Level equivalent education, and low to no qualifications or leaving school at the minimum age.

The Changing Shape of the Class Structure

The last half-century has seen a pronounced growth in the size of the middle class. Although this transition is well known, it is useful to map out what it looks like in terms of our class categories. This is shown in Figure 1.1. The top graph in the figure contains census data back to 1931.[12] The bottom graph presents the patterns of change captured in survey data from the British Election Study (BES) surveys which run from 1963 to 2015, and the British Social Attitudes (BSA) surveys which cover the period from 1983 to 2015. Given that the latter are social survey estimates based on a few thousand people, there is a reassuring degree of similarity in the trends from these different sources. The growth of the middle class, and especially the new middle class, is clear, as is the steady decline of the working class. By 2000 the new middle class had become larger than the working class in both the BES/BSA and census series.

The rise of the new middle class is closely linked to educational changes. Many new middle class jobs are primarily professional or semi-professional in nature and have increasingly required formal qualifications for entry. The attainment of educational qualifications, especially a degree, has risen accordingly. This is, in part, because of deliberate government strategies to improve skill levels in Britain's increasingly knowledge-based economy. As with occupational class, we display these trends using both official sources of data and the survey data used for most of our analyses in later chapters of the book. We show the changes in our high, medium, and low categories of education in Figure 1.2 using data from the Labour Force Survey (LFS) from 1979–2015 and the BES/BSA data from 1964–2015.[13] The first and last of those groups have changed in size enormously over time. In the 1960s the number

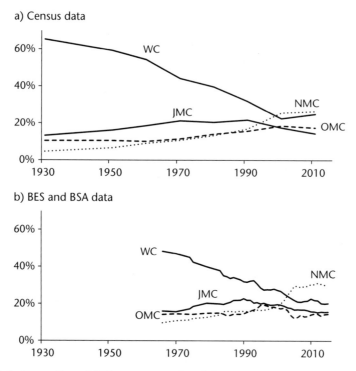

a) Census data

b) BES and BSA data

Figure 1.1. Proportion of different occupational class groups

Note: The figures here show the proportion of people in different occupational class groups. The top graph shows occupational class from UK census data; the bottom graph shows occupational class from combined BES and BSA data (three period moving average). Four occupational class groups are displayed: old middle class (OMC), new middle class (NMC), junior middle class (JMC), and working class (WC).

Source: UK Census 1931–2011; British Election Studies 1963–2015; British Social Attitudes Surveys 1983–2015.

of people with a degree was tiny, a few per cent of the population, and around two thirds of people had left school at the minimum age (which for most people then would mean fourteen). Today, around a quarter of the electorate has a degree, and a quarter have no qualifications. As with occupation the educational structure of Britain has been transformed.

The Politics of Class

What do these changes mean for politics? Most discussions of the changing nature of class politics have talked about the transformation of society and the demise of class divisions. We agree that there has been transformation, but not because class divisions have disappeared. The changing politics of class has resulted from the 'top down' influence of politicians and the media. This book

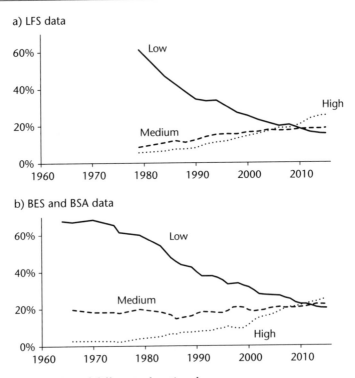

Figure 1.2. Proportion of different educational groups

Note: The figures here show the proportion of people in different educational groups. The top graph shows education from LFS data; the bottom graph shows education from combined BES and BSA data (two period moving average). Three educational groups are displayed: people with degree-level education (high), people with A Level equivalent education (medium), and people who left school at the minimum school leaving age for their cohort or have no qualifications (low).

Source: UK Labour Force Surveys 1979–2015; British Election Studies 1963–2015; British Social Attitudes Surveys 1986–2015.

develops our case with evidence on two contrasting features of British society: social continuity and political change. By social continuity we mean objective inequalities between classes, perceptions of class identities, and class divisions in social and political attitudes. These social divisions have remained remarkably unchanged despite Britain's transition from an industrial to a post-industrial society. Britain remains a class-divided society. By political change we refer to change, not among voters, but among parties, politicians, and the media. The media's representation of class, the policies the mainstream parties offer, the groups that parties talk about, and the composition of party elites have all changed dramatically.

Social Continuity

An emphasis on the decline of class is usually part of a theoretical focus on the decline of structural divisions more broadly. Changes in the class basis of politics are thought to have derived from general economic developments leading to the emergence of less structured societies. The argument runs that increased social mobility, affluence, and educational expansion have weakened the distinctiveness of classes in a globalized world. This has meant that traditional social groups, such as classes, have declined in political significance (Clark and Lipset 1991; Pakulski and Waters 1996a; Clark 2001a, 2001b).[14] Underlying much of this work is the key assumption that classes are no longer monolithic sources of identity and interests and that 'few individuals now possess exclusively middle-class or working-class social characteristics, and the degree of class overlap is increasing over time' (Dalton 2008, p.156). At its most extreme this process has been thought of as a form of 'structural dissolution'. This means a process of individualization, where society is composed of individuals whose identities and interests are so multi-layered as to render social categories redundant (Beck and Beck-Gernsheim 2002). Similarly, Beck's earlier (1992) formulation of the 'risk society' proposes that risk is ubiquitous in modern societies and the differential experience of risk between classes has weakened. Ultimately all of these depictions of bottom up change are about social blurring, social atomization, and increasing social heterogeneity.

Why might these influential ideas be wrong? One answer is that the assumption that classes are more alike is simply incorrect. The blurring assumed in terms of income and quality of life has not happened. As we shall see in Chapter 2, claims about the demise of class differences and divisions do not fit with the plentiful evidence of continuing class-based inequalities of resources, opportunities, and risks. In this chapter we examine trends of inequalities in income, unemployment, health, and educational achievement, as well as levels of inter-generational social mobility between classes. Across these many areas an extensive body of research confirms the continuation of pronounced class inequalities. Chapter 2 also shows that people are aware of these inequalities, both in their own lives and more generally.

Interestingly, perceptions of the incomes of different occupations actually underestimate the extent of inequality and the degree to which it has increased. This does not, however, mean that people are unaware of class or lack a sense of being in a class. Nonetheless, the assumption that the working class, in particular, has lost its identity runs through many recent narratives. One strand focuses on the idea of 'dis-identification' and another on the idea that everyone now thinks that they are middle class. Given the evidence on continuing class inequality presented in Chapter 2, it would be surprising if people did think in that way and in Chapter 3 we show the resilience of class identities and people's persistent awareness of class division. Levels of class identification remain robust over more than fifty years and people remain aware of class in both societal and everyday contexts. There has been little change in perceptions of class conflict and barriers between classes, or even in the difficulty of having friends from other social classes. People also seem to define classes in fairly similar terms. There is almost the same strong emphasis on occupation as there was in the 1960s, and both income and education are at least as important as then. In short, class awareness remains a part of British society. Changing class sizes and increased upward mobility have not weakened people's sense of class position and class division.

This pattern of continued distinctive classes is also evident when considering social and political attitudes, as we do in Chapter 4. Persistent class divisions in resources, risks, opportunities, and educational attainment foster continuing differences in political preferences. That inequality, insecurity, and limited opportunities should lend themselves to continued class divisions in support for different economic policies is unsurprising from a rational choice perspective. Likewise, when we consider issues and policies associated with socially liberal values, the idea that the middle class is less authoritarian than the working class is not new (Lipset 1959), and has been established across many societies (Napier and Jost 2008). Overall we find that economic issues are still related to class, with the middle classes wanting less interventionist and redistributive policies, and issues such as immigration and the EU are also powerfully divisive along class and education lines.

The message from all of these chapters is one of continuity. Objective inequalities, perceptions of those inequalities, awareness of class position and divisions, and the political ideologies of the different classes largely remain unchanged in Britain. The changes in the sizes of classes, however, have had dramatic consequences.

Political Change

While the differences between social classes may not have changed, the changing size of those classes has had a pronounced impact on the political parties. Labour decided in the 1990s that it could no longer base its electoral success primarily on working class support. This led to the party attempting both to change perceptions of itself as a working class party, and also to move its policy stance rightwards towards the Conservatives. This convergence process had at its heart a strategic focus on the median voter as the basis for electoral success. In addition, the higher ranks of the political parties have altered. Both have become increasingly dominated by professional career politicians with middle class backgrounds and a university education (Heath 2015).

These changes have also been accompanied by a shift within the most political branch of the media: the national newspapers. Information about politics and how it relates to people's own positions in society is obtained primarily from the mass media. How newspapers portray class and its relationship to politics is therefore important. This is not to say that newspapers tell people what to think: readers to a large degree select what they want to consume and inevitably this process will be more about reinforcement than persuasion.[15] But the media can still shape the way in which people understand the relationship between politics and class through the messages they see on a daily basis.

In this section of the book we therefore describe 'a perfect storm' whereby electoral strategy has resulted in the convergence of political parties on the middle class voter and the exclusion of the preferences of working class people from the political mainstream, which in turn has been amplified by the disappearance of class politics from the press. In Chapter 5 we analyse how the newspapers have changed their representation of class. We show that they have moved from a portrayal of the working class as the main reference group, with an acceptance of class as a fundamental aspect of society, to the newspapers of today that rarely mention class. In effect, the structuring of the political world in class terms by the newspapers no longer exists.

In Chapter 6 the convergence of the main parties' ideology and political rhetoric is described in detail via systematic examination of manifestos and leader speeches since 1945. These primarily quantitative analyses reveal consistent patterns of change in policy and group appeals. In terms of policy, we show that while there was similarity between the parties at the end of the 1960s, this is sometimes exaggerated, and that policy convergence in the post-war period only really happened in the 1990s. Class group appeals show an even clearer pattern. References to the working class were standard practice by Labour (and even the Conservatives) in the post-war era, but started to fall dramatically from the late 1980s onwards. After that point class effectively disappeared from the lexicon of party politics. As with policy convergence, these changes were part of the re-branding of Labour as 'New' in the early 1990s. Finally, we show that at this time political recruitment started to be dominated on both sides of Westminster by degree-educated members of the middle class. The two parties grew alike in policy, in their rejection of class appeals, and in their social composition. Crucially Chapter 6 also shows that the electorate noticed these changes as they happened. As a result of these combined transformations, the connection among policy, party, and class is now almost absent in mainstream British politics.

In direct contrast to the pronounced stability of economic, social, and attitudinal divisions between classes, Chapters 5 and 6 show that the party messages to voters, and their mediation via the press, changed enormously. Class was consigned to political history not by the blurring of classes, but by the actions of politicians.

The Consequences of Social Continuity and Political Change

What does the combination of bottom up social continuity and top down political change mean for class voting? Traditionally, class occupied a central position in British voting behaviour (Alford 1964; Butler and Stokes 1969). Indeed much effort was spent in trying to explain the specific phenomenon of anomalous 'working class Conservatives' (Nordlinger 1967; McKenzie and Silver 1968). This emphasis on the potentially powerful role of class fell quickly under attack, however, as scholars pointed to dealignment as a distinguishing feature of partisan divisions in the 1970s (Crewe et al. 1977b; Sarlvik and Crewe 1983). The intensity of the academic dispute over the role of class in politics in the 1980s almost paralleled the political disputes in the real world (Heath et al. 1985, 1987; Dunleavy 1987; Crewe 1987, Franklin 1985; Rose and McAllister 1986). The conflict in academia focused on whether class voting had actually declined, with some arguing that we had seen 'trendless fluctuation', not real change. Yet, by the late 1990s, those on the trendless fluctuation side of the argument effectively conceded that class had declined as an influence on party choice. The question is why?

Some have argued that class no longer matters for party choice because there are no longer meaningful class divisions. Unfortunately, this is typically asserted with no serious analysis of the accuracy or otherwise of this assumption. Clarke et al. (2004), for example, reiterate the claim that the decline of class voting in Britain is due to the fact that 'class boundaries have become increasingly fluid' (Clarke et al. 2004, p.2) without at any point demonstrating this is actually the case. We instead emphasize the role of the political elite in the structuring of class divisions in political choices. Sometimes referred to as the top down, or supply side, approach, the argument here is that the strength of social divisions in political preferences derives from the choices offered to voters by politicians and parties. This is not a new thesis. Przeworski and Sprague (1986) were influential advocates of this idea, and Converse argued in the 1950s that when parties failed to adopt distinct positions on class-relevant issues voters would be unable to use their class positions as bases for voting (Converse 1958, pp.395–9). Nonetheless, it is only recently that there has been thorough empirical analysis of the impact of the choices offered by parties on social divisions in voting.[16]

There are two aspects to political change that we might care about. The first is whether parties take different policy positions. Policy convergence weakens the motivation for choosing parties as a result of class interests or values. Party policy polarization should in turn accentuate class voting. Voter responses depend upon the choices voters are offered (the supply side), as well as the presence of differences in ideological and value preferences within the electorate (the demand side).[17] Modern Britain exemplifies the consequences of a top down political process of change. Labour's rightward shift in policy in the 1990s resulted in a constrained set of choices for voters, and thus less class voting. There is a second type of political change, however. Politics is not just about policy; it is about less instrumentally obvious signals. It concerns the kinds of people or groups that parties refer to and are seen to represent. Labour's shift to being a party of the middle class was not just about policy; it was also about the party's image. That image derives from policy stances, but also from the rhetoric and social background of politicians.

In Chapter 7 we examine the first electoral consequence of these changes: the demise of class voting. Combining different sources of data, we show that levels of class voting were largely static from the 1940s to the 1990s. Only then did the relationship between class and party collapse, and in the space of a few years. These dramatic changes correspond with the pronounced political changes that we discuss in Chapters 5 and 6. As shown in Chapter 6, policy, group appeals, and party elites all changed at the end of the 1980s and beginning of the 1990s. Following this, class voting fell for the first time since the end of the Second World War.

Moreover we directly link these party changes to people's individual voting decisions. We show that the core political issues of ownership and redistribution, which Chapter 4 reveals to be still fundamentally class-based, lost much of their power to account for vote choice during the 1990s. Equally important were changing perceptions of the parties as class parties. The short-lived policy convergence in the 1960s did not change voters' images of the parties. People still thought that both the main parties were *class* parties. This completely altered under New Labour. In Chapter 7 we use class perceptions of the parties to predict vote choices, and find that it is the combination of changing policy and changing perceptions of the parties that explains the decline of class voting in Britain.

Chapter 7 illustrates the fact that while parties can change policy, if that change does not affect people's perceptions of the parties, both in policy and class image terms, then policy change alone will not lead to dramatic and persistent changes in class voting. Images in that sense are 'sticky'. Large, abrupt changes by a party are required to reshape perceptions, and only multiple concurrent changes produce a transformation of the political equilibrium. In Britain in the 1990s there was such a shock to the system. Labour radically changed its nature in a short space of time. Not unrelated to this transformational signal from the party, the newspapers stopped talking about the politics of class. As a result of these policy and image changes, class voting was fundamentally undermined.

There is a further consequence of Labour's recasting as a party of the middle classes. Chapter 8 shows how these political changes have caused a new phenomenon in British politics: class-based abstention from voting. Although there have always been class differences in turnout in Britain, these differences have been very small. As we show, working class people were almost as likely to turn out to vote in the second half of the twentieth century as middle class people. Britain has therefore differed historically from the US, where occupation and education have traditionally had strong influences on political participation (Hout et al. 1995; Leighley and Nagler 2014).[18] This began to change in the 2000s in Britain and is directly due to the lack of political choice. With Labour no longer representing them and their views, working class people have increasingly chosen not to vote. Labour has followed the earlier path of the Democrats in the US and effectively created new inequalities in political participation. These inequalities work to reinforce the declining representation of working class people since parties are less likely to care about the preferences of people who do not vote.

There are some political processes that might be thought to counteract this gloomy prognosis. As the major parties have become more similar we have seen increasing electoral volatility and an increasing vote for minor parties. This was brought into focus by the 2014 European Parliament elections and 2015 General Election, which saw the emergence of the United Kingdom Independence Party (UKIP). As in other European countries, the presence of a radical right party in Britain is providing a new political voice for the working class (Ford and Goodwin 2014). Chapter 8 shows that the arrival of these new political choices has indeed increased class voting, as UKIP, and to a lesser extent the SNP in Scotland, have a strong appeal to the working class. Nonetheless, few of the voters drawn to either insurgent party were previously non-voters and, in that sense, these new party options have failed to renew working class electoral participation.

The Evidence

Any book is only as good as the evidence it uses to support its arguments. To test our ideas we need comparable long-term data on many aspects of social structure, social identities, political attitudes, the mass media, and parties. This distinguishes this book from others about class in general and the working class in particular. Journalists and social commentators such as Owen Jones (2011) and Ferdinand Mount (2004) have illustrated the extent of continued social snobbery and the neglect of the working class by politicians, while others such as David Goodhart (2013) have examined the negative consequences of immigration for the working class, but they do not systematically examine what the mass of the population thinks, nor do they test mechanisms that explain the outcomes to which they refer. A similar limitation characterizes renewed interest in the working class among British sociologists, which has usually involved small-scale, impressionistic studies (Skeggs 2004; Lawler 2005; Irwin 2015).

In contrast, our evidence is systematic, comparable over time, and allows us to test each of the explanatory processes we have proposed. It covers the experiences, beliefs, and actions of the electorate, as well as the claims and actions of the parties and the media. Most of the survey evidence is taken from the BES and BSA surveys. These are high-quality, representative probability samples of individuals living in private households in Britain. Both involve face-to-face interviews with several thousand people in most waves. The BES began in 1963 with a pre-election survey, and has been repeated at every general election since, and the BSA is an almost annual survey starting in 1983.[19] Both surveys are weighted to take into account both differential probability of selection and known patterns of non-response.

We complement these by introducing pertinent evidence from one-off surveys such as the Marshall et al. (1988) survey on class in Britain undertaken in 1984, and a module on social class included in the 2005 BSA survey that we examine in our analyses in Chapter 3. We also make use of the large sample size and high quality of the government's Labour Force Surveys to examine occupational changes in Chapter 2. Chapter 7 uses Gallup surveys that allow us to track class voting back to the 1940s, with three surveys from 1945 and 1946 as well as a run of nearly annual surveys from 1955 to 1968. We have also collected new survey data specifically for this book: this includes a module on class and politics in the 2015 BSA survey that features in Chapter 3 and a module of questions on class and representation embedded within the 2015 BES survey that is used in Chapter 6.

In addition to this vast array of survey evidence on the experiences, opinions, and actions of the public, we have coded what politicians, parties, and the media say. These quantitative and qualitative analyses examine references to class in three major newspapers, party leaders' conference speeches, and the content of party manifestos all stretching back to 1945. We have also obtained detailed biographical data about individual MPs across the period and link this information with the perceptions of the voters in their constituencies.

By integrating these extensive sources of systematic comparable data we hope to demonstrate our argument authoritatively. As noted earlier, when social scientists have referred to the changing relationship of class and politics in Britain they have not usually examined evidence that might explain this change. This is no longer the case.

Conclusions

In the 1960s the working class were pre-eminent demographically, and to a large degree politically. Their views were those of the majority and the political parties competed for their affections. Since then many have argued that class no longer matters, that the distinctions between classes have blurred and that individualization is the key attribute of modern, post-industrial societies. As a result, parties no longer need to connect with differences in interests between classes: the blurring of social divisions has produced a blurring of political divisions. In direct contrast, we demonstrate in the chapters which follow that the most significant feature of the post-industrial class structure is not its disappearance, but the changing sizes of its classes. Inequalities have not only survived but have in some respects actually increased.

Whereas the point of division in the past was between a large and fairly homogenous working class and a small middle class, now it is between a larger group of middle classes and a much smaller working class. At its simplest our thesis is that class divisions in social attitudes and political preferences remain robust. It is the political parties that have chosen not to represent these class differences. This has led to a decline in class voting, but also an accompanying accentuation of class divisions in non-participation. This is a new class divide that is unlikely to be reversed.

Notes

1. These were complemented by numerous studies of working class images of society (Bulmer 1975) and oral histories (Roberts 1984). Jackson and Marsden's *Education and the Working Class* (1966) told of the often uncomfortable relationship between children from working class backgrounds and grammar schools, and Willis's *Learning to Labour* (1977) focused on less academic groups. Work-place ethnographies also focused on working class job experiences (Fraser 1968/9; Beynon 1973), while the landmark study of 'the affluent worker' (Goldthorpe et al. 1969) convincingly disconfirmed the idea that the working class was becoming more like the middle class.
2. Since then there has been renewed interest in class amongst British sociologists, though often with respect to subjective elements of class identification and typically using small-scale ethnographic studies: e.g. Skeggs (2004), the various contributions to a special issue on 'Class, Culture and Identity' (*Sociology* 2005), a report from the Runnymede Trust (Sveinsson 2009), the work of Savage and colleagues (Savage et al. 2010) and, most recently, Irwin's (2015) interviews with people about job insecurity and the cost of living.
3. Arguably, measures of socio-economic position that combine education and occupation, and often income, into a composite measure of class raise as many questions as they answer in order to understand the various interconnections between them (Evans and Mills 1998).
4. Most recently, the BBC's 'Great British class survey' (Savage et al. 2013) garnered a lot of attention. Most commentators were of the view that class divisions were pronounced and of great public interest, but there was also scepticism about whether the classes defined in the BBC study were valid (Mills 2015a).
5. This also avoids the problems of subjectivity that plague self-reported measures of class position. We treat class identity as a possible product of occupational class position and education (see Chapter 3).
6. High levels of income churn from year to year also mean that income is unlikely to measure consistently more or less advantaged social positions within

the economic structure. Occupation-based measures are more stable (Connelly et al. 2016).

7. The Goldthorpe schema class categories have consistently been shown to be related to differences in employment conditions, job autonomy, income, and life-time expected earnings (Evans 1992, 1996; Evans and Mills 1998, 2000; Goldthorpe and McKnight 2006). This has led to its adoption as the primary component of the National Statistics Socio-economic Classification (NS-SEC) now used in the UK Census (Rose and Pevalin 2003), and as the basis for cross-national European research using the European Socio-economic Classification (Harrison and Rose 2006). It has been used extensively to study the class basis of social and political preferences in Britain (Heath et al. 1985, 1991, 2001; Marshall et al. 1988; De Graaf et al. 1995; Evans et al. 1999; Evans and Tilley 2012a, 2012b) and elsewhere (Weakliem 1989; Nieuwbeerta 1995; De Graaf et al. 2001; Evans and Whitefield 2006; Brooks et al. 2006; Elff 2007, 2009; and various contributions to Evans 1999 and Evans and De Graaf 2013).

8. SEGs are an occupational classification that measures employment status rather than skill or social standing. SEGs are derived from a combination of occupational groups, employment status (self-employed or employee) and size of establishment.

9. Where there have been criticisms of the Goldthorpe schema they have often been in relation to divisions within the middle class and the rise of a potentially more left-wing, liberal group of socio-cultural specialists (Butler and Savage 1995; Oesch 2006; Guveli et al. 2007a). These criticisms can be overstated with respect to the validity of the schema itself (Evans and Mills 2000), and there has been a debate on whether these distinctions identify class divisions or sectoral ones (Goldthorpe 1995), but they are useful for understanding the occupational bases of political preferences.

10. Others have proposed various versions of the old and new middle classes. The terminology and exact occupational specification vary—see Parkin (1968), Kriesi (1989), and Heath et al. (1991) among other early discussions. Recent work on this subject (Oesch 2006; Guveli et al. 2007b) has focused mainly on distinctions between 'technocrats' (typically managers) and 'socio-cultural specialists' (typically professionals).

11. Indeed recent British research finds that growth in own account work has typically been among people who were previously unemployed. This has been described as 'bad self-employment', which functions as a more or less short-term alternative to employment when jobs are scarce (Baumberg and Meager 2015).

12. The census data from 1971, 1981, 1991, 2001, and 2011 is available directly, and for 1971, 1981, and 1991 the SEG can be used to code our class categories. For 2001 and 2011 we use the NS-SEC measure of occupation to code into our class categories. For 1931, 1951, and 1961 the figures come from Price and Bain (1988). We have applied a small correction of 5 per cent, calibrated against their estimates for 1971 and 1981, to the Price and Bain proportion of 'manual workers' for those years as they contain people who we would have classified as personal service workers.

13. For the LFS data, we include those with 'trade apprenticeships' as people with no qualifications as they are not categorized separately for some early surveys. We also combine 'A Level equivalent' and 'some higher education' for the medium category for both datasets as it maintains more consistency over time for both the LFS and the combination of the BES and BSA data. The proportions of people in educational

categories not shown in the figure are, in total, quite static from the early 1980s onwards at a bit over a third of the population. There are some changes within these other categories, however. Taking the 1985–2015 end points of the BSA for which we have the full range of educational qualifications coded, the number of people with apprenticeships drops from about 7 per cent of people to 2 per cent and the numbers with CSE equivalent qualifications increases from around 4 per cent to over 7 per cent. The main group not shown in the figure, those with O Level equivalent qualifications, forms a stable quarter of the population.

14. There are many others who have taken related positions, from early writings on the end of ideology and the end of class politics (Bell 1960; Nisbet 1959) through Lipset's reformulation of the politics of class in his revised edition of *Political Man* (1981), Inglehart and Rabier's move from class-based to post-materialist politics (1986), Eder's 'new politics of class' (1993), and Kitschelt's analysis of the rise of centralist social democracy (1994), to name but a few.

15. It is generally accepted that the media help to shape the public's opinions by agenda setting (focusing on some issues at the expense of others) rather than by directly changing people's views. Early studies of media effects (Lazarsfeld et al. 1948; Berelson et al. 1954; Klapper 1960) emphasized its role in partisan reinforcement. Most research since has also identified an indirect campaign influence reinforcing prior opinions (Gelman and King 1993; Andersen et al. 2005), or modest effects on areas of political behaviour such as turnout (Iyengar and Simon 2000; Goldstein and Ridout 2004).

16. Evidence on these propositions using British data was originally presented in Evans et al. (1999) and Evans and Tilley (2012a, 2012b, 2013). Oskarson (2005) and Elff (2009) have expanded this approach cross-nationally, while Janssen et al. (2013) demonstrate the relationship across a large number of countries.

17. Some have argued that voters' preferences are shaped by the way parties frame choices and talk about politics. If parties adopt certain positions, voters will tend to follow suit. Sartori (1969, p.84) even argued that the politicization of class divisions by parties not only influences voters' party choices but actually produces class consciousness and an awareness of class-related economic interests. This 'preference shaping' approach to understanding class politics implies that parties directly influence the attitudes of their supporters. In this case we would expect class differences in ideology and values to reflect the shifting positions taken by the parties associated with different social classes. This implies that working class voters should have followed 'their' Labour party to the centre and become more like the middle classes. As with other recent studies (Baldassarri and Gelman 2008; Adams et al. 2012), we find limited evidence for this and, as we show in Chapter 4, the classes remain distinct in their policy preferences even when the parties converge.

18. Unsurprisingly, American political scientists developed the influential 'resource model' of turnout, in which participation is facilitated by the reduced costs of gaining information about politics and of voting itself, for middle class, higher-income, and more highly educated people (Verba and Nie 1972; Verba et al. 1978; Verba et al. 1995).

19. The BSA was not fielded in 1988 and 1992. For some of the analyses presented in later chapters we are unable to use the BES from 2005 and 2010 as it did not ask occupational class in a way that can be fully compared with previous surveys.

Part I
Social Continuity

2

Inequality

As the twentieth century ended many believed that social classes were a thing of the past. Social divisions based on economic inequality were disappearing as 'post-material' values concerning quality of life issues grew. Yet, at the same time as some talked of the death of class, others were revealing that class divisions not only remained but that social inequalities were becoming more pronounced. The United States was in the midst of the greatest expansion of income inequality for a century and although many advanced post-industrial societies witnessed economic growth this was accompanied by pronounced increases in inequality (Bartels 2008; Pierson 2001; Beckfield 2003; Alderson et al. 2005; Fischer and Hout 2006; Neckerman and Torche 2007; Moller et al. 2009; Reardon and Bischoff 2011; Piketty 2014). As a result of globalization and regional integration, the real wages of low-skilled workers stagnated or even declined (Brady 2005; Beckfield 2006).

In Britain there has also been a resurgence of interest in class inequality. Governments and NGOs have expressed repeated concern about their continued presence. A report from the Runnymede Trust in 2009 suggested that working class people are increasingly separated from the majority by inequalities of income, housing, and education (Sveinsson 2009). The Sutton Trust (2009) exposed the role of educational institutions in inhibiting upward mobility and reproducing class inequality. The Labour government formed the National Equality Panel, followed a few years later by the Conservative/ Liberal government's appointment of Alan Milburn to chair the Social Mobility and Child Poverty Commission (SMCPC). On taking up the post, the former Labour minister expressed the view that 'sadly, we still live in a country where, invariably, if you're born poor, you die poor. Just as if you go to a low-achieving school, you tend to end up in a low-achieving job'.[1] The SMCPC, still on-going, has an explicit brief to monitor progress in improving social mobility and reducing child poverty in the hope that Mr Milburn's observations will eventually be shown to be wrong. As we shall see, there is little sign of this hope being realized in the foreseeable future.

In this chapter we focus on this contemporary renewal of research into class inequality in Britain. We include studies of trends in inequalities in income, unemployment, health, and educational achievement, as well as levels of social mobility between classes. We show both the continuation, and in some cases exacerbation, of class inequalities. Evidence of 'the death of class' is in short supply. We also look at how ordinary people make sense of these inequalities. Are people aware of the extent of inequality and how it has developed over time? How do people explain unequal outcomes? Such subjective perceptions complement objective inequalities. First, we consider research on trends in objective inequalities between occupational classes: economic, health-related, and educational.

The Reality of Inequality

Class and Pay

It is common knowledge that wage inequality has been increasing in Britain in recent decades. General interest has focused on changes at the top end of the salary range. For example, the National Equality Panel report concluded that 'between 1999 and 2007 the real earnings of the CEOs of the top 100 companies more than doubled (reaching £2.4 million per year)' (National Equality Panel 2010, p.42). However, showing that earnings have spiralled at the top is not in itself evidence that wider class inequalities have become exacerbated. For this we need to look more broadly at class divisions in earnings.

Various pieces of evidence are available to examine this question. Gallie (2015) has recently conducted a detailed examination of changing class inequalities in pay between 1986 and 2012 using the Skills and Employment Surveys. These constitute six national samples of between approximately 2,000 and 5,000 people. To measure class position he uses the National Statistics Socio-Economic Classification (NS-SEC) which was developed from, and is very similar to, the Goldthorpe class schema (Rose and Pevalin 2003). Using gross hourly pay adjusted to 2012 prices, Gallie finds that pay inequalities polarized across all classes when compared to higher managerial and professional workers. The working class, classified as semi- and unskilled routine workers using NS-SEC terminology, were clearly the most disadvantaged at the start of the period and became increasingly more so over time.

A more nuanced picture of changing patterns of earnings inequality can also be obtained from the New Earnings Survey/Annual Survey of Hours and Earnings (NES) which we have for the period from 1975–2008. This covers all of the period of marked growth in pay inequality identified by Gallie, and also allows us to examine trends from the 1970s to the 1980s. Most significantly, the NES is a compulsory survey covering more than 1 per cent of the labour force. This vast array of data provides arguably the most robust available

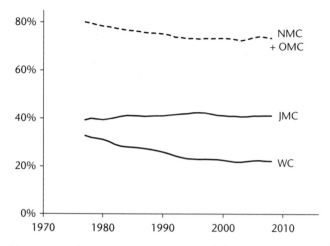

Figure 2.1. Mean percentile income by occupational class

Note: The figure here shows mean percentile income by occupational social class for full-time and part-time workers, aged 18–65 whose earnings were not affected by absence (three period moving average). Three occupational class groups are displayed: middle class (MC), junior middle class (JMC), and working class (WC).

Source: New Earnings Survey.

evidence on earnings and class in modern Britain. What does it tell us? Figure 2.1 shows mean percentile wage positions of the different classes over time. The mean percentile wage is the proportion of workers in each social class who are paid more than the average hourly wage. This is intrinsically a relative measure as it is estimated in relation to the average wage in a given year. For example, approximately around a third of the working class were paid more than the average hourly wage in 1975, but this dropped to around a quarter by 2008. We are forced to combine the old and new middle classes here, and show the comparison between them, the junior middle class (the intermediate class in NS-SEC) and the working class (semi- and unskilled routine workers in NS-SEC). In essence, occupational class differences in income are fairly stable across more than three decades, although the gap between the working class and the junior middle class moderately increased between the 1970s and the 1990s.[2]

We can also see the extent to which these class differences in income are evident in the BES and BSA datasets that form the core of our analysis of political attitudes and behaviour in later chapters. These surveys have measures of household income. This means that they do not allow hourly rates to be calculated and we are not necessarily linking people's own jobs to their own incomes. The sample sizes are also far smaller, and the measurement categories of income are far cruder. Nonetheless, they show a similar pattern of stability to the NES data. Figure 2.2 shows the proportion of each class that falls within the top 40 per cent of the income distribution since the 1960s. The proportion of the old and new middle occupational classes in the top

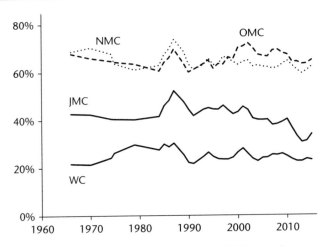

Figure 2.2. Proportion in top 40 per cent of the income distribution by occupational class

Note: The figure here shows the proportion of people in the top two quintiles of the income distribution by occupational social class (three period moving average). Four occupational class groups are displayed: old middle class (OMC), new middle class (NMC), junior middle class (JMC), and working class (WC).

Source: British Election Studies 1963–1979; British Social Attitudes Surveys 1984–2015.

40 per cent of the income distribution remains stable and very high, about 70 per cent across fifty years. The proportion of the working class with high incomes remains much lower than those in the new and old middle classes. Someone in the new or old middle class is about three times as likely to be in the top 40 per cent of the income distribution as someone in the working class. The junior middle class falls somewhere in between, and has actually edged closer to the working class in recent years, possibly since a higher proportion of junior middle class jobs are now part-time and, unlike in Figure 2.1, we do not measure hourly rates.

Labour Market Insecurity

Income is only one indicator of advantage and disadvantage. One of the key distinctions between occupational classes is in their provision of other desirable features of jobs, such as employment security, sick pay, pensions, health insurance, and other benefits. For Beck (1992), the notion of the 'risk society' involves the spreading of risks across the class structure. The insurance approach (Iversen and Soskice 2001; Moene and Wallerstein 2001) likewise focuses on cleavages based on risk exposure that are thought to be uncorrelated with traditional class divisions. While not necessarily claiming that class inequalities have disappeared, these approaches suggest that risk, especially of unemployment, is now more evenly spread across the different classes. However, as we will see, evidence on class differences in unemployment rates actually shows little change over time.

Figure 2.3 shows unemployment rates by class position using the LFS and BES/BSA.[3] We can see that the old and new middle classes have extremely low

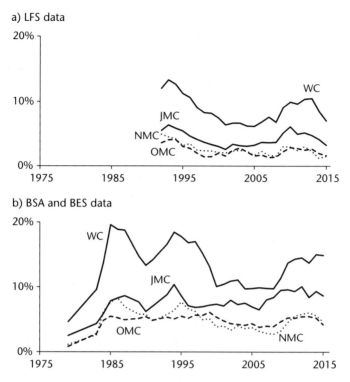

Figure 2.3. Unemployment rate by occupational class

Note: The figures here show the proportion of people who are unemployed as a percentage of those in the labour force (including those who are in education or training) by occupational class. The top graph shows unemployment rates from LFS data; the bottom graph shows unemployment rates from BSA and BES data (three period moving average). Four occupational class groups are displayed: old middle class (OMC), new middle class (NMC), junior middle class (JMC), and working class (WC).

Source: Labour Force Survey 1992–2014; British Social Attitudes Surveys 1984–2015; British Election Studies 1974–1983.

unemployment rates, always fewer than 5 per cent in the LFS and around that level in the BES/BSA surveys. The junior middle class is similar. In contrast, the gap between the middle classes and working class is always substantial. In fact, unemployment rates for the working class are on average three times higher than those of the new middle class. Beyond this, it is clear that unemployment rates among the working class move up and down with the economic cycle. Both sets of data indicate that changes in overall unemployment rates disproportionately affect the working class.

Health

Continuing class differentials in health are evident across a variety of measures, including self-rated general health (Drever et al. 2004), physiological gauges such as blood pressure (Atherton and Power 2007) and healthy diet and exercise (Roberts et al. 2013). The same holds true for mortality. White et al. (2003) analysed class differentials in mortality during the 1990s using data from the ONS Longitudinal Study: a 1 per cent sample of the UK population for which data from censuses has been linked to death registrations. They observed that mortality fell in all classes; but relative class differentials actually increased for men.[4] Similarly Langford and Johnson (2010) examined trends in class differentials in male mortality during the 2000s finding, again, that while mortality fell in all classes over time, relative class differentials increased slightly. Johnson and Al-Hamad (2011) report a similar pattern for women.

Psychological measures such as depressive symptoms (Atherton and Power 2007) also show pronounced class differentials. A recent analysis of children's dysfunctional behavioural conduct, negative emotional symptoms, and hyper-activity comparing three nationally-representative UK birth cohort studies (1958, 1970, and 2001/2) finds growing class inequalities over several decades (Anderson 2016). The general pattern across all three outcomes is of striking rises in class inequality since 1969, which was the starting point for comparison (at this point the 1958 cohort were ten to eleven years of age). Given the links between such symptoms and educational success (McLeod and Kaiser 2004; Kantomaa et al. 2010), these also carry implications for continuing class inequalities in educational attainment.

Educational Attainment

The contemporary labour market places greater emphasis on educational credentials than was typically the case in the mid-twentieth century. The dramatic expansion of higher education since the 1980s has brought with it an increasing tendency for employers to emphasize degree-level qualifications as entry hurdles for many posts. Previous generations may not have needed to succeed in education to gain promotion, but we live in a more credentialist society than we did in the 1960s and 1970s. Differential educational success is likely to play a larger role in consolidating class inequalities than used to be the case.

It is well established that there are sizable and persistent class differences in educational attainment (Erikson et al. 2005; Crawford 2014; Stuart et al. 2014). This inequality starts early. The government's own report (Stuart et al. 2014) into the outcomes of white British children who are eligible for free school meals (FSM) finds that they are consistently the lowest-performing group. Even at age five, only 32 per cent of children on FSM achieve the expected benchmark for their age, compared with 56 per cent of children who are not on FSM. By sixteen the gap is even wider: 32 per cent on FSM achieve five C-grade GCSEs or above, compared to 65 per cent not on FSM (IPPR 2014). Mills' (2015b) analysis of data from the Labour Force Survey found that the class gradient in GCSE performance decreased slightly between the mid-2000s and 2012, but just as with the FSM analysis, it is white British children from working class backgrounds that are the worst performers.[5]

As an aside, most academic studies focus on the state education sector, but a remarkably effective supplier of recruits to the best positions in our society is not part of that system. English public (i.e. fee-paying) schools have excellent international reputations for their ability to carve out success for their pupils. For good reason: although just 7 per cent of people attend independent schools, they make up 70 per cent of High Court judges and 54 per cent of CEOs of FTSE 100 companies (Sutton Trust 2009). Moreover, as we have shown elsewhere, the extent of the social divisions associated with private schooling runs far beyond differences in access to rarefied elite jobs (Evans and Tilley 2011). Even taking into account many other differences, private schooling is a key predictor of subsequent occupational and educational attainment.[6]

More importantly for our purposes, a further area of continued class inequality is in advancing beyond the minimum school leaving age and going on to further and higher education. Children whose parents have working class jobs are less likely to progress to A Levels, even conditional on their performance at the GCSE stage (Erikson et al. 2005). This inequality continues to university admissions. Bolton (2010) reports that university intake is heavily influenced by parental occupational class. Changes since the 1970s have been very modest, although from 2002–2008 there was a slight increase in the relative representation of children from working class backgrounds.[7]

Overall, class divisions in educational outcomes show little sign of weakening. Unsurprisingly, this differential educational attainment is consequential for inequalities in outcomes such as income and unemployment. People who complete more years of education go on to earn substantially more during the course of their working lives, and there are also pay premiums from postgraduate degrees over and above that conferred by an undergraduate degree (Leary and Sloane 2005; PWC 2005; PWC 2007; Kirby and Riley 2008; Conlon and Patrignani 2011).[8] People who complete an undergraduate degree earn about double the wage of those who do not attain any formal qualifications (Conlon and Patrignani 2011). Analysis of unemployment rates from 1992–2014 by educational level finds similarly strong effects (Busch 2015). Busch shows that throughout this period the unemployment rate for those with degrees or other forms of higher education was no more than 5 per cent. People educated to GCSE level were significantly more likely to experience unemployment, though they were far less likely to do so than those with no educational qualifications. Moreover, the differences in risks of unemployment between people with different educational levels widened after the economic crisis of 2008. From 2009 onwards, people with no qualifications had unemployment rates of around 17 per cent while unemployment rates among those with degrees remained only 3 per cent.

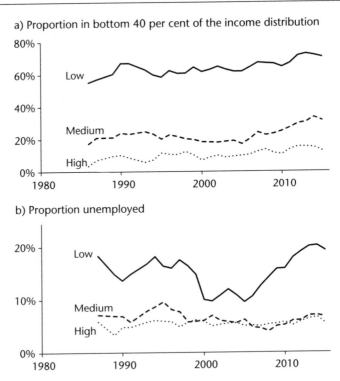

a) Proportion in bottom 40 per cent of the income distribution

b) Proportion unemployed

Figure 2.4. Income and unemployment by education

Note: The top graph here shows the proportion of people in the bottom two quintiles of the household income distribution by educational level (two period moving average). The bottom graph shows the proportion of people who are unemployed as a percentage of those in the labour force (including those who are incapacitated and in education or training) by educational level (three period moving average). Three educational groups are displayed: people with degree level education (high), people with A Level equivalent education (medium), and people with no qualifications (low).

Source: British Social Attitudes Surveys 1985–2015.

As we might therefore expect, in the BSA data differing levels of education are associated with substantial income and unemployment disparities. Figure 2.4 shows the proportion of people in the bottom 40 per cent of household incomes and those who are unemployed by the three levels of education identified in Chapter 1. As with social class, our survey data indicate a pattern of fairly constant and predictable educational inequalities in income. The evidence on unemployment also mirrors the patterns for occupational class: those with the lowest level of educational qualifications are more vulnerable to unemployment during difficult economic times, and the differences between educational groups are marked.

Social Mobility

Education is the single most important influence on occupational attainment (Breen and Jonsson 2005). Educational reform has therefore been seen as a major lever for governments attempting to increase social mobility. However, educational changes, of all types, appear to have proved ineffective in ameliorating class differences in mobility chances (Bukodi and Goldthorpe 2016; Goldthorpe 2016).[9] Given that educational disadvantages may be more important in the contemporary labour market than they were before higher education expansion, we might even expect social mobility to have fallen. This has certainly been prominent in the arguments of influential economists: Blanden and Machin (2007) and Ermisch and Nicoletti (2007) have claimed that intergenerational income mobility has declined in recent decades. Interestingly, however, this research focuses specifically on intergenerational *income* mobility, not occupational class mobility. And the case for decline is not straightforward. Goldthorpe and Mills (2008) argue that intergenerational occupational mobility (defined as relative chances of upward and downward mobility) has in fact been fairly stable over the last thirty years.[10] Goldthorpe and Mills contrast this with the middle decades of the last century when upward mobility actually increased.

Upward mobility chances for both men and women have also been estimated over the long term using the 1946, 1958, and 1970 Birth Cohort studies (Bukodi et al. 2015). For men the picture is clear: there are constant levels of upward mobility with no significant change across the three cohorts. For women, there is evidence of an increase in upward mobility in the most recent cohort.[11] However, this is only found among women who work part-time. Among full-time workers the picture is the same as it is for men.

Putting this together, there is little evidence that parental class has a weaker impact on people's own occupational trajectory. Indeed, the debate is largely between those who think social mobility has decreased versus those who think it is largely stable. This is broadly true of class inequality across the many areas that we discuss. Occupational class and education shape the reality of people's lives, in terms of incomes, instability, health, and social mobility much as they did fifty years ago.

The Interpretation of Inequality

In some respects class inequality appears to have got worse and in others it has remained stable. However, the social and political responses to such objective inequalities are likely to be conditioned by how people interpret them. In this section we examine evidence on beliefs about inequality and how unequal outcomes are achieved.

We should first note that objective evidence of class inequalities in pay, job security, and health are clearly apparent to the people who experience them: working class people are more fearful of unemployment, enduring poverty,

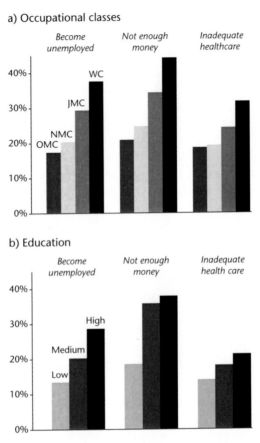

a) Occupational classes

Figure 2.5. The experience of various risks by occupational class and education

Note: The figures here show the proportion of people who think that it is likely that they will suffer the following over the next twelve months: unemployment, not having enough money for household necessities, and not receiving necessary health care in the event of becoming ill. The top graph shows this by occupational social class; the bottom graph shows this by educational level. Four occupational class groups are displayed: old middle class (OMC), new middle class (NMC), junior middle class (JMC), and working class (WC). Three educational groups are displayed: people with degree-level education (high), people with A Level equivalent education (medium), and people with no qualifications (low).

Source: European Social Survey 2008.

and facing health problems than middle class people. This can be seen from a recent BSA survey that asked people whether they thought it was likely that they would be unemployed, not receive adequate health care if they became ill, or not have enough money to cover household necessities. Figure 2.5 presents responses by occupational class and education.

Almost 40 per cent of the working class think that it is likely they will become unemployed in the next twelve months, compared with less than 20 per cent of the middle classes. Likewise over 45 per cent of the former are concerned about not having enough money to cover necessities compared with less than 25 per cent of the latter.[12] Concerns about adequate health care are connected with class position in similar, though less pronounced, ways. That they are still clearly linked despite the presence of the National Health Service could well relate to the ability of middle class people to afford private health care, or perhaps to live in areas where the postcode health lottery is more favourable. Educational differences in such perceived risks again mirror the patterns of differences between classes. The more education that someone has, the lower their level of perceived risk.

These perceptions tell us something about the fears associated with vulnerable labour market positions: the psychological costs of the risk of unemployment and the risk of not having enough money to make ends meet, accompanied by concerns about inadequate health care should the worst happen. But what of people's beliefs about how inequality works in society more generally? First, we examine whether people are aware of how unequal society has become with respect to pay levels. We then look at how people explain why some end up with the best jobs.

Awareness of Pay Inequality between Classes

Earnings inequality has been growing, but are people aware of this? The BSA surveys in 1987, 1999, and 2009 asked respondents to estimate the amounts earned by people in a range of jobs, including middle class (or above) positions such as GPs, company chairmen, or cabinet ministers, as well as working class jobs such as unskilled factory workers or shop assistants. People are asked how much people in each type of job 'usually earn each year before taxes'. Table 2.1 presents the answers to these questions.

We can see that people underestimate the actual salaries of high earners though less so in some cases than others. Cabinet ministers' salaries in 2009 were £144,500, and GPs in England typically earned around £110,000.[13] People underestimated these amounts, but nowhere near as much as they

Table 2.1. Perceived mean earnings of different jobs

	1987	1999	2009
Chair of large national company	£90,903	£179,870	£224,283
Cabinet minister	£39,455	£71,641	£109,352
GP	£21,187	£38,105	£75,957
Unskilled factory worker	£6,072	£10,859	£15,313
Shop assistant	–	£9,265	£13,297

Note: These figures are the mean amount each type of occupation is believed to 'usually earn each year before taxes'.
Source: British Social Attitude Surveys 1987, 1999, and 2009.

31

underestimated the salaries of heads of large national companies. In 2008 the average remuneration package of the CEOs of the FTSE top 100 companies was £2.4 million a year, while that of the next largest 250 companies was £1.1 million (Heath et al. 2010). By comparison, at the lower end of the wage scale perceptions are more accurate. The 2009 LFS indicates that the average earnings of female shop assistants were roughly £13,000 per year and unskilled male factory workers earned around £15–16,000 per year.

The perceived gaps between the earnings of occupations have changed over time, but only modestly. Whereas cabinet ministers were seen as earning 6.5 times a factory worker's wages in 1987, in 2009 it was just over 7. Whereas GPs were seen as earning 3.5 times a factory worker's wages in 1987, in 2009 it was 5 times. The earnings ratio for CEOs and factory workers was effectively unchanged over twenty-two years.[14] Awareness of the growing inequality discussed earlier in this chapter is surprisingly muted.

Are these perceptions shared across the class structure? Table 2.2 presents estimates of wages by class position. The earnings estimates for working class people given as a percentage of the three middle classes are shown at the bottom of the table. From Table 2.2 it appears that people from different classes have rather similar perceptions of the wages for different jobs, and there is little evidence of change over time.

The closeness of the different classes' estimates of earnings for the working class jobs may well reflect the limited variance in earnings among such jobs, as well as a 'floor effect'. However, working class respondents are generally more likely to underestimate how much those in middle class professions earn. This downward bias may serve to mitigate resentment about highly paid middle class jobs by working class people. This possibility can be examined by

Table 2.2. Perceived mean earnings of different jobs by occupational class

	1987				2009				
	CEO	Cab Min	GP	US Man	CEO	Cab Min	GP	US Man	Shop Asst
Earnings in £1,000s									
Old middle class	101	39	21	6	257	103	81	14	14
New middle class	90	35	22	6	252	110	80	18	14
Junior middle class	91	39	22	6	207	103	77	14	13
Working class	87	42	21	6	188	114	71	14	13
Comparisons to Working Class									
WC/OMC	86	108	100	100	73	111	88	100	93
WC/NMC	97	120	95	100	75	104	89	78	93
WC/JMC	95	107	97	96	91	111	93	102	101

Note: Entries in the first four rows are the mean amounts each occupation is believed to 'usually earn each year before taxes', rounded to the nearest thousand. Entries in the last three rows are group comparisons given as percentages.

Source: British Social Attitude Surveys 1987 and 2009.

Table 2.3. Gap between perceived and deserved earnings by occupational class

	1987				2009				
	CEO	Cab Min	GP	US Man	CEO	Cab Min	GP	US Man	Shop Asst
Differences in £1,000s									
Old middle class	38	9	–1	–1	82	24	7	–3	–3
New middle class	36	7	–	–1	103	33	3	–1	–4
Junior middle class	35	11	–1	–1	65	36	10	–4	–4
Working class	45	14	–	–2	73	51	1	–4	–4
Differences as ratio									
Old middle class	0.4	0.2	–	–0.2	0.3	0.2	0.1	–0.2	–0.2
New middle class	0.4	0.4	–	–0.2	0.4	0.3	–	–	–0.3
Junior middle class	0.4	0.3	–	–0.2	0.3	0.4	0.1	–0.3	–0.3
Working class	0.5	0.4	–	–0.3	0.4	0.4	–	–0.3	–0.3

Note: Entries in the first four rows are differences between the average amounts it is believed each occupation earns each year versus the average amount it is believed that occupation should earn, rounded to the nearest thousand. Entries in the last four rows are fractions of over/underpayment. Negative values indicate underpayment.

Source: British Social Attitude Surveys 1987 and 2009.

comparing beliefs about what jobs are perceived to be paid, with beliefs about what they *should* be paid. This gives us a measure of the perceived injustice of occupational differences in pay (Kelley and Evans 1993).

Table 2.3 indicates that the gap between perceived and deserved pay is surprisingly constant across different classes. Levels of deserved pay are shown in the top half of the table and the disparity between that and perceived pay is shown as a proportion in the bottom half. All classes think that CEOs are substantially overpaid; all think that the two working class jobs are underpaid. All see GPs' salary as about right. The only class differences are in the tendency for the working class to believe that cabinet ministers are overpaid to a greater extent than do the middle classes, though this is only a matter of degree. Generally, the classes are in remarkable agreement on both the levels, but particularly the fairness, of pay between different types of occupations.

Explaining Success

Maybe more important than perceptions of the extent of class differences in incomes is the way in which they are explained. Explanations for success and failure are argued to be shaped by an individualistic ideology pervasive in Western societies (Ichheiser 1949; Huber and Form 1973; Kluegel and Smith 1986). This holds that people believe society to be relatively open and that equality of opportunity, if not of outcome, is widespread. In short, people are responsible for their own fate. Accordingly, success is attributed to personal characteristics regardless of social origins. Such attributions are correlated with a set of beliefs emphasizing personal responsibility and the perception that people 'get what they deserve', including ideas of a just world (Cozzarelli et al. 2001), the Protestant work ethic (Furnham 1988), social dominance (Lemieux and Pratto 2003), and political conservatism (Zucker and Weiner 1993). This set of beliefs, which Huber and Form (1973) refer to as 'the dominant ideology', and which Ichheiser (1949) talks of as 'the success ideology' has been thought to provide a legitimation of widespread social inequalities in Western societies (Huber and Form 1973; Kluegel and Smith 1986).[15] Its generic presence has led to it being labelled 'the fundamental attribution error' (Ross 1977).

The BSA also has a set of questions that look at how people explain who 'gets ahead' in life. These ask how important different factors are in 'getting ahead', namely: coming from a wealthy family; having well-educated parents; knowing the right people; having a good education yourself; having ambition and hard work. 'Ambition' and 'hard work' attribute success to the individual rather than social circumstance, and could be thought to be endorsing meritocracy,[16] whereas 'coming from a wealthy family', having 'well-educated parents', and 'knowing the right people' emphasize the role of social background and connections. These are typically thought of as structural, or non-meritocratic, factors. As we have seen, the chances of obtaining a good education are in fact strongly influenced by class background. This could perhaps also be seen as non-meritocratic. It does not appear that people understand it in this way, however, as 'having a good education' correlates far more closely with individualistic attributions than structural ones.

It is clear from Table 2.4 that people believe that 'hard work', 'ambition', and 'having a good education' are the most important explanations of success. On average, three quarters of people or more think these are very important or essential, a level which has stayed fairly constant over time despite the noticeably worse economic circumstances in which the later survey was undertaken.

Table 2.4. Beliefs about what is important for 'getting ahead'

% saying essential or very important	1987	1999	2009
Individualistic or meritocratic			
Hard work	84%	84%	84%
Ambition	79%	74%	71%
A good education	72%	74%	74%
Structural or non-meritocratic			
Wealthy family	21%	15%	14%
Knowing the right people	39%	35%	33%
Well-educated parents	27%	28%	31%

Note: These are the proportions of people who said these characteristics are either 'very important' or 'essential' 'for getting ahead'.

Source: British Social Attitude Surveys 1987, 1999, and 2009.

Structural factors are seen to be important by only a minority of people. There has also been a decline since the 1980s in the proportion believing that these are very important or essential, although this is accompanied by a slight increase in the proportion believing that 'having well-educated parents' is an important factor. This reflects, perhaps, the extensive growth of higher education during this period and its consequences for access to good jobs. Generally, however, people believe that individuals themselves, rather than their circumstances, are responsible for their success. But are these views

a) Structural explanations

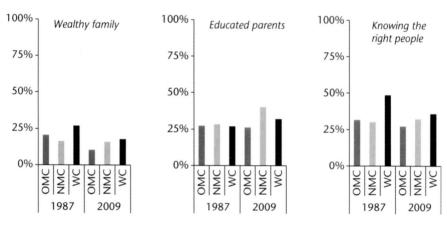

b) Individualistic explanations

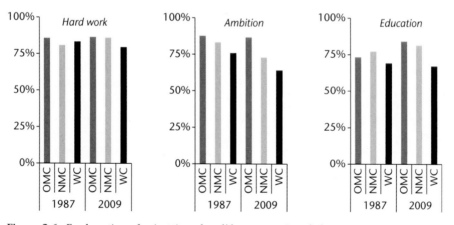

Figure 2.6. Explanations for 'getting ahead' by occupational class

Note: The figures here show the proportion of respondents who said each characteristic is either 'very important' or 'essential' 'for getting ahead'. The top graphs display structural characteristics; the bottom graphs display individual characteristics. Three occupational class groups are displayed: old middle class (OMC), new middle class (NMC), and working class (WC).

Source: British Social Attitudes Surveys 1987 and 2009.

shared across the class structure? While we might expect the socially disad-vantaged to reject individualistic accounts of success, this is not the case.

Figure 2.6 shows there is very little difference at all in the weight given to the individualistic factors of education and ambition. The working class are less likely to emphasize ambition and education than the middle classes in 2009, but the differences are outweighed by the similarities: more than 60 per cent of all classes thought that these attributes were very important or essen-tial for getting ahead. Interestingly, in 1987 respondents were also asked about the importance of 'natural ability' for explaining who gets ahead. The working class were actually *more* likely to emphasize the importance of natural ability than the middle classes. Among the structural explanations for success, the most noticeable class difference, in the higher importance given to 'knowing the right people' by working class people in 1987, had weakened by 2009. The increase in emphasis on educated parents in 2009 was most marked in the new middle class, yet among all classes structural factors were far less likely to be seen as important or essential for getting ahead than individual attributes.

Explanations of who gets ahead seem to a fair degree to be shared across society, and do not appear to have changed very much. Heath et al. (2010) conclude that even personal mobility experiences have only a 'very modest' relationship with people's explanations of success. Using an experimental design and indirect measures of attributions, Evans (1997) found a similarly closely shared view of the importance of structural versus individualistic influences on social mobility between people on the left and right of the political spectrum.[17]

Conclusions

In the introduction to the 1989 edition of *The Road to Wigan Pier*, Richard Hoggart notes Orwell's disdain for those who thought class divisions in 1937 were dead, and points out that the same assertions continued to be incorrectly made. As he rightly said, 'each decade we shiftily declare we have buried class: each decade the coffin stays empty' (Hoggart 1989). His words are no less resonant another thirty years later. The fact is that modern Britain has strong and pervasive class inequalities. Pay differences between the classes have not diminished, and may have increased. All our data shows that patterns of unemployment are strongly related to class and education, and those groups that are more likely to be unemployed are also those hit harder by fluctuations in the economy.

Major studies of health inequalities point to widening not declining class differences in relative mortality and in psychological indicators of dysfunctional behavioural conduct, negative emotional symptoms, and hyper-activity. Class inequalities in educational attainment start at age five and as children go through the education system the gap gets wider. Even when controlling for differences in GCSE performance, working class children fail to progress relative to their middle class peers and under-representation at higher educational levels shows no sign of abating. Education itself retains its significant and substantial impact on earnings, risk of unemployment, and other aspects of life-chances including, of course, the attainment of class positions themselves. Social mobility opportunities have remained at best constant, and some have argued they are in decline. In short, it is better to be middle class than working class, and it is better to be highly educated than poorly educated.

People are also aware of these social inequalities. Working class people perceive more insecurity in their lives, while people in all social classes think pay differences between some highly paid jobs and typical working class jobs are too high. At the same time, these views on inequality are accompanied by a general perception that the achievement of unequal outcomes is a result of ambition and effort rather than social advantage. Such beliefs about achievement underpin to some degree the perception that class position is based on merit; one implication being that inequality between classes is acceptable as long as mobility between classes is possible.

These patterns of stability in both inequality and perceptions of inequality differ from the US experience. Upward social mobility in the US has not increased, but 40 per cent of Americans believe it has (Scott and Leonhardt 2005). Thus large increases in class inequality in the US have been accompanied by the strengthening of belief in the American Dream: that it is possible to start out poor, work hard, and become rich. While British people do endorse aspects of this philosophy, for example most people think hard work is important for success, there is little evidence of change over time. Inequalities remain constant, and perceptions of those inequalities remain constant.

Notes

1. Alan Milburn talking to the BBC in April 2011 (http://www.bbc.co.uk/news/mobile/uk-politics-12962487).
2. There has been more income polarization by class in the USA, where Weeden et al. (2007) use the US Current Population Survey to show that not only is the amount of earnings inequality increasing between classes but the share of total inequality occurring *within* occupations has declined. As they note: 'the well-known take off in inequality has generated a "lumpier" earnings distribution with relatively stronger class and occupational distinctions' (Weeden et al. 2007, p.702).
3. It is not possible to directly create our class categories using the LFS data, so old middle class in Figure 2.3 for the LFS data refers to NS-SEC analytic category 1.1 (large employers and higher managerial), new middle class refers to 1.2 (higher professional), junior middle class refers to 3 (intermediate), and working class refers to 6 and 7 (semi-routine and routine).

4. When assessing changes in class differentials in death rates over time, a distinction can be drawn between absolute inequality and relative inequality (Langford and Johnson 2010; Johnson and Al-Hamad 2011). The former refers to the absolute difference in number of deaths (age standardized) per 100,000 per year between two classes; the latter refers to the ratio. For example, if class X has a death rate of 600 and class Y has a death rate of 400, the absolute difference is 200, while the ratio is 1.5.

5. These class differentials in educational achievement occur even when taking into account differences in ability. On the basis of extensive UK birth-cohort data, Bukodi et al. (2015) find that class differences in cognitive ability have only modest effects on the continued impact of parental occupational class on educational attainment.

6. Given that a privately-educated person is also seven times more likely to be married to another privately-educated person than is someone who is state-educated, and 65 per cent of these privately-educated couples send their children to fee-paying schools, it is unsurprising that private schools are seen as 'perpetuating the apartheid which has so dogged education and national life in Britain since the Second World War' (Seldon 2008).

7. On entering higher education yet another set of class disparities emerge. Crawford (2014) found that individuals from higher socio-economic groups were less likely to drop out, more likely to graduate, and more likely to graduate with an upper second or first-class degree.

8. There does not appear to be much evidence that the pay premium from an undergraduate degree changed during the period of higher education expansion that began in the late 1980s (PWC 2007, p.6; Conlon and Patrignani 2011, pp.37–9). One possible explanation for the apparent stability of the undergraduate pay premium over the last few decades is that countervailing forces have cancelled one another out. On the one hand, the automation of mid-skilled service jobs, the outsourcing of comparatively high-paying manual jobs, and the influx of low-skilled immigrants may have increased the undergraduate pay premium. On the other hand, the rising higher education enrolment rate, and the corresponding decrease in the skill level of the marginal graduate may have dampened it.

9. Goldthorpe (2016) makes the point that educational attainment is a 'positional good': where someone stands in the educational hierarchy relative to others is likely to be more consequential for their occupational attainment than simply their level of qualifications. It is not how much education an individual has but how much he or she has relative to others. In terms of people's ranking in the educational hierarchy, class inequalities have remained largely constant over time.

10. We should note that these contrasting findings are not necessarily incompatible if, as we have observed earlier, there have been changing patterns of earnings within occupational classes. Erikson and Goldthorpe (2010) consider the discrepancies and present the case against using income in more detail.

11. Using Bukodi's data we find that long-range, upward mobility from the working class (classes 6 and 7 in the Goldthorpe schema) into the middle class (classes 1 and 2 in the Goldthorpe schema) is stable for men: in each of the cohorts it is, respectively, 26 per cent, 24 per cent, and 28 per cent. For women the equivalent figures were: 17 per cent, 17 per cent, and 30 per cent. Heath et al. (2009) use

somewhat different data, taken from the General Household Survey for 1987, 1992, and 2005, and from the British Household Panel Study for 1999, to estimate measures of long-range and short-range upward mobility. They report modest increases in upward mobility between 1987 and 2005. However, they used occupational data from respondents aged eighteen and over, which might well lead to an underestimate of some aspects of intergenerational reproduction as many people in the professional and managerial classes do not attain destination jobs until much later in their careers.

12. Whether members of these classes have different expectations with regard to what might be thought of as necessities cannot be ascertained from these questions, but we might expect a higher level of expectation among the more advantaged classes, so these are likely to be rather conservative estimates of differences in the likelihood of equivalent financial hardship.

13. This figure refers to contractor GPs (partners at a practice). Salaried GPs earn considerably less (£58,000 in 2009 on average).

14. As Heath et al. (2010) note, comparing change over time in actual earnings for specific jobs is not straightforward. However, we know that cabinet ministers' salaries increased by 30 per cent between 1999 and 2009. GPs' salaries increased substantially following the Labour Government's re-negotiation of their contracts in 2004: NHS information centre figures that are available for the period 2002/3 to 2008/9 show an increase of approximately 50 per cent in just six years. Similarly, the National Equality Panel report (p.42) indicates that the remuneration of CEOs of large companies rose by much more between the 1990s and 2009 than did that of the average employee, which was generally static.

15. Such attributions are not limited to explanations of success. In one of the first large-scale studies of attributions for poverty, Feagin (1975) found that individualistic attributions were supported more strongly than other explanations, a finding that is indicative of a tendency to view poverty as a sign of personal and moral failure (Katz 1989; Shirazi and Biel 2005). Feagin's work was replicated in Britain by Furnham (1982, 1988). He found that even during a period of large-scale unemployment people tended to hold the poor responsible for their own fate.

16. The term meritocracy was coined by Michael Young in *The Rise of the Meritocracy* (1958), a dystopian vision of the future referring to the negative consequences that follow when achievement is based purely on a formula of 'IQ plus effort'. Typically, a meritocracy is now seen as a society where rewards derive from indicators of achievement such as educational success, and motivational factors expressed through hard work. This is generally contrasted with a society in which factors such as family background, such as parents' income and social connections, or characteristics ascribed at birth, such as race or sex, are more important for success.

17. Although expectations associated with *implicit* assumptions about class have a pervasive influence on people's understanding of who gets where in society, who becomes unemployed, who votes for which party, and even upon who marries whom (Evans 1993a), these assumptions do not fundamentally alter the individualistic bias in *explicit* attributions for success and failure, again testifying to the power of this ideology.

3

Identity

In this chapter we follow up on Chapter 2's examination of inequalities between the classes by considering class identities: whether people still see themselves and others in class terms. Following the influential approach of Cantril (1943), Centers (1949), Hodge and Treiman (1968), Jackman and Jackman (1983), we distinguish between 'class identification' and 'class awareness'.[1] Class identification refers simply to the tendency for people to place themselves in social classes. This involves recognizing the existence of classes, but does not require people to attribute importance to these classes. Class awareness is usually seen as separate from class identification (Vanneman and Cannon 1987). If people are class aware, they should have a broader understanding of how class position influences people's lives. An awareness of class at the very least implies a connection between someone's objective occupational class and their subjective class identification.

So do people in Britain still have class identities and are they aware of the impact of class on their own and others' lives? Our focus on these questions is a response to claims that class position no longer influences how people see themselves or others. In the mid- and late twentieth century researchers typically found that most people understood class labels and believed that social classes existed (Butler and Stokes 1969; Bulmer 1975; Jackman and Jackman, 1983; Vanneman and Cannon, 1987; Marshall et al. 1988; Argyle 1994). People were able to describe their own and others' social class positions. They placed far greater weight on characteristics such as occupation, education, and income, than on characteristics such as race, gender, marital status, and age when judging social status (Coleman and Rainwater 1979). Recently, however, it has been argued that such expressions of class identity and awareness are more historical than contemporary. Many social and political scientists now believe that even the most elementary aspect of class-related beliefs, class identity, is a 'relic of a bygone age' (Eidlin 2014, p.1045).

One theme centres on the idea that, regardless of the persistence of inequality, the distinctiveness and implications of class identity have been lost.

Traditional notions of class simply do not resonate with ordinary people's experience of social life. As a result some researchers (Savage 2000; Skeggs 1997; Savage et al. 2001; Irwin 2015) have argued that class position no longer generates a deep sense of identity and belonging. Apparently we have seen a 'paradox of class' (Bottero 2004), in which the continued role of class position in shaping life chances is nevertheless accompanied by a declining level of class identification. This work has been interpreted through Beck and Beck-Gernsheim's (2002) theory of individualization and the risk society, which asserts that individuals have been 'disembedded' from traditional communities and the inherited identities associated with them. People now choose their own identities so that if 'you are interested in what is going on in people's minds and the ways of life they are leading, you have to get away from the old categories' (Beck and Beck-Gernsheim 2002, p.207). Notwithstanding their nuances, all of these arguments centre on the idea that class identity is divorced from class position and has lost its meaning.

Other researchers have claimed that rather than class identity disappearing, middle class identification has now become the new norm in modern society. This change is principally attributed to increasing affluence leading to people in working class jobs seeing themselves as middle class. The benefits of economic prosperity in the post-war era have been spread more equally across social classes, while the welfare state has also served to reduce the more extreme hardships associated with class inequality (Andersen and Curtis 2012). Inglehart's influential interpretation of value change asserts that affluence has 'brought a shift in the political agenda throughout advanced industrial society...a shift from political cleavages based on social class conflict towards cleavages based on cultural issues and quality of life concerns' (Inglehart 1997, p.237). Class matters less because class-related poverty and inequality are no longer such pressing concerns.

A somewhat different version of the affluence thesis relies on ideas taken from reference group theory (Shibutani 1955; Merton 1957; Siegel and Siegel 1957) and assumes that perceptions of social structure are conditioned by the character of the immediate social environment. The literature on 'working class images of society' (Bulmer 1975) took this perspective as its starting point, as did Runciman's (1966) influential analysis of working class attitudes towards inequality in the early 1960s. More recently, however, it has been used to understand the prevalence of a middle class identity. Pahl et al. (2007) argued that by the end of the last century the relatively narrow income range of the population led to most people seeing themselves as in the middle. This was argued to reflect a 'reasonably accurate view that the material lifestyle of the households geographically and socially close to them is simply not that different' (Pahl et al. 2007, p.18).

Kelley and Evans (1995, Evans and Kelley 2004) generalized this proposition, arguing that people consider their own position in comparison with those around them and this homogeneity of reference groups shapes perception of the class structure and where people place themselves in this structure. Although their thesis is tested across many countries, it suffers from a rather serious limitation in that it does not measure class identity. It employs an 11-point scale of 'position in society'. This scale is labelled only 'top' and 'bottom' and makes no reference to what a self-placement of '4' or '7', for example, might mean. Nor is it clarified what 'top' and 'bottom' might refer to, so it is not clear what their scale is measuring. By comparison, research employing measures of class identity found that in most countries there are predictable patterns of working class and middle class identification (Evans 1993b; Andersen and Curtis 2012; Curtis 2016). Even in the US, Hout (2008) shows that just over two thirds of people think of themselves as belonging to one of those two classes, with no trend in this proportion between the 1950s and the 2000s. There was a predictable shift towards a higher proportion of middle class identifiers in line with changes in class sizes, as might be expected, but nowhere near enough to suggest that everyone now sees themselves as middle class.[2]

So has class identity in Britain changed? The dis-identification argument suggests that despite continued inequality class is simply no longer meaningful to people, the affluence argument predicts increasing middle class identification during periods of growth but a fall during downturns, while the reference group argument suggests that predominantly middle class perceptions are both generated and insulated by comparison processes.[3] In the rest of this chapter we refute each of these arguments. We show that people still see themselves as belonging to social classes and that these identities still relate to people's objective characteristics, both past and present. Moreover, working class identities are still prevalent. We also show that people see others in class terms and still believe that class has an important impact on people's lives. There is as much social continuity in class identities as there is in class inequalities.

How People See Themselves

Class identity was one of the central concerns of the early BES surveys (see Butler and Stokes 1969) and questions about this have appeared in almost all of the BES surveys that followed, as well as a few of the later BSA surveys. First we examine the most basic aspect of class identity: how many people were willing to say yes when asked whether they thought of themselves as belonging to a class. The left-hand graph in Figure 3.1 breaks people down into three

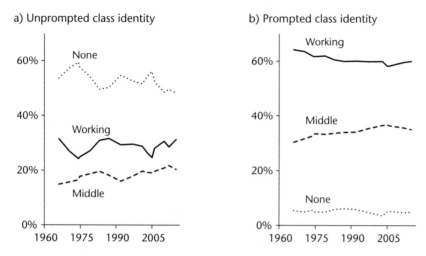

Figure 3.1. Unprompted and prompted class identities

Note: The figures here show the proportion of individuals who identify with particular classes. The left-hand graph show unprompted class identity and the right-hand graph a combined unprompted and prompted class identity. Three class identities are displayed: middle class identity (middle), working class identity (working), and no identity (none).

Source: British Election Study 1964–2015; British Social Attitudes Surveys 2003–2015.

categories: those with no identity, those who said they thought of themselves as working class, and those who thought of themselves as middle class. There has been no decline in these unprompted class identifications. In 1964, when class was ostensibly the defining theme of British society, just under 50 per cent of people volunteered that they were middle or working class; in 2015 the figure was almost identical. Both middle class and working class identities are also very stable over time. There has been a slight increase in the number of people saying that they were middle class (about 5 per cent between 1964 and 2015), but it is still only 20 per cent of the population. Clearly, we are *not* all middle class now.

Those who did not volunteer a class identity were prompted to choose between being working class or middle class. Specifically, they were asked: 'Most people say they belong to either the middle class or to the working class. Do you ever think of yourself as being in one of these classes?' Almost no one appears to have found this excessively difficult to answer across the entire period. The right-hand graph in Figure 3.1 shows class identity after this prompting is included. Again we find little support for the idea that class identity has declined, let alone disappeared. In 1964 fewer than 10 per cent of people chose not to give a class identity, and this figure was, if anything, lower in 2015. Interestingly, as with the unprompted question, although the proportion of working class jobs has declined over time, the proportion of people who identify themselves as working class is still clearly a majority.

Being class aware is usually seen as more than simply being able to use labels for self-identification. There are various ways of examining this issue, but the most commonly adopted method is to examine the link between objective and subjective class position. If class identification connects with occupational class, it is likely to be more firmly grounded in experience. Figure 3.2 presents evidence on changes in the relationship between occupational class and unprompted class identity across time. We can see that among all the occupational groups, levels of overall class identity remain fairly stable. Among those who have an identity, people with working class jobs clearly express a working class identity, which remains constant from the 1960s to 2015: at no point do more than a trivial proportion of the working class see themselves as middle class. Equally, people in middle class jobs are clearly more likely to regard themselves as middle class. Levels of identification in the old and new middle classes are very similar to each other, although rates of middle class identification are somewhat lower for the junior middle class group. It is also interesting to note that there is actually a pattern of gently increasing working class self-identification among all three of the middle class occupational groups.

If we examine levels of class identification after combining prompted and unprompted class identification we see similar patterns. As Figure 3.3 shows, a working class identity is both constant and dominant among people with working class jobs. Over more than fifty years around 80 per cent of people with working class occupations have consistently identified themselves as working class. The dominance of a middle class identity is less pronounced among those with middle class jobs, and again we see a pattern of gradually increasing working class self-identification among the middle classes.

So contrary to the 'we're all middle class now' thesis, middle class identifiers are the ones who are in short supply. Substantial minorities of people with middle class jobs see themselves as working class and have always done so. Although the working class have retained a solidly working class identity, the middle classes have actually become slightly more likely to express a working class identity. The reasons for people with middle class jobs seeing themselves as working class are worth examining a little further. One possibility is that class identities are shaped in childhood and are as much to do with where someone comes from as where they end up. This is suggested by various studies of class identity that have found an effect of occupational class background in addition to people's current jobs (Heath et al. 2009; Jackman and Jackman 1983; Pérez-Ahumada 2014; Curtis 2016), and can be seen in Figure 3.4 which shows the percentage of people who identified themselves as working class or middle class by their father's occupational class.

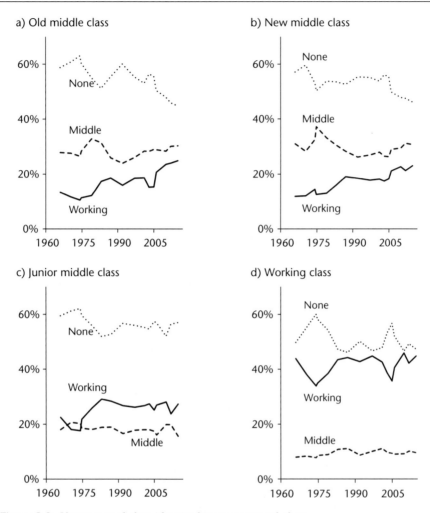

Figure 3.2. Unprompted class identity by occupational class

Note: The figures here show unprompted class identity by occupational social class. The top-left graph shows values for members of the old middle class; the top-right shows values for the new middle class; the bottom-left shows values for members of the junior middle class; the bottom-right shows values for the working class. Three class identities are displayed: middle class identity (middle), working class identity (working), and no identity (none).

Source: British Election Study 1964–2015; British Social Attitudes Surveys 2003–2015.

These effects are very stable. Class background matters for someone's current class identity just as much now as it did in the 1960s. The effect of someone's own occupational class has about the same effect on identity as their father's occupational class. This means that across all years, people with middle class jobs whose fathers had working class jobs are quite likely to think

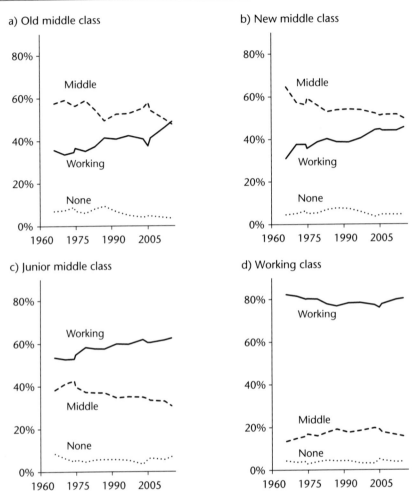

Figure 3.3. Prompted class identity by occupational class

Note: The figures here show prompted class identity by occupational social class. The top-left graph shows values for members of the old middle class; the top-right shows values for the new middle class; the bottom-left shows values for members of the junior middle class; the bottom-right shows values for the working class. Three class identities are displayed: middle class identity (middle), working class identity (working), and no identity (none).

Source: British Election Study 1964–2015; British Social Attitudes Surveys 2003–2015.

of themselves as working class. In 1964 44 per cent of people with middle class (new and old) occupations whose fathers had a working class job had a working class identity compared with 22 per cent of similar people whose father had a middle class job. In 2015 these figures were 58 per cent and 29 per cent respectively. The effect of class background on class identity is

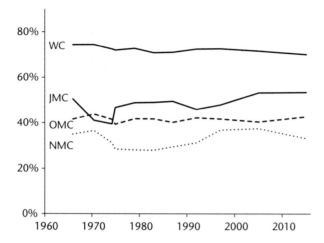

Figure 3.4. Working class identity by father's occupational class

Note: The figure here shows the proportion of respondents identifying as working class (prompted and unprompted combined) by father's occupational social class. Four occupational class groups are displayed for fathers: old middle class (OMC), new middle class (NMC), junior middle class (JMC), and working class (WC).

Source: British Election Study 1964–1997; British Social Attitudes 2005 and 2015.

remarkably constant across fifty years; in both 1964 and 2015 exactly twice as many middle class people who have a working class father also see themselves as working class compared with those who have middle class fathers.

Background clearly matters and helps us to understand why so many people with middle class jobs see themselves as working class. It does not help explain growing levels of working class identification among people with middle class jobs however. The proportion of people in middle class (old and new) jobs who have a working class background has remained constant (35 per cent in 1964; 38 per cent in 2015), as has the proportion of people in working class jobs from middle class (old and new) backgrounds (14 per cent in 1964; 15 per cent in 2015). A more likely explanation for the increase in working class identity among some groups is the dramatically changing distribution of educational qualifications. Education has long been recognized as an important influence on class identification (Robinson and Kelley 1979). However, as we saw in Chapter 1, far more people now go on to further and higher education than was the case in the mid- and late twentieth century. One implication of this is that the importance for social identity of having obtained further and higher educational qualifications has declined as educational expansion reduces the social distinctiveness of higher levels of education. This can be seen in Figure 3.5, which shows the class identity of people with low, medium, and high educational qualifications over time.

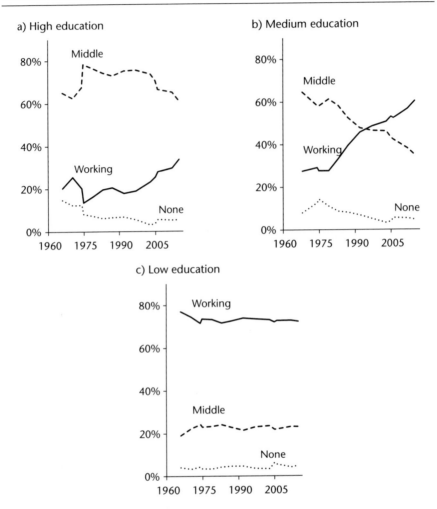

Figure 3.5. Class identity by education

Note: The figures here show combined prompted and unprompted class identity by education. The top-left shows values for those with a high level of education; the top-right shows values for those with a middle level of education; the bottom shows values for those with a low level of education. Three class identities are displayed: middle class identity (middle), working class identity (working), and no identity (none).

Source: British Election Study 1964–2015; British Social Attitudes Surveys 2003–2015.

People with the lowest level of education are solidly working class in their identity throughout the period examined. Among people with medium levels of education and degree-level qualifications, there has been a shift towards a more working class identity in recent decades. It could be that the growth in the proportion of the population obtaining educational qualifications has reduced the social distinctiveness of having these qualifications. It is not because the income returns to education have declined. As we saw in Chapter 2, they have not. Controlling for any changes in income levels by different educational levels has no noticeable effect on the pattern of overtime change in education's effects on class identification. Educational attainment simply appears to have become less consequential than it used to be for a person's sense of being middle class.[4] This same idea could perhaps also explain why levels of middle class identification have declined slightly among the occupational middle classes. If the social distinctiveness of educational qualifications has declined, so has the social distinctiveness of having a middle class job. If most people are middle class, maybe it is less easy to feel that sense of community and identity that characterized the much smaller middle class of the 1960s.[5]

Class Closeness

Overall we find a great deal of continuity in the relationship between occupational class and subjective class identification. We can, however, examine a further aspect of class identity: closeness to others with the same identity. In the 1963 pre-election wave of the BES, Butler and Stokes tried to measure the strength of belonging to a class community: in other words, a sense of closeness to one class and distance from another. This was followed up in 2005 and in the latest wave of the BSA in 2015 to give a long-term, if not very regular, insight into such perceptions. People were asked whether they felt that 'they have a lot in common with other people of their own class'? People could say that they felt 'pretty close to other [middle/working] class people' or that they didn't 'feel much closer to them than to people in other classes'.

The patterns are shown in Table 3.1. There is some change over time. This is most noticeable in the proportion of people seeing themselves as 'working class and close to other working class people'. This drops by 16 percentage points between 1963 and 2005, although it then increases again by 5 percentage points in 2015. Among the middle class there is an increase in the number

Table 3.1. The closeness of class identity

	1963	2005	2015
Close to middle class	15%	15%	15%
Middle class but not close	12%	22%	23%
Neither	8%	6%	5%
Working class but not close	25%	35%	29%
Close to working class	39%	23%	28%

Note: The numbers here are percentages giving each type of response to the question of whether 'they have a lot in common with other people of their own class'.

Source: British Election Study 1963; British Social Attitudes Surveys 2005 and 2015.

of people who feel middle class 'but not close' between 1963 and 2005 that does not decline in 2015. This change could be seen as a result of the rapidly growing size of the middle class groups. In both 1963 and again in 2015, the average level of closeness of people who identify with the working class is greater than it is for those who identify with middle class.[6] Overall, expressions of class identity seem to be a little less about class solidarity than they were in the 1960s, but these are rather modest changes.[7]

How People See Others

So far we have focused on possible changes in the levels and sources of a person's own class identity. But it is also important to see whether people's views of others have changed. In his post-war study, Zweig noted: 'As soon as a man opens his mouth everyone knows to which class he belongs' (Zweig 1952, p.204). Is this still true? Unfortunately we do not have the same long-running series of questions here, but in some respects we can still compare responses informatively across long periods of time.

What sorts of people are thought to belong to the middle and working classes? If the meaning of class has changed in the ways suggested by the various authors discussed previously, we might expect people to have changed their beliefs about what it is that divides classes. Indeed, they might not have views on classes and how they are distinguished at all. Typically, twentieth-century research into this issue found a consistent range of criteria were used by people to understand where people stood in the class structure. In the US the early work of Centers (1949), showing that occupation, education, and income were key, was replicated and developed by Coleman and Rainwater (1979) and Jackman and Jackman (1983). In British studies, Goldthorpe et al. (1969), Butler and Stokes (1969), Moorhouse (1976), and Marshall et al. (1988) also show that these same three criteria dominate, a similarity further confirmed by comparative work (Bell and Robinson 1980). Evidence on possible changes in the meaning of class can be obtained by simply asking people what sorts of attributes they think of when they think about people in the middle and working classes (Centers 1949; Goldthorpe al. 1969; Moorhouse 1976; Bell and Robinson 1980).

We have four waves of these questions that ask people 'what sort of people would you say belong to the middle class?', and 'what sort of people would you say belong to the working class?'. These appear in the 1963 BES (Butler and Stokes 1969), the 1984 Class in Britain survey (Marshall et al. 1988), and the 2005 and 2015 BSA surveys. The response options for these questions are, unusually for survey research, open-ended. People provide their own answers which are recorded verbatim. They are then coded *post hoc* by researchers. The coding of all such data can always be open to dispute, although some of these data are publicly available for re-analysis.[8] Moreover, they allow us to see if people's ideas about what sorts of people are working class and middle class have changed without constraining their options.[9] Table 3.2 presents the main categories of responses: occupation, income, education, and 'cultural' characteristics. These are the proportions of people who mentioned any of these characteristics. Since some people mentioned more than one thing, and we do not show all characteristics mentioned here anyway, these percentages do not add up to 100 per cent.

We can see that in 1963 62 per cent of people thought that occupation defined middle class people, and 71 per cent thought that occupation defined working class people. Jump forward forty or fifty years and we can see that occupation remained the primary characteristic associated with class membership, but less so. In general, people seem a little less inclined to judge class on the basis of occupation, but not noticeably a lot more willing to use other factors like education or income except with respect to a possible increase in references to income in relation to being working class. The same three criteria also remain dominant. In 1963 the combined total of references to occupation, income, and education was 89 per cent for the middle class and 83 per cent for the working class. Similar figures for 2015 were 79 per cent and 80 per cent.

Although interesting in themselves, these broad categories do not tell us what sorts of jobs, education, and income status are associated with being middle class or working class. We can look more closely at the responses to the Marshall et al. and BSA surveys from 1984 and 2015. For these we have comparable disaggregated coding schemes and can separate out the sorts of characteristics associated with class. We distinguish between high and low levels of education, high and low levels of income, and different types of jobs. We also show two other common responses: 'workers' and 'ordinary people'. The distributions of these in 1984 and 2015 are shown in Table 3.3.

Table 3.2. The meaning of class

	1963		1984		2005		2015	
	Middle class	Working class	Middle class	Working class	Middle class	Working class	Middle class	Working class
Occupation	62%	71%	52%	80%	50%	64%	44%	54%
Income	22%	9%	19%	18%	36%	27%	26%	20%
Education	5%	3%	3%	1%	10%	6%	9%	6%
Manners and morals	5%	6%	5%	4%	2%	2%	5%	5%

Note: The numbers here are percentages of people who mentioned particular types of characteristics when describing people in the working and middle classes.

Source: British Election Study 1963, Social Class in Modern Britain 1984; British Social Attitudes Surveys 2005 and 2015.

Here we see very clear-cut patterns of association. Middle class people are associated with white-collar jobs and good incomes. The opposite is the case for the working class: associations here are with manual workers and those with low incomes. Education has a similar pattern of class polarization to income and occupation, but this is not a pattern that features as strongly in these associations. Jobs and money dominate in very clearly class-structured ways. Again we can see the weakening of occupation as a defining characteristic, especially for the working class, but little evidence of its replacement with anything else. This declining reference to work as a characteristic of class, and thus the relative increased importance of income and education, might hint at a declining status of the working class, as might the increase in references to income noted in Table 3.2. If being working class is a more 'stigmatized' identity associated with low incomes, we might expect people to find it less easy to acknowledge class pride. Unfortunately we do not have over time survey evidence on this topic. We do, however, have two questions that ask about this issue in the 2015 BSA survey and which explicitly contrast the current situation with that of earlier periods. The first asks, 'How proud do you think people are of being working class nowadays?' and the second, 'Thinking about when you were growing up, how proud were people of being working class then?'

Table 3.4 suggests that there has been a decline in the perceived pride associated with being working class. Among everyone, as well as those with a working class identity, there was a drop in 'very proud' responses for the working class now compared to when they were growing up. These differences are not dramatic, but they are consistent with the idea of work, and its associated merits, being a less salient indicator of working class status than it used to be.

Table 3.3. Specific types of people associated with classes

	1984		2015	
	Middle class	Working class	Middle class	Working class
Business owner	17%	1%	4%	0%
White-collar job	44%	8%	32%	2%
Blue-collar job	2%	42%	1%	25%
High income	18%	0%	23%	2%
Low income	1%	17%	1%	18%
High education	3%	0%	6%	1%
Low education	0%	1%	0%	5%
'Worker'	8%	26%	6%	17%
'Ordinary people'	10%	11%	14%	11%

Note: The numbers here are percentages of people who mentioned particular types of characteristics when describing people in the working and middle classes.

Source: Social Class in Modern Britain 1984; British Social Attitudes Survey 2015.

Table 3.4. Pride in being working class

	All		Working class identifiers	
	Nowadays	When you were growing up	Nowadays	When you were growing up
Very proud	20%	30%	23%	38%
Quite proud	57%	53%	58%	51%
Not very proud	21%	16%	17%	11%
Not at all proud	2%	1%	2%	1%

Note: The table presents responses to two questions. The first asks: 'How proud do you think people are of being working class nowadays?', and the second: 'Thinking about when you were growing up, how proud were people of being working class then?' The left-hand side presents responses to these questions for all respondents and right-hand side just for those expressing an unprompted working class identity.

Source: British Social Attitudes Survey 2015.

How People See Society

The literature on the dissolving of class assumes that class divisions do not matter any more to people. But there is little actual survey evidence on this. We have therefore replicated questions first asked many years ago in the early BES surveys, to see if responses have changed on these issues. We start with the boldest of claims, that class conflict itself is in some sense inevitable. At various points in the BES and also in the 2015 BSA people were asked whether they think 'there is bound to be some conflict between different social classes' or whether 'they can get along together without any conflict'? Figure 3.6 shows the percentage of people who think that there is bound to be class conflict. The primary conclusion across the fifty years covered by these questions must be one of no clear change. There is certainly no evidence of a decline in perceptions of the inevitability of class conflict.

Class conflict is arguably a quite extreme and rare event. However, as we have seen in Chapter 2, divisions between classes can still exist in many forms and constitute more or less permanent constraints and barriers in society. It is therefore helpful to look at people's beliefs about such differences between classes, as well as perceptions of how those differences have changed. In 1970 the BES asked people 'how wide are the differences between social classes in this country' and whether they thought that 'these differences have become greater or less or have remained about the same'. We replicated these questions in the 2015 BSA. The responses in the two years are shown in Table 3.5.

In 2015 77 per cent thought class differences were fairly or very wide, compared with 51 per cent in 1970. This is a fairly substantial change. If we look at perceptions of change, we likewise see that people believe class divisions are becoming more polarized in 2015 (31 per cent) than in 1970 (12 per cent).

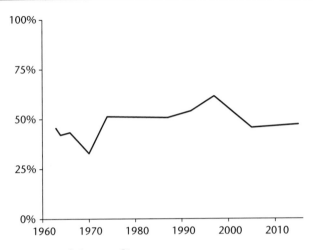

Figure 3.6. Perceptions of class conflict

Note: The figure shows percentages of respondents agreeing that 'there is bound to be some conflict between different social classes'.

Source: British Election Studies 1963–1997; British Social Attitudes Surveys 2005 and 2015.

On this evidence, in 2015 people believe we live in a more class-divided society than we used to almost half a century earlier. If the classes are divided, does this make traversing class boundaries difficult? If transitions between classes are commonplace, then it might also be less consequential that there are wide class divisions. It is important to know whether people believe it is hard to move between classes and whether classes are thought to be more permeable than in the past. We examine this issue via a question in the 1963 BES that was replicated in the 2005 and 2015 BSA which asked people, 'how difficult would you say it is for people to move from one class to another?' The responses are shown in Table 3.6. It seems that people think it is, if anything, harder to move classes than they did ten years ago. Responses are distributed somewhat differently in 1963, perhaps as a result of question framing, but the 58 per cent who thought moves between classes were hard in 1963 had increased to 65 per cent in 2005 and 73 per cent in 2015.

There are also more day-to-day indicators of class boundaries in society in terms of how people interact with people from other social classes. This is what we might call the micro-world of class divisions. There are a couple of very useful questions here too. Firstly, in 1979 the BES asked, 'When you first meet someone, how aware are you of their social class?' and 'how easy do you think it is to have friends in other social classes?'. Again we replicated these questions in 2015. Table 3.7 shows the results. In both 1979 and 2015 only one third of people say they never really notice someone's class on first

Table 3.5. Perceptions of differences between classes

The differences between classes are . . .	1970	2015
Very wide	27%	24%
Fairly wide	24%	53%
Not very wide	40%	21%
No differences	9%	2%

The differences between social classes have become . . .	1970	2015
Greater	12%	31%
About the same	59%	44%
Less	28%	24%

Note: The table shows responses to questions on 'how wide are the differences between social classes in this country' and 'whether these differences have become greater or less or have remained about the same' ('no differences between classes' includes an additional category of 'not wide' in 1970).

Source: British Election Study 1970; British Social Attitudes Survey 2015.

Table 3.6. Difficulty of moving between social classes

Moving between classes is . . .	1963	2005	2015
Very difficult	30%	19%	21%
Fairly difficult	28%	46%	52%
Not very difficult	42%	36%	26%

Note: The table shows responses to the question: 'how difficult would you say it is for people to move from one class to another?'

Source: British Election Study 1963; British Social Attitudes Surveys 2005 and 2015.

meeting. And even this is not quite a statement that they '*don't* notice a person's class' on first meeting. Either way, there is little evidence of change. Most people are aware of class when meeting people. With regard to friends, most people in both years say there is 'no difficulty' in having friends from other classes. But there is certainly no evidence that this number is increasing; in fact, it is falling. In 2015 there are 10 per cent fewer people who say cross-class friendships are easy than in 1979.

Despite the social desirability biases that are likely to affect responses to both of these questions, the difference between the years tells us that awareness of class barriers is, if anything, a little stronger now than it was in the late 1970s. This appears generally true of class perceptions. Some perceptions suggest more constancy: class conflict and social contact. Some perceptions suggest a little more class division: perceptions of wider gaps between classes and the greater difficulty of moving between classes. None suggests less division.

Table 3.7. Awareness of social class and difficulty of having friends from other social classes

Aware of someone's class...	1979	2015
Usually notice	27%	22%
Sometimes notice	40%	45%
Never really notice	33%	33%
Having friends from other classes is...	1979	2015
Hard	6%	7%
A little difficult	23%	32%
No difficulty	71%	61%

Note: The table shows responses to two questions: 'when you first meet someone, how aware are you of their social class?', and 'how easy do you think it is to have friends in other social classes?'

Source: British Election Study 1979; British Social Attitudes Survey 2015.

Conclusions

In this chapter we have shown the resilience of class identities and the persistence of people's awareness of class as a source of division. Most people still express class identities and these show no evidence of decline over the last fifty years. Moreover, unlike research in the US that has found a growing proportion of the public holding middle class identities, British people with middle class jobs are quite likely to see themselves as working class. In part, this is because class identity reflects where someone comes from as well as where they end up, and many people in middle class jobs come from working class backgrounds. Over time this tendency has even increased slightly, as educational qualifications have lost some of their power to convey a sense of being middle class. Despite fifty years of transition from an industrial to post-industrial society, expressions of a working class identity remain important. The idea that we are 'all middle class now' is very far removed from the reality of class identity in contemporary Britain.

Furthermore, it is not just in their self-perceptions that people express the persistence of class. Evidence on beliefs about the meaning of class and the extent of class divisions is less extensive, but the various indicators we have examined echo the resilience of class identities: the nature of classes, the likelihood of class conflict, whether people notice a person's class, the impact of class on friendships, the extent of class boundaries, the possibility of moving between classes, are all at least as pronounced in 2015 as they were back in the 1960s and 1970s.[10]

People are a little less likely to consider class membership to be defined by the job that someone does. This may reflect the growth in income inequality between the working class and others documented in Chapter 2. If the working class are becoming 'the poor' rather than 'the workers', then it might mean that the term could also be socially stigmatizing. Some journalists seem to have assumed this is strongly the case, and have written as though the word 'chav' is broadly synonymous with 'working class' (Jones 2011). But this seems a dramatic overstatement. The changes that we find are small, and in fact, working class identities, and class identities more generally, appear to be remarkably robust over time.

In summary, class awareness is, if anything, higher now than it was forty or fifty years ago. Changing class sizes and increased upward mobility have not weakened these indicators of social division. This pattern of continued distinctiveness is also evident when considering policy attitudes, as we do in Chapter 4. Persistent class divisions in resources, risks, opportunities, and educational attainment foster continuing differences in political ideology.

Notes

1. These are distinct from 'class consciousness', in which 'an awareness of common interests . . . leads to action through political representation' (Oddsson 2010: 293). Typically, this form of class-based political action has been expressed via class voting—'the democratic class struggle' (Anderson and Davidson 1943). We examine this in Chapters 7 and 8.
2. In the 1950s 40 per cent of people who gave a class identity in the US placed themselves in the middle class and 60 per cent in the working class. By 2000 59 per cent said middle class and 41 per cent working class.
3. It is unclear whether the recent recession might have influenced social comparisons. Evans and Kelley (2004) argue that higher unemployment might exert a downward force on self-placement in the social hierarchy as people feel worse about their position because of employment insecurity. Others have suggested that experiences of distress are cushioned because people feel themselves 'to be in the same boat' (Ragnarsdottir et al. 2013), while Oddsson (2010) believes the pressures associated with recession might increase class awareness.
4. This pattern is confirmed by multivariate logistic models of class identity that include people's own occupational class and education, and their father's occupational class. Across the period as a whole, the effects of these three factors are more or less equivalent in affecting class identity. However, by 2015 the effects of education had declined. In 2015 the impact of higher education compared to a low level of education fell to only two thirds of the overall average for the combined surveys. By contrast, the effects of own occupational class and fathers' class were indistinguishable from the average for the combined dataset.
5. A further interesting possibility is that the high proportion of working class identifiers in the middle classes may be due to such people seeing society as composed of a small privileged elite that is distinct from everyone else, including themselves, who are by comparison 'working class'. Systematic evidence on such images of the structure of society is unfortunately rather limited. However, we were able to look

at this issue using quite recent BSA data (2009), in which respondents were presented with several different distributions of inequality and asked for their views on which of them Britain was most like. There was an indication that people who described themselves as working class were more likely to see society as divided between a large disadvantaged group and a smaller privileged elite (for further analysis see Evans and Mellon 2016b).

6. This fits with Surridge's (2007, p.213) recent analysis of class identity using data from 2003, which found that working class identities are a little more salient than middle class ones when asked as part of a larger battery of different social identities: '24 per cent selected a working-class identity as one of their three primary identities, a very similar proportion to those who said they were working class in the "standard" identity question. However, only 8 per cent gave middle class as one of their three identities, compared with 19 per cent on the more usual identity question'.

7. We should also be slightly cautious about interpreting some of these changes because the 1963 answers are based on an initially prompted class question and the 2005/2015 answers are based on an initially unprompted question. This means that more people say that they are middle or working class in 1963 after the first question and may therefore feel that they 'should be' close to their class.

8. Sadly the original uncoded responses to the 1963 survey are no longer obtainable.

9. These open-ended questions also assume that people are able to access and articulate their beliefs. This assumption reflects the standard problem of recall versus recognition in survey measurement (Vanneman and Cannon 1987, pp.102–6). As it happens, indirect approaches to eliciting class-based expectations employed to address this concern (Evans 1993a, 1997; Stubager et al. 2016) produce reassuringly similar results.

10. Heath et al. (2009) found some evidence of decline in some aspects of class identity in their comparison of data from 2005 with earlier periods. It is possible that this reflected the optimism of the long-disappeared economic boom of the 'noughties'. If so, it appears to have been quickly reversed.

4

Ideology

This chapter moves away from looking at what class means to people, both objectively and subjectively, to how class shapes political ideology. Given the way in which class influences people's lives at every stage, it is unsurprising that people's occupation and education are a strong determinant of how people think that the world should be organized. In this chapter we show that occupational class and educational attainment provide a structure to views on long-standing economic issues, like redistribution and public ownership, but also non-economic moral issues and conflicts over EU integration and mass immigration. Moreover, we also show that most of this structure has remained unchanged over the last fifty years. Class, in its broader sense, still determines how people think about fairness, what the role of the state should be, and how they define what is right or wrong.

As always, there is some devil in the detail. First, while differences between classes over economic policy are largely stable there have been some changes. For economic issues, we show that differences were most pronounced during the 1980s. This means that while there was a degree of convergence during the 1990s, this still left class differences much as they were in the 1960s. Second, while economic issue positions are largely driven by occupational class, education is as important for predicting non-economic positions. It is the intertwined nature of education and occupation that generates positions towards EU integration and immigration. Other non-economic attitudes are largely divorced from people's economic situation. Issues of moral 'rights' and 'wrongs', such as attitudes towards homosexuality and child rearing, are almost exclusively driven by education.

Nonetheless, while some of the trees might be a bit different to one another, the shape of the wood is clear: people's position in society affects how they view political issues in a way that has not changed very much over the last five decades. People today may be generally less keen on privatization than they were in the 1980s, or for that matter less keen on criminal executions than they were in the 1960s, but the class distinctions that mark both of these issues are just as prevalent. At the end of this chapter we show that the broad positioning of the classes, defined in terms of occupation and education, on economic left–right issues and social authoritarianism-liberalism is remarkably consistent over time. The professional classes are centrist economically and socially liberal; the managerial and bourgeois classes are right-wing economically and socially authoritarian; the working class is left-wing economically and socially authoritarian. Just as people's experiences and views of class have not really changed, nor have class positions on the big political issues.

This chapter is organized by issues and we start with the dominant conflict within post-war British politics: the organization of the economy. Where do people stand on public ownership versus private ownership; on whether income should be redistributed; and how conflicts between employers and employees should be resolved? The second section looks at issues that are broadly separate from this major economic left–right dimension: attitudes towards immigration; the EU; law and order; and 'moral' issues such as tolerance of homosexuality and attitudes towards child rearing. The final section then imposes a structure on these disparate attitudes to show how class generally matters for political ideology.

A Bit to the Left, a Bit to the Right

Many political issues boil down to issues of ownership and equality. Should industries be privately owned? Do workers get a fair deal compared to owners? Should wealth be redistributed from those who currently own it to those who do not? These are typically what we think of as economic left–right issues and are thought to be informed by self-interest. People with less want more, and people with more want to hang on to what they already have.[1] These are therefore precisely the kind of issues that we might expect to be shaped by social class. Indeed there is plenty of evidence, from Britain and other countries, that this is the case. People in working class jobs are typically more economically egalitarian than the middle classes (Evans 1993c; Bartels 2008; Houtman et al. 2008; Weakliem and Heath 1994; Corneo and Gruner 2002; Hayes 1995; Linos and West 2002; Kalmijn and Kraaykamp 2007). As Lipset puts it: 'In all democratic nations...there has been a correlation between socioeconomic status and political beliefs and voting. The less privileged have supported parties that stood for greater equality and welfare protection, through government intervention, against the strain of a free enterprise economy' (Lipset 1991, p.208).

The problem is that most of this previous work treats these economic left–right values and attitudes rather crudely and most importantly examines just a single point in time.[2] Moreover there are divisions within the middle class that are often not taken seriously (see, however, Kalmijn and Kraaykamp 2007). People more closely connected to the marketplace (employers) and people in positions of authority (managers) are more likely to side with free market principles than the professional middle classes who are more isolated from the marketplace and managerial responsibilities. Here we take a more nuanced approach and look at the same, or very similar, questions over long periods of time, carefully identify different occupational groups, and finally separate these economic issues into three distinct elements. The first is about ownership and control. How do people think industries should be run and who benefits from capitalist institutions? The second is about equality. How do people think income and wealth should be distributed and what kind of power does wealth bring? The third is about labour relations. What role should trade unions play in society and to what extent are management and employee interests opposed to one another?

The Means of Production

We start by looking at questions of ownership and control. We focus on occupational class here, as it is by far the strongest predictor of left–right attitudes in Britain (as it is comparatively, Kalmijn and Kraaykamp 2007). Throughout this chapter, and mainly to keep the number of lines on graphs to a manageable level, we just show the old middle class, new middle class, and working class groups in all the figures. Tables also show the other major middle class group: the junior middle class. As in Chapter 3, we use a combination of data from the BES surveys (1963–2015) and the BSA surveys (1983–2015).

The left-hand graph in Figure 4.1 shows how many people support further privatization[3] from 1963 through to 2005 for the old middle class, the new middle class, and the working class. There are two obvious points to make. Support for privatization is highest in the 1980s, particularly 1983. Second, the differences between the class groups are very constant, albeit exaggerated somewhat in the early 1980s when the issue is most salient. The working class are consistently the most opposed to privatization (even in 1983 fewer than a third support further sell-offs of publically owned industries) and the old middle class are the most supportive. There is a very similar pattern when we look at who is seen to benefit from the capitalist economy. The right-hand graph in Figure 4.1 shows the proportion of people who think that 'big business benefits owners rather than workers'. The working class are quite

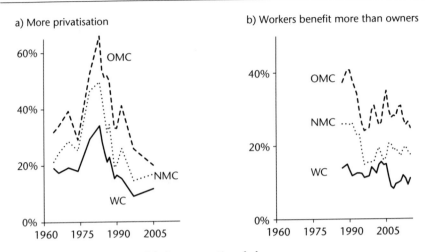

Figure 4.1. Views on ownership by occupational class

Note: The left-hand graph here shows the proportion of people who agree that there should be 'more privatization of companies by government'. The right-hand graph shows the proportion of people who disagree that 'big business benefits owners rather than workers' (two period moving average). Three occupational class groups are displayed: old middle class (OMC), new middle class (NMC), and working class (WC).

Source: British Election Studies 1963–2005; British Social Attitudes Surveys 1986–2015.

obviously the least likely to think that workers benefit, and the old middle class the most likely to think that workers benefit. Again these differences are remarkably constant over time.

Overall, it is quite clear that there are substantial differences in how people view the costs and benefits of public ownership and identify the winners and losers from the free market. These differences are primarily driven by occupational class. Table 4.1 shows results from a logit regression analysis, pooling the data by decade, for the effects of occupational class (this time for all four major occupational class groups) holding constant education level and a large number of other variables. These are: region, age group, trade union membership, sector of work, agricultural employment, housing tenure, religious denomination, gender, year, and ethnicity.[4] Controlling for all these other factors, including education, occupation still obviously matters for both attitudes towards privatization and more general views of private ownership.[5] The old middle class are most supportive of private enterprise and the working class least supportive, with the new and junior middle class groups somewhere in between. These differences are greatest in the 1980s, but are clearly present before and after then. Holding constant lots of other facets of people's lives that might be related to their occupational class does not get rid of these consistent, and substantial, differences between people in different class positions on how the economy should be organized.

Table 4.1. Impact of occupational class on attitudes towards ownership

Want more privatization	1960s	1970s	1980s	1990s	2000s	
Old middle class	24%	42%	50%	50%	18%	
New middle class	18%	41%	40%	39%	17%	
Junior middle class	21%	44%	40%	39%	15%	
Working class	17%	32%	30%	30%	12%	
Old middle class - working class	7%	10%	21%	19%	6%	
Think workers benefit from big business			1980s	1990s	2000s	2010s
Old middle class			52%	37%	39%	33%
New middle class			40%	25%	29%	25%
Junior middle class			39%	24%	26%	20%
Working class			30%	19%	21%	19%
Old middle class - working class			22%	17%	17%	14%

Note: The numbers here are predicted probabilities from logit regression models using pooled data by decade that predict agreement with the statement that there should be 'more privatization of companies by government' and disagreement with the statement that 'big business benefits owners rather than workers'. As well as occupational class, these models include controls for education, housing, trade union membership, gender, age, region, agricultural employment, religion, race, and year. Employment sector is also included in the second set of models. The predicted probabilities are for a white Anglican man in his forties, who is a homeowner, has middling educational attainment, lives in the south east of England, and is not a trade union member. Year is set as close as possible to the middle of each decade.

Source: British Election Studies 1964–2005; British Social Attitudes Surveys 1986–2015.

Some Animals Are More Equal Than Others

The second pillar of left–right ideology concerns equality, and especially equality of income and wealth. To what extent are there clear class differences in how people see inequality and in support for policies designed to rectify those inequalities? The left-hand graph in Figure 4.2 shows how opposition to the redistribution of income and wealth has changed since 1974.[6] Again it is striking how large the differences are between the occupational class groups. The old middle class is typically about 20 per cent more likely to oppose redistribution than the working class, with the new middle class generally in between. There is some evidence of small changes here as well. The gaps between groups after the mid-1990s are somewhat smaller than in the 1970s and 1980s. There is less change over time when we look at underlying notions of inequality and unfairness. The middle and right-hand graphs in Figure 4.2 show responses to questions about whether people agree that there 'is one law for the rich and one law for the poor' and whether 'ordinary people get a fair share of the wealth'. There are large differences between occupational groups from when the data starts in 1986 through to 2015. Interestingly, the differences here are much more clearly between the working class and the two middle class groups.

Table 4.2 shows estimates from a logit regression model which allows us to look at the effects of occupational class over time, controlling for all sorts of other variables. Again the data is pooled separately for each decade in order to

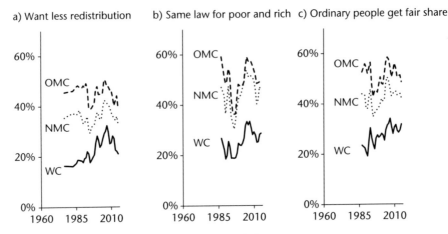

a) Want less redistribution   b) Same law for poor and rich   c) Ordinary people get fair share

Figure 4.2. Views on equality by occupational class

Note: The left-hand graph here shows the proportion of respondents who disagree that 'income and wealth should be redistributed to ordinary people' (two period moving average). The middle graph shows the proportion who agree that there is 'one law for the rich and one law for the poor' (two period moving average). The right-hand graph shows the proportion who agree that 'ordinary people get a fair share of the wealth' (two period moving average). Three occupational class groups are displayed: old middle class (OMC), new middle class (NMC), and working class (WC).

Source: British Election Studies 1974–2015; British Social Attitudes Surveys 1985–2015.

allow us to track any changes, and we include the same long list of control variables as in the previous models in Table 4.1. The story here is rather similar to the one regarding ownership. Holding everything else constant, occupational class still clearly matters. People with working class jobs consistently perceive more inequality, and want more measures to reduce inequality, than people in either the old or new middle class. While these differences are fairly stable, it is interesting that they also appear to peak in the 1980s, just as they did for attitudes towards privatization.

I'm Alright, Jack

Finally we turn to labour relations. The left-hand graph in Figure 4.3 shows how people's views of trade union power have changed since 1963.[7] And they certainly have changed. When people were asked whether trade unions had too much or too little power in the 1960s, almost everybody thought unions had too much power, but over the course of the 1980s, people's perceptions changed rapidly as the unions were defanged by a combination of mass unemployment and government legislation. In the 1960s and 1970s there was also a clear distinction between the classes as to whether unions were too powerful. The working class were considerably less likely than the two middle class groups to think unions had too much power. This divide narrowed considerably in the 1980s and although it remains the case that the old middle class

Table 4.2. Impact of occupational class on attitudes towards equality

Want less redistribution	1970s	1980s	1990s	2000s	2010s
Old middle class	35%	51%	48%	53%	47%
New middle class	31%	42%	38%	46%	40%
Junior middle class	31%	40%	39%	43%	37%
Working class	18%	28%	27%	36%	32%
Old middle class - working class	*17%*	*23%*	*21%*	*17%*	*15%*
Ordinary people get a fair share		1980s	1990s	2000s	2010s
Old middle class		70%	61%	63%	62%
New middle class		64%	52%	55%	55%
Junior middle class		62%	53%	52%	49%
Working class		48%	43%	46%	47%
Old middle class - working class		*21%*	*17%*	*18%*	*15%*
Rich and poor treated equally		1980s	1990s	2000s	2010s
Old middle class		63%	51%	61%	59%
New middle class		54%	45%	55%	54%
Junior middle class		50%	44%	51%	49%
Working class		39%	34%	45%	44%
Old middle class - working class		*24%*	*17%*	*17%*	*16%*

Note: The numbers here are predicted probabilities from logit regression models using pooled data by decade that predict a) disagreement that 'income and wealth should be redistributed to ordinary people', b) agreement that there is 'one law for the rich and one law for the poor', and c) agreement that 'ordinary people get a fair share of the wealth'. As well as occupational class, these models include controls for education, housing, trade union membership, gender, age, region, agricultural employment, religion, race, and year. Sector of employment is also included in the second and third set of models. The predicted probabilities are for a white Anglican man in his forties, who is a homeowner, has middling educational attainment and lives in the south east of England, and is not a trade union member. Year is set as close as possible to the middle of each decade.

Source: British Election Studies 1974–2015; British Social Attitudes Surveys 1986–2015.

are more worried about union power than the working class, the differences today are smaller. If we look at more underlying attitudes to employer/employee relations, we see almost no change, both in terms of absolute beliefs and also divisions between the classes. The right-hand graph in Figure 4.3 shows whether people disagree that 'management will always try to get the better of employees given the chance'. Very few working class people disagree with this, but a sizable minority of the old middle class take a more benevolent view of how those at the top of the hierarchy deal with those at the bottom. There is little change in this difference when we compare 1985 (when this question was first asked) with today. In fact, the 25 per cent gap between the old middle class and the working class in 1985 had actually increased to 28 per cent by 2015.

This divergence in underlying attitudes about labour relations from specific views on union power is not surprising, given the radical change in the nature and scale of unionization in Britain over the last fifty years. Figure 4.4 shows the proportion of people who are members of a union by their occupational class from 1963 to today. In the 1960s over 40 per cent of working class people were in

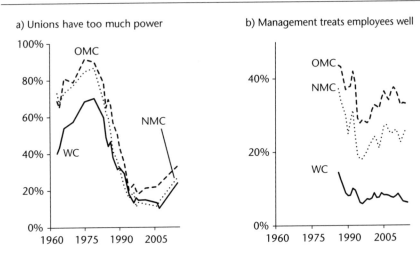

a) Unions have too much power

b) Management treats employees well

Figure 4.3. Views on labour relations by occupational class

Note: The left-hand graph here shows the proportion of people who agree that 'trade unions have too much power'. The right-hand graph shows the proportion of people who disagree that 'management will always try to get the better of employees given the chance' (two period moving average). Three occupational class groups are displayed: old middle class (OMC), new middle class (NMC), and working class (WC).

Source: British Election Studies 1974–2005; British Social Attitudes Surveys 1985–2015.

a union, but less than a quarter of the new middle class were unionized and very few members of the old middle class were affiliated with a union. Given the relative size of the working class, this meant that most union members had working class jobs. In fact, if we include foremen as well, the working class made up well over three quarters of union members in 1964. By the end of the 1990s this position was completely changed. Today, around half of union members are located in the new middle class. It is not surprising then that people outside the working class are less likely to see unions as too powerful, since any power that they do retain is increasingly used to help their predominantly middle class, and often degree-educated, membership.

In fact, once we control for education and, particularly, trade union membership, we see much less change in how unions are perceived. Table 4.3 shows percentages, derived from a model that holds constant the long list of other variables mentioned previously, of people thinking unions have too much power and who think that management does not take advantage of employees by occupational class. For the latter, the differences between the occupational groups shrink, but remain large and constant over time. More interestingly, once we hold constant some of these other factors (and, unsurprisingly, trade union membership is a particularly good predictor of how people view unions), the differences between the classes' views of union power change a

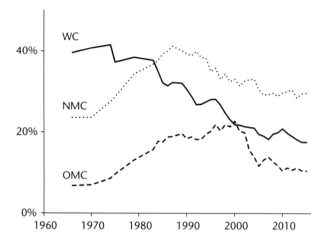

Figure 4.4. Union membership over time by occupational class

Note: The figure here shows the proportion of people who state that they are currently a member of a trade union or staff association (three period moving average). Three occupational class groups are displayed: old middle class (OMC), new middle class (NMC,) and working class (WC).

Source: British Election Studies 1963–2015; British Social Attitudes Surveys 1983–2015.

Table 4.3. Impact of occupational class on attitudes towards labour relations

Think unions have too much power	1960s	1970s	1980s	1990s	2000s	2010s
Old middle class	80%	88%	69%	39%	32%	35%
New middle class	84%	88%	61%	33%	24%	32%
Junior middle class	80%	87%	64%	34%	25%	39%
Working class	66%	77%	56%	33%	18%	26%
Old middle class - working class	*14%*	*11%*	*13%*	*6%*	*15%*	*9%*

Think management does not take advantage of employees	1980s	1990s	2000s	2010s
Old middle class	45%	36%	40%	41%
New middle class	38%	24%	28%	30%
Junior middle class	34%	24%	22%	24%
Working class	21%	14%	16%	15%
Old middle class - working class	*24%*	*22%*	*24%*	*26%*

Note: The numbers here are predicted probabilities from logit regression models using pooled data by decade that predict a) agreement that 'trade unions have too much power' and b) disagreement that 'management will always try to get the better of employees given the chance'. As well as occupational class, these models include controls for education, housing, trade union membership, gender, age, region, agricultural employment, religion, race, and year. Sector of employment is also included in the second set of models. The predicted probabilities are for a white Anglican man in his forties, who is a homeowner, has middling educational attainment and lives in the south east of England, and is not a trade union member. Year is set as close as possible to the middle of each decade.

Source: British Election Studies 1963–2015; British Social Attitudes Surveys 1985–2015.

lot less over time. The gap between the middle classes and the working class now looks almost constant. Nonetheless, it does seem that the new middle class is slightly more favourable towards unions now than it was fifty years ago. This should not surprise us given that unions look more and more like a series of professional organizations than the labour movement of old.

Different aspects of left–right economic ideology have been more or less important, and more or less divisive, at different points over the last fifty years. This means that while there does appear to be some convergence in the attitudes of occupational class groups since the 1980s, this is probably a return to the differences that existed in the 1960s and 1970s. In fact, this pattern of gently increasing difference from the 1970s to 1980s and then gently decreasing differences from the 1990s onwards is true for both support for privatization and support for redistribution. Nonetheless, we should not let these changes overshadow the most important point. What is most notable is not change, but the consistent, large differences between occupational class groups on these attitudes, even when holding constant a huge variety of other characteristics such as housing, region, age, and, importantly, education. To argue that classes are now indistinguishable from one another in terms of attitudes towards the free market is simply incorrect.

Beyond Left and Right

Although British politics is often thought to have been dominated by economic left–right issues, there are other divisions within society and within the political system. These are issues that are often thought to form a second dimension in most political systems, sometimes called the 'new politics' or the authoritarian–libertarian dimension (Kitschelt 1994, 1995; Flanagan 1987). We divide these other issues into three different policy areas. The first element concerns issues that are still related to economic concerns, but are also clearly separate from the classic capitalism versus socialism debate. This includes attitudes to EU integration and immigration. Positions on both are related to economic interests, but also wider notions of national identity and culture.

The second and third policy areas are largely separate from the economic world, however. Here we are less concerned with people's views on the rights and wrongs of the market economy and more concerned with how they see right and wrong in a moral sense. Stubager (2008, 2009, 2010) makes an extremely useful distinction between attitudes towards social hierarchies and attitudes towards social tolerance. Our second policy area taps into ideas about hierarchy and authoritarianism. How much importance should we attach to order and how much power should we give to those who uphold that order? This particularly includes attitudes towards people who break the law and subvert that order. In other words, to what extent should the state focus on punishing criminals for their crimes? The third of our policy areas is about social tolerance. This is perhaps best thought of as moral conservatism. Should people with 'unconventional' lifestyles be tolerated or should they be forced to conform?

These are all important issues in the political realm, and there is a great deal of evidence that occupation and education matter for how people weigh their pros and cons. For EU membership and immigration, these are differences that are partially motivated by the same economic concerns as we have already seen: further immigration and EU integration is less appealing to people who do not economically benefit. More generally, there is a long-standing body of research that suggests that occupation and education matter for both authoritarianism and tolerance. Lipset's famous maxim that 'the more well-to-do are more liberal, the poorer are more intolerant' (Lipset 1959, p.102) sums up much early research that built on Adorno et al.'s classic, albeit now somewhat discredited, work *The Authoritarian Personality* (1950). There is further nuance to Lipset's findings, however. He actually shows repeatedly the now standard finding that, on a ladder of tolerance and liberalism, it is those in professional jobs, our new middle class, who are at the top, with the working class at the bottom and the old middle class somewhere in the middle. Later work has questioned the universalism of this relationship, often suggesting that education, not occupation, is the most important factor (Dekker and Ester 1987; Houtman 2003; Ray 1983; Weakliem 2002).

There are different models for how education shapes attitudes, although it seems that socialization within the educational system is most important (Stubager 2008). It is less clear exactly how this happens. Some argue for a direct impact of the educational curriculum. Supporting this claim, there is evidence that field of study is important in shaping attitudes; people with humanities and social sciences degrees are more socially liberal due to the nature of their courses than those with natural science or business degrees (van de Werfhorst and de Graaf 2004; van de Werfhorst and Kraaykamp 2001; Surridge 2016). Others claim that most of these education effects are due to selection into different educational trajectories by people with different views (Lancee and Sarrasin 2015). There is undoubtedly also a reinforcing effect of tutors' predominantly liberal views and conformity with fellow students' liberal views (Jacobsen 2001).

Regardless of the exact mechanisms, there is no doubt that education, and maybe occupation, are linked to social liberalism. In the next section we disentangle the different aspects of this dimension of politics into three: attitudes towards other nationalities and supra-national cooperation; attitudes towards authoritarianism, especially with regards to crime; and moral conservatives, especially attitudes towards tolerance of particular groups.

Bloody Foreigners

We start by looking at attitudes towards immigration and EU membership. These are in some ways closest to economic issues. After all, they involve economic costs and benefits that affect different types of people in different ways. Indeed, historically, attitudes towards the EU were generally thought to be shaped by people's levels of human capital. This meant that people in professional jobs with lots of education (who were well placed to benefit from the market opportunities that flowed from the EU integration process) were broadly supportive of the EU, while people with fewer marketable skills who occupied a more vulnerable economic position were more sceptical about EU integration (Anderson and Reichert 1995; Gabel and Palmer 1995; Gabel 1998a; Gabel 1998b; Balestrini 2012; Hobolt 2014). This is a direct way of thinking about how self-interest, embodied in social class, affects attitudes. There is also a more indirect way, however, because while attitudes towards these issues are affected by economic concerns, 'cultural' concerns are also very important. It is now widely recognized that support for EU integration is partially a function of group loyalties and cultural threat (McLaren 2002, 2004, 2006, 2007; Hooghe and Marks 2004, 2005; Garry and Tilley 2009; van Klingeren et al. 2013). Since views of national identity and cosmopolitanism are often produced by educational and occupational experiences,[8] both these external economic and cultural threats to people are likely to be shaped by their social class. Very similar arguments about both economic and cultural threats are typically made for how people think about immigration policy.[9]

The above points to a greater role for education in determining these attitudes. Occupational class certainly matters for economic threat, but less so for cultural threat, whereas education matters for both economic and cultural threat. Figures 4.5 and 4.6 therefore show how attitudes towards these two issues have changed since the 1960s by both occupational class and education. As there has been no continuously asked series of questions over this period of time, Figure 4.5 uses a number of different questions to measure opposition to immigration.[10] This means that changes in the average level of opposition to immigration are not necessarily easy to interpret. Even if it were the same question over time, since the most common formulation asks whether there is 'too much immigration', this could simply reflect changes in actual levels, or types of, immigration.

More important for our purposes are the differences among groups. The occupational class markers we use are the same as those discussed previously, but we also show the effects of education. As discussed in Chapter 1, we mainly show the differences among the three main groups of high education (people with a degree), medium education (left school at 17/18 or A Level equivalent qualifications), and low education (left school at minimum leaving age or no qualifications).

As Figure 4.5 shows, people's views on immigration are related to both education and occupational class. People in working class jobs with low levels of education are most opposed to immigration, and people in new middle class jobs with degrees are the least opposed. Note that it is the new middle class group that is most enthusiastic about immigration, as we expected. These differences are relatively large, especially for education, and very constant. While opposition to immigration has generally risen over time, whether due to real increases in immigration rates, changing views about immigration, or changed question wording, the differences among groups have remained the same or actually increased.

There is a similar story for opposition to EU membership, shown in Figure 4.6. Here we show opposition to joining the Common Market prior to the 1970s and then subsequently support for withdrawal from the EEC/EC/EU.[11] Clearly levels of opposition to EU membership vary quite dramatically over time, peaking in the 1970s and early 1980s, then falling dramatically, before rising again towards the end of the 2000s. While it is almost always the case that the same groups are most opposed to EU membership (the working class and the least educated), the differences between people do change a little over time. In particular the gaps between class and educational groups are larger in the early 1980s and 2010s.

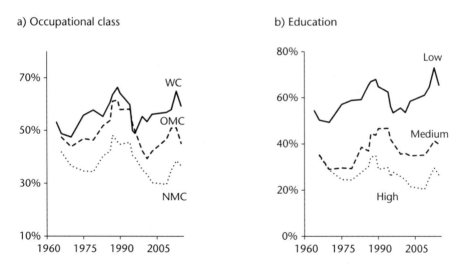

Figure 4.5. Strongly against more immigration by occupational class and education

Note: The figures here show the proportion of people who strongly agree that immigration should be reduced, or a close variant of this question (two period moving average). The left-hand graph disaggregates the results by occupational class; the right-hand graph disaggregates the results by education. Three occupational class groups are displayed: old middle class (OMC), new middle class (NMC), and working class (WC). Three educational groups are displayed: people with degree-level education (high), people with A Level equivalent education (medium), and people who left school at the minimum school leaving age for their cohort (low).

Source: British Election Studies 1963–2015; British Social Attitudes Surveys 1986–2013.

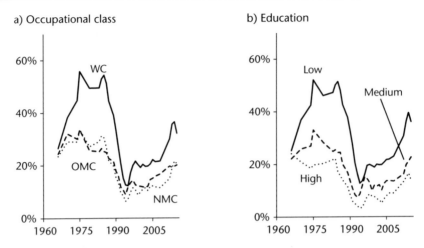

Figure 4.6. Against EU membership by occupational class and education

Note: The figures here show the proportion of people who agree that Britain should leave the EU, or not join the EEC in earlier years (three period moving average). The left-hand graph disaggregates the results by occupational class; the right-hand graph disaggregates the results by education. Three occupational class groups are displayed: old middle class (OMC), new middle class (NMC), and working class (WC). Three educational groups are displayed: people with degree-level education (high), people with A Level equivalent education (medium), and people who left school at the minimum school leaving age for their cohort (low).

Source: British Election Studies 1963–2015; British Social Attitudes Surveys 1986–2013.

Tables 4.4 and 4.5 back up these conclusions. Here we show the effects of occupation controlling for education, and vice versa, on opposition to immigration and EU membership respectively. We also hold constant the litany of other factors mentioned previously such as ethnicity, trade union membership, and age group. Both occupational class and education matter, although here it is education that dominates, and both have a constant effect over time. It is the two groups that are shrinking—the working class and those with low levels of education—that are most opposed to immigration and EU membership. These patterns are fairly constant, especially for immigration, but it is also clear that the divisions today between educational and class groups are some of the largest that we have seen in the post-war period.

Crime and Punishment

Although Lipset (1959) makes little direct reference to how class shapes attitudes towards law and order, the clear implication is that the working class and people with less education have more punitive views towards criminals. Many authors have conceptualized authoritarianism in terms of attitudes towards criminals (Ray 1982). In Britain, Heath et al. (1985, 1991) argue that

Table 4.4. Impact of occupational class and education on attitudes towards immigration

Want less immigration	1960s	1970s	1980s	1990s	2000s	2010s
Old middle class	44%	40%	67%	54%	63%	57%
New middle class	42%	34%	69%	51%	48%	54%
Junior middle class	42%	43%	68%	54%	52%	59%
Working class	42%	44%	61%	56%	59%	63%
Old middle class – working class	− 1%	−11%	−9%	−5%	−11%	−8%
High education (degree)	36%	27%	47%	32%	28%	29%
Medium education (A Level)	41%	30%	63%	43%	42%	46%
Low education (school leaving age)	53%	49%	72%	56%	61%	62%
High education – low education	−16%	−22%	−25%	−24%	−33%	−33%

Note: The numbers here are predicted probabilities from logit regression models using pooled data by decade that predict agreement that immigration should be reduced (or a close variant of this question). As well as occupational class and education, these models include controls for housing, trade union membership, gender, age, region, agricultural employment, religion, race, and year. The predicted class probabilities are for a white Anglican man in his 40s, who is a homeowner, has middling educational attainment and lives in the south east of England, and is not a trade union member. The predicted education probabilities are for the same type of person in the junior middle class category. Year is set as close as possible to the middle of each decade.

Source: British Election Studies 1963–2015; British Social Attitudes Surveys 1986–2013.

Table 4.5. Impact of occupational class and education on attitudes towards the EU

Support leaving EU	1960s	1970s	1980s	1990s	2000s	2010s
Old middle class	33%	22%	28%	22%	22%	26%
New middle class	31%	22%	32%	20%	22%	33%
Junior middle class	38%	28%	33%	24%	26%	34%
Working class	36%	34%	42%	28%	28%	38%
Old middle class – working class	−3%	−12%	−14%	−6%	−6%	−12%
High education (degree)	32%	38%	19%	12%	14%	19%
Medium education (A Level)	29%	41%	26%	18%	22%	27%
Low education (school leaving age)	31%	53%	42%	26%	28%	42%
High education – low education	1%	−15%	−23%	−15%	−14%	−23%

Note: The numbers here are predicted probabilities from logit regression models using pooled data by decade that predict agreement that Britain should leave the EU (or not join in earlier years). As well as occupational class and education, these models include controls for housing, trade union membership, gender, age, region, agricultural employment, religion, race, and year. The predicted class probabilities are for a white Anglican man in his forties, who is a homeowner, has middling educational attainment and lives in the south east of England, and is not a trade union member. The predicted education probabilities are for the same type of person in the junior middle class category. Year is set as close as possible to the middle of each decade.

Source: British Election Studies 1963–2015; British Social Attitudes Surveys 1986–2013.

attitudes towards crime and the death penalty form a core part of the second dimension of politics in Britain and education is a key part of explaining divisions on issues within the middle class occupational groups. This is echoed by more recent work that focuses on education and how the educational system instils 'in students a set of libertarian values that continue to influence their thinking long after they have completed their education' (Stubager 2008, p.331; see Surridge 2016 on the British case).

a) Occupational class   b) Education

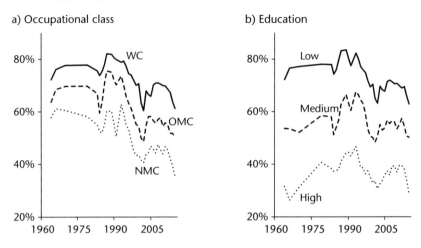

Figure 4.7. Support death penalty by occupational class and education

Note: The figures here show the proportion of people who agree that the death penalty should be reintroduced, or retained in earlier years (two period moving average). The left-hand graph disaggregates the results by occupational class; the right-hand graph disaggregates the results by education. Three occupational class groups are displayed: old middle class (OMC), new middle class (NMC), and working class (WC). Three educational groups are displayed: people with degree-level education (high), people with A Level equivalent education (medium), and people who left school at the minimum school leaving age for their cohort (low).

Source: British Election Studies 1963–2001; British Social Attitudes Surveys 1983–2015.

It is therefore not surprising that Figures 4.7 and 4.8 show that support for the death penalty[12] and stiffer sentences for criminals in Britain over time are strongly related to occupational class and education. People in the working class are about 20 percentage points more likely to support the death penalty than people in the new middle class, and while overall support has dropped a little since the 1990s, this gap is actually larger today than it was fifty years ago. These differences are even bigger by education, with 30–40 percentage point gaps between the most and least educated groups. Similar points can be made about the proportion of people who strongly agree with the statement, 'people who break the law should be given stiffer sentences'; the working class and those with the least education consistently favour the harshest measures against criminals. These differences are large (10–20 per cent gaps between the working class and the new middle class and 20–30 per cent gaps between the most and least educated) and barely change over time.

Interestingly, while the differences by occupational class are reduced when we hold constant other characteristics of people (the same long list as before including education), the differences by education remain almost the same. Table 4.6 shows that occupational class still affects how people view the death penalty, but there is now less than a ten percentage point gap between the

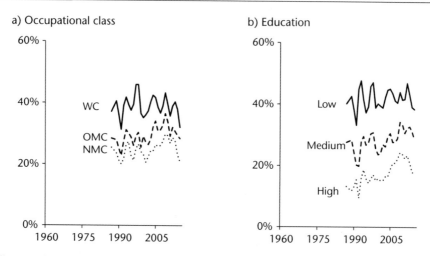

a) Occupational class

b) Education

Figure 4.8. Strongly support stiffer sentences by occupational class and education

Note: The figures here show the proportion of people who strongly agree that 'people who break the law should be given stiffer sentences' (two period moving average). The left-hand graph disaggregates the results by occupational class; the right-hand graph disaggregates the results by education. Three occupational class groups are displayed: old middle class (OMC), new middle class (NMC), and working class (WC). Three educational groups are displayed: people with degree-level education (high), people with A Level equivalent education (medium), and people who left school at the minimum school leaving age for their cohort (low).

Source: British Election Studies 1987–2001; British Social Attitudes Surveys 1986–2015.

new middle class and the working class. The differences on sentencing by occupational class are almost zero and we do not show them here. By contrast education matters for both attitudes. The differences between those with medium and low levels of education are at least ten percentage points for both sentencing and the death penalty, and are unchanged over fifty years. There are even larger gaps between those with high and low levels of education.

There is some change over time. While people with degrees are consistently the most relaxed about punishment, this group is more authoritarian than it used to be. The gap on support for the death penalty between the least and most educated has dropped by about 10 percentage points since the 1960s, although it remains at nearly 30 per cent. This is almost entirely due to the increasing illiberalism of those with degrees. This is perhaps not surprising since those with degrees in 2013 are a larger and more heterogeneous group than they were in 1963. If we think of the ways that higher education may liberalize people, then it is likely to prove less effective when higher education is no longer such an immersive experience. As more students work and study part-time, or live at home rather than on campus, it seems likely that these socialization effects may weaken.[13]

Table 4.6. Impact of occupational class and education on attitudes towards the death penalty and stiffer criminal sentences

Support death penalty	1960s	1970s	1980s	1990s	2000s	2010s
Old middle class	70%	62%	70%	71%	72%	66%
New middle class	67%	56%	63%	66%	69%	61%
Junior middle class	74%	61%	68%	71%	72%	66%
Working class	73%	65%	71%	74%	76%	70%
New middle class – working class	−7%	−10%	−7%	−8%	−7%	−10%
High education (degree)	36%	34%	39%	44%	46%	44%
Medium education (A Level)	65%	59%	60%	63%	63%	62%
Low education (school leaving age)	76%	71%	76%	75%	74%	72%
High education – low education	−40%	−37%	−37%	−32%	−28%	−29%

Strongly support stiffer sentences			1980s	1990s	2000s	2010s
High education (degree)			12%	15%	20%	17%
Medium education (A Level)			24%	25%	28%	27%
Low education (school leaving age)			33%	34%	41%	35%
High education – low education			−21%	−20%	−21%	−19%

Note: The numbers here are predicted probabilities from logit regression models using pooled data by decade that predict a) agreement with the reintroduction (or retention in earlier years) of the death penalty and b) strong agreement that 'people who break the law should be given stiffer sentences'. As well as occupational class and education, these models include controls for housing, trade union membership, gender, age, region, agricultural employment, religion, race, and year. The predicted class probabilities are for a white Anglican man in his forties, who is a homeowner, has middling educational attainment and lives in the south east of England, and is not a trade union member. The predicted education probabilities are for the same type of person in the junior middle class category. Year is set as close as possible to the middle of each decade.

Source: British Election Studies 1963–2001; British Social Attitudes Surveys 1983–2015.

Nowt as Queer as Folk

The final set of attitudes that we are interested in relate to what might be termed moral questions: how people think about questions to do with sex and 'traditional values'. Here the recent emphasis has also been on the role of education (for example, Lottes and Kuriloff 1994; Kalmijn and Kraaykamp 2007). Nonetheless, there is also a tradition of thinking about how occupational class matters for these attitudes, with the presumption that middle class people are typically more tolerant of certain groups.[14] There is some cross-national evidence for this when it comes to attitudes towards homosexuality (Andersen and Fetner 2008) and we find similar patterns in Britain. When people are asked whether they agree that 'sexual relations between two adults of the same sex is always wrong', there are substantial differences by occupational class and education. Figure 4.9 shows these differences from the early 1980s until today. The rate and scope of change is quite striking: while a substantial majority of people thought homosexuality was always wrong in the 1980s, this compares to only a small minority now. Of all the attitudes that we look at in this chapter it is probably the one for which we see the most far-reaching and most consistent change over time.[15] Just as importantly, there are clear and consistent effects of class and education. The new middle class and those with degrees are the most tolerant, and this remains unchanged over time.

This pattern is not entirely replicated when we look at other 'moral' issues. People's views about censorship and whether young people are respectful enough are shaped by education, but not by occupational class. Figure 4.10 therefore just shows differences by education in support for the statements that 'censorship of films and magazines is necessary to uphold moral standards' and 'young people today don't have enough respect for traditional British values'.[16] There are huge differences by educational attainment in relation to whether young people are respectful enough, and sizable effects for how education shapes attitudes towards censorship. More education means that you are less worried about young people's lack of respect and less willing to endorse censorship, or at least censorship of a particular kind that 'upholds moral standards'.

Of course, all these differences seem likely to be related not just to education but to religiosity and age which are themselves correlated with education. If anything is a constant of history it is older people complaining about the youth of today. Nonetheless, Table 4.7 shows that even controlling for religion and birth cohort, alongside the long list of other variables that we used before, differences by education for both questions remain. These

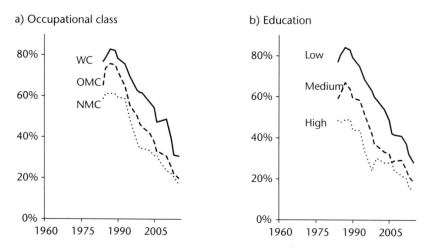

Figure 4.9. Agree homosexuality is wrong by occupational class and education

Note: The figures here show the proportion of people who agree that 'sexual relations between two adults of the same sex is always wrong' (two period moving average). The left-hand graph disaggregates the results by occupational class; the right-hand graph disaggregates the results by education. Three occupational class groups are displayed: old middle class (OMC), new middle class (NMC), and working class (WC). Three educational groups are displayed: people with degree-level education (high), people with A Level equivalent education (medium), and people who left school at the minimum school leaving age for their cohort (low).

Source: British Social Attitudes Surveys 1983–2015.

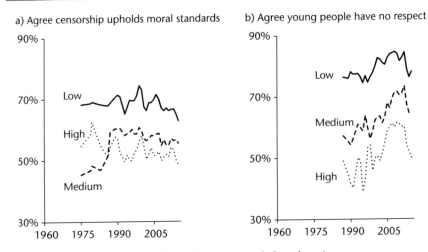

a) Agree censorship upholds moral standards

b) Agree young people have no respect

Figure 4.10. Views on censorship and young people by education

Note: The left-hand graph here shows the proportion of people who agree that 'censorship of films and magazines is necessary to uphold moral standards' (two period moving average). The right-hand graph shows the proportion who agree that 'young people today don't have enough respect for traditional British values' (two period moving average). Three educational groups are displayed: people with degree-level education (high), people with A Level equivalent education (medium), and people who left school at the minimum school leaving age for their cohort (low).

Source: British Election Studies 1974–2015; British Social Attitudes Surveys 1986–2015.

differences are very constant over time and still large. There are about 20 percentage points separating those with high and low levels of education for both the question about homosexuality and the question about young people's levels of respect.

Putting It All Together

What the above discussion, and associated tables and figures, illustrates is that class mattered, and continues to matter, for how people view political and social issues. Occupational class is a good predictor of how people view all aspects of how the market should be constrained. Education, and to a lesser extent occupation, shape how people view other political issues from immigration to the death penalty. The public as a whole have changed their minds on some of these issues: few people think homosexuality is wrong or that unions are too powerful today. What remains constant are the differences in how people think about these questions with regard to their own formative and current circumstances. Someone's place in the occupational structure and their educational experiences shape how they see the world just as much today as they did fifty years ago.

Table 4.7. Impact of occupational class and education on attitudes towards homosexuality, young people, and censorship

Agree homosexuality is wrong		1980s	1990s	2000s	2010s
Old middle class		76%	58%	38%	35%
New middle class		73%	58%	39%	35%
Junior middle class		76%	60%	37%	38%
Working class		77%	64%	49%	49%
New middle class – working class		−5%	−7%	−10%	−14%
High education (degree)		61%	36%	24%	19%
Medium education (A Level)		77%	52%	31%	25%
Low education (school leaving age)		86%	69%	44%	37%
High education – low education		−26%	−32%	−20%	−18%
Agree young people have no respect		**1980s**	**1990s**	**2000s**	**2010s**
High education (degree)		63%	57%	69%	57%
Medium education (A Level)		75%	71%	78%	73%
Low education (school leaving age)		82%	78%	86%	78%
High education – low education		−19%	−21%	−17%	−22%
Agree censorship upholds moral standards	**1970s**	**1980s**	**1990s**	**2000s**	**2010s**
High education (degree)	69%	71%	56%	57%	60%
Medium education (A Level)	57%	75%	63%	64%	69%
Low education (school leaving age)	69%	78%	69%	72%	72%
High education – low education	–	−7%	−13%	−15%	−12%

Note: The numbers here are predicted probabilities from logit regression models using pooled data by decade that predict a) agreement that 'sexual relations between two adults of the same sex is always wrong', b) agreement that 'censorship of films and magazines is necessary to uphold moral standards', and c) agreement that 'young people today don't have enough respect for traditional British values'. As well as occupational class and education, these models include controls for housing, trade union membership, gender, age, region, agricultural employment, religion, race, and year. The predicted class probabilities are for a white Anglican man in his forties, who is a homeowner, has middling educational attainment and lives in the south east of England, and is not a trade union member. The predicted education probabilities are for the same type of person in the junior middle class category. Year is set as close as possible to the middle of each decade.

Source: British Election Studies 1974–2015; British Social Attitudes Surveys 1986–2015.

This can be seen most clearly if we group some of these issues to make two ideological dimensions on which people can be placed. This is a common strategy in Britain (Heath et al. 1994; Evans et al. 1996), the US (Ansolabehere et al. 2008; Fleishman 1988) and other Western countries (Grunberg and Schweisguth 1993; Middeldorp et al. 1993) and typically assumes that political systems have divisions along economic and 'new politics' lines (Kitschelt 1994; Flanagan 1987). We reduce political placements to a position on economic issues and a position on a set of moral/authoritarian issues. We are thus looking at the long-standing economic cleavage, largely driven by occupational class, and the 'new politics' cleavage, largely driven by education. We exclude, for the moment, the issues of immigration and EU integration.

Creating scales to measure people's positions on these two dimensions is not a straightforward task as there are few questions that actually span the entire time period consistently. For the 1960s–1980s, we measure someone's left–right position using the questions on trade unions and privatization and their position on the second dimension using the question on the death penalty. For 1986–2015 we have a much better set of measures. These are composed of five questions for economic left–right ideology and five questions for social conservative–liberal ideology. Variations of these scales are widely used and have been extensively validated (Heath et al. 1994; Evans et al. 1996; Evans and Heath 1995; Sturgis 2002; Cheng et al. 2012).

For the left–right scale for the earlier period, we add up positive responses and divide by two. The left–right score is thus the average number of people who agreed with more privatization and that unions have too much power, and the conservative–liberal score is simply the number of people who agreed that the death penalty was wrong. High scores on the left–right measure mean that someone is more right-wing, and high scores on the conservative–liberal measure mean that someone is more liberal. We do something similar for the later period. Here we have five questions that relate to left and right with responses from 'strongly agree' to 'strongly disagree', and five questions that relate to conservative and liberal with responses from 'strongly agree' to 'strongly disagree'. The first five are all questions that we have looked at individually: whether people want less redistribution, whether there is the same law for rich and poor, whether ordinary people get a fair share of the wealth, whether workers benefit more than owners and whether management treats employees well. These are added together and transformed to give a 0–1 scale. 1 on this scale represents people who said 'strongly agree' to all of these statements (the most right-wing response); 0 represents people who said 'strongly disagree' to all these statements (the most left-wing response). For the conservative–liberal scale we again use five questions. These relate to: opposition to the death penalty, opposition to stiffer sentences, support for gay rights, opposition to censorship, and support for young people. These are the same questions discussed earlier in the chapter. Again we scale the answers, with 0 the score for people who strongly disagreed with all the statements (the most conservative response) and 1 the score for people who agreed with all the statements (the most liberal response).[17]

Given these scales we can track different groups over time in a 2-dimensional space. In order to make these easier to visualize we show three groups that combine educational and occupational characteristics. With apologies to Marx, these are the *proletariat* (people in working class jobs with low levels of education), the *intelligentsia* (people in new middle class jobs with high levels of education), and the *bourgeoisie* (people in old middle class jobs with middling educational levels). These groups represent different sections of society, one growing rapidly in the last few decades (the intelligentsia) and one declining in recent decades (the proletariat). The actual number of people in these precise groups may not always be huge, but they allow us to see how education and occupation combine to produce different kinds of attitudes.[18] Figure 4.11 shows how these groups have changed over time on the two scales; the first graph shows the 1960s–1980s and the second the 1980s–2010s. Note that these figures come from statistical models that hold constant all other variables that we have used previously, for example, trade union membership and age.[19]

Focusing on the underlying attitudinal structure, across multiple attitudes, throws the patterns that we have already found into starker relief. Figure 4.11 shows distinct groups of people with distinct attitudes and these never overlap. In every decade, the proletariat are always the most left-wing and always the most socially conservative. The intelligentsia is always the most socially liberal, and always more right-wing than the proletariat. The bourgeoisie is always the most right-wing and is always less liberal than the intelligentsia. These differences are remarkably consistent over a long period of time. These differences are also large. For the more reliable measures of both dimensions in the second graph, the difference between the intelligentsia and the proletariat is almost a standard deviation on the conservative-liberal scale and the difference between the bourgeoisie and the proletariat is about three quarters of a standard deviation on the economic left–right scale.

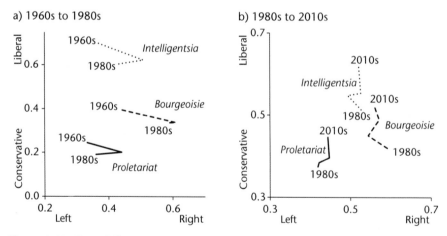

Figure 4.11. How different groups have moved positions on the economic left–right and social conservative–liberal dimensions

Note: The figures here show predicted probabilities from linear regression models using pooled data by decade that predict scores on left–right and social liberal–conservative 0–1 scales. The left-hand graph shows results from the 1960s to the 1980s; the right-hand graph shows results for the 1980s to the 2010s. Higher scores indicate more economically right and socially liberal responses. As well as occupational class and education, these models include controls for housing, trade union membership, gender, age, region, agricultural employment, religion, race, sector of employment, and year. The three groups are low education and a working class occupation (proletariat), medium education and an old middle class occupation (bourgeoisie), and high education and a new middle class occupation (intelligentsia).

Source: British Election Studies 1963–1987; British Social Attitudes Surveys 1986–2015.

Of course, this is not to say that nothing changes. Looking at the 1980s onwards, the most noticeable change is that people have become a little more socially liberal (about a third of a standard deviation of the scale). This is despite holding constant religion and race. Interestingly, this move towards a more liberal world view is least pronounced among the proletariat. Class differences on this dimension have actually slightly increased. There is less change in terms of left and right over the same period, although the 1990s stand out as a slightly more left-wing period, especially with regard to the two middle class groups. It is more difficult to talk about change in the earlier period since we are reliant on very few questions. It does appear that people became more right-wing in the 1980s compared to the 1960s, or at least they became fonder of privatization and less fond of trade unions, but this altered the differences between the three groups only marginally. People also became less opposed to the death penalty between the 1960s and 1980s as well, a change we already saw in Figure 4.7.[20]

This analysis leaves out two issues where we saw the most change: the EU and immigration. While these are related to the second dimension, in that people who are less socially liberal are typically more opposed to EU membership and further immigration, they are also separate in terms of their policy implications and the more economic mechanisms that underpin these beliefs. How did the attitudes of the three archetypes discussed above change with regard to these issues? Figure 4.12 shows this. Here we combine the two questions on the EU and immigration to give a similar 0–1 scale, where 0 indicates people who strongly disapprove of further immigration and wish to withdraw from the EU and 1 indicates people who advocate neither of these positions. Again, these figures come from regression models that hold constant the same wide variety of other factors used before. It is interesting to examine the three groups separately. The bourgeoisie's position is fairly static. The intelligentsia becomes steadily more pro-EU and pro-immigration over the period, with a slight reverse in the 2010s. But it is the proletariat group which changes its views most distinctively. The proletariat always have the most Eurosceptic and anti-immigration views, but this disparity between them and the two middle class groups is widest in the 1970s and particularly in the 2010s. On at least these two issues, class differences actually appear to have widened slightly.

Conclusions

Chapters 2 and 3 have emphasized that people's experiences and perceptions of class in Britain have changed remarkably little over the last fifty years. It is therefore not that surprising that the way in which class and education influence political ideology has also remained the same. There is little

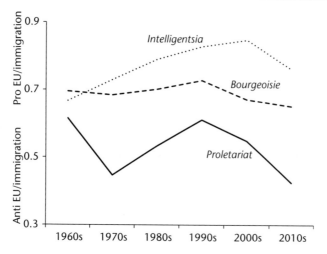

Figure 4.12. How different groups have moved positions on the immigration/EU dimension

Note: The figure here shows predicted probabilities from linear regression models using pooled data by decade that predict scores on an EU/immigration 0–1 scale. Higher scores indicate greater support for EU integration and immigration. As well as occupational class and education, these models include controls for housing, trade union membership, gender, age, region, agricultural employment, religion, race, and year. The three groups are low education and a working class occupation (proletariat), medium education and an old middle class occupation (bourgeoisie), and high education and a new middle class occupation (intelligentsia).

Source: British Election Studies 1963–2015; British Social Attitudes Surveys 1986–2013.

evidence in this chapter of the declining importance of class. People in working class jobs still think that the market economy does not benefit them as much as it does the middle classes, and are more supportive of public ownership, trade unions, and redistribution than anyone else. Equally, education and occupation still shape people's views of right and wrong: middle class people with more education are systematically the most socially liberal group and most in favour of EU integration and mass immigration.

This lack of change in the differences between educational and occupational groups disguises one important fact, however. The differences between the *average person* and different educational and occupational groups have changed because the number of people in those different groups has changed. When people who had a working class job and left school with few, if any, qualifications were the majority of the population, the average position of British society was similar to people in this majority. As this group, our stylized proletariat, shrinks, it starts to look rather different to the average person. If we assume no change over time *within* groups then the average person is constantly moving away from the proletariat over time. Assuming there is no change within groups for the high-quality scale measures of left–right and conservative–liberal attitudes, the proletariat are about one quarter of a standard deviation more left-wing and about a tenth of a standard deviation more socially conservative than the average person in the 1960s. By the 2010s the proletariat group are a half of a standard deviation more left-wing and a third of a standard deviation more socially conservative than the average person. Differences between the groups may have remained rather static, but the position of the working class group has become more dissimilar from the typical voter, because the typical voter is now more educated and more middle class. Why does this matter? It matters because rational politicians, especially when faced with a first past the post electoral system, should change their policies to match the average voter. As the average voter moves away from the working class, so should the parties. As we see in Chapter 6, this is broadly what has happened.

It is also important to make clear that there have been some changes. In particular, there has been modest convergence between occupational classes on some of the economic left–right issues since the 1980s. Nonetheless, this essentially entails a return to the status quo of the 1960s, rather than a long run convergence of views between classes. There have also been modest increases in class and education disparities in terms of attitudes towards immigration and the EU in recent years. In that sense, aspects of underlying class conflict appear to be greater now than they were previously. Of course, for that to be politically salient, parties need to do something about it, and voters need to know about that class conflict and party responses to it. For most people, a key source of information about society and politics is the media. And so in Chapter 5 we look at how media coverage of class and politics has changed, before in Chapter 6 turning to how parties themselves have changed.

Notes

1. Some have argued that self-interest does not drive political attitudes. Rather, what matters is people's 'conditioning in their pre-adult years, with little calculation of the future costs and benefits of these attitudes' (Sears et al. 1980, p.671). Although this work on 'symbolic politics' by Sears has been very influential (Sears et al. 1980; Sears 1975, 1983, 1993), it is in practice very difficult to separate out conditioning and socialization factors from social characteristics. It is also worth noting that Sears finds that education and income (a weaker measure of class than occupation anyway) are strong predictors of attitudes, even holding constant what he terms symbolic attitudes, such as party identification.

2. For example, in Bartels' 2008 book *Unequal Democracy*, he provides various rich sources of evidence about how income inequality affects, and is affected by, politics in the US, but he is only able to track consistently one attitudinal question about economic issues, specifically whether 'the government should see to it that every person has a job'. Even that is only for 1972–2004, and he can only compare broad

income groups over time. Those looking at Britain have typically had access to a wider range of repeated questions, and better measures of class, but what work there is over time in Britain is now also rather out of date. Heath et al. (1991) look at both economic and non-economic values for the four British general election studies from 1974–1987, but given this time period is barely more than a decade, it seems insufficient to make lasting judgements about long-term change. While Evans (1993a) covers a longer time period (1964–1987), his data ends almost thirty years ago and is a comparison of only two cross-sectional surveys.

3. The question is worded slightly differently depending on the survey, but essentially asks whether people would prefer 'more nationalization of companies by govern-ment', 'more privatization of companies by government', or for things to stay the same. In some years people are also asked whether they would like a lot more or a little more nationalization/privatization. We compare here people who say they want more privatization to everyone else.

4. These control variables are measured slightly differently for the 1963–2005 period that covers the privatization measure and 1986–2015 period that covers the ques-tion about who benefits. In general, the measures that cover a longer time period are somewhat weaker, and those from the mid-1980s onwards are somewhat stronger. For example, the regional measure for the full 1963–2015 data has six categories, whereas the regional measure for the period that starts in 1986 has eleven categories. Full details of the control measures used are included in Appen-dix A4.1.

5. Sector of work cannot be measured before the late 1970s and so is not included in the models that predict privatization attitudes. Interestingly, if we model attitudes towards privatization from the 1980s onwards we see that while employment sector does shape people's attitudes about the merits of the free market, it has less effect than occupational class. This rather puts the lie to the claim made in the 1980s that sectoral divisions would become the most important source of conflict in British politics (Dunleavy 1980, 1986; Dunleavy and Husbands 1985).

6. The exact question is almost identical from year to year and asks whether people agree that 'income and wealth should be redistributed to ordinary working people' with 'strongly agree' to 'strongly disagree' as possible responses. We show the proportion of people who disagree with the statement (either somewhat or strongly).

7. The exact wording of the question varies slightly over the time period. The BES surveys, apart from 1987, give people the options of answering that trade unions have too much or too little power (with a 'don't know' option as well), and the BSA surveys allow people to say that the power that unions wield is far too little, too little, about right, too much, or far too much. We combine these to just contrast people who think unions have too much power compared to any other answer.

8. For example, Tilley and Heath (2007) show that occupational class and education, along with religion and generation, are two of the best predictors of the strength of pride in Britishness over the 1984–2003 period (see also Dowds and Young 1996).

9. Since most immigration to Britain is low-skill, this has a much more negative effect on people in working class jobs with low levels of education, and since attachment

to national culture is generally weakened by higher education, cultural threats are perceived as lowest among the most highly educated (Schneider 2008; McLaren and Johnson 2007; Sides and Citrin 2007). There is also a large, and ever-growing, literature examining these arguments in relation to radical right party support across Europe (for example, Oesch 2008; Ivarsflaten 2008; Lucassen and Lubbers 2012). Two recent books deal with immigration policy and views in Britain in detail: *Revolt on the Right* by Ford and Goodwin (2014) talks about the factors that affect UKIP support and *Immigration and Perceptions* by Lauren McLaren (2015) focuses on how views about immigration link to national identity. We return to this debate in Chapter 8.

10. Most questions focus on whether immigration rates should be increased or decreased, and we look at the proportion of people who think immigration should be decreased a lot/very strongly agree it should be decreased. For the period from 1983–1996 we also used a question that asks whether people think controls on immigrants' relatives joining them should be stricter and for a couple of years in the early 2000s we used a question that asks whether people agree that immigrants take jobs from British people. Some of these questions are asked in the same survey in certain years and the correlation between them is typically high, suggesting that they tap into a general underlying positive or negative view of immigration.

11. Some of the response options given to people vary over time. For example, in 1974 people were asked whether they thought Britain should 'stay in the EU', 'stay and change the EU', 'change the EU or leave', or simply 'leave', whereas in the 1980s, the only options given to people were to 'stay' or 'leave'. In later years, people were also given options of a 'single European government' or 'increasing EU powers'. What is common is the option to leave the EU, and that is what we report here.

12. Before 1970, the question on the death penalty refers to whether the death penalty should be kept (the death penalty for murder was formally abolished at the end of 1969), from 1979–1985 whether it should be re-introduced, and from 1986–2015 whether 'for some crimes, the death penalty is the most appropriate sentence'.

13. It is difficult to get good quality figures on many of these changes, but even between 1995 and 2005 the number of students living with their parents nearly doubled from 12 to 20 per cent (Universities UK 2006).

14. It is important to note that increased tolerance of *all groups* for those with more education or in a higher occupational social class is not the expectation. It is not tolerance in and of itself that education or a professional job brings, but rather support and opposition to certain types of people. For example, more highly educated people are often less tolerant of racist or religious groups, and sometimes more willing to curtail their freedom of speech, than people with lower levels of education (Davis 1975; McCutcheon 1985).

15. See Turner (2015, pp.215–30) for an account of changing attitudes towards sexuality in 1990s Britain, which puts those changes in a political and cultural context. Perhaps most revealing in terms of attitude change is the leader column from *The Sun* in 1994 about gay men serving in the military that Turner cites: 'the British soldier needs to worry about the enemy ahead. Not some queer behind him' (p.217). It is impossible to imagine *The Sun* running this editorial today.

16. For 1974 and 1979 we use a slightly different question that asks whether the 'right to show nudity and sex in films and magazines' has gone too far. This captures something similar, and is correlated at 0.5 with the standard question when both are asked in 1992. The direct mention of 'nudity and sex' perhaps explains the difference in how this question is answered by degree holders in the 1970s, which could be picking up on feminist, rather than socially conservative, objections to pornography.

17. For the whole dataset, the economic left–right five-item scale has an alpha score of 0.82 which remains very consistent over time. The conservative–liberal five-item scale has an, again unchanging, alpha score of 0.62.

18. These are relatively common pairings of the education and full seven-category occupational class variables. A clear majority of people in working class occupations have the lowest level of education in every decade. Equally people in the new middle class occupational group are consistently the most likely to have a degree, with nearly half having some sort of higher education in every decade apart from the 1960s. The old middle class occupational group is unsurprisingly more mixed, but this is the group in which someone is most likely to have intermediate qualifications.

19. We run separate linear regression models for each decade and for each scale, including survey year as a series of dummy variables along with the control variables of region, age group, trade union membership, sector of work, housing tenure, religion, agricultural employment, sex, and ethnicity. The points for the proletariat are the actual values for that group as a whole in each decade, and the points for the other two groups are thus the scores they would have if they were identical to the proletariat group in every way apart from their education and occupational class.

20. This shows the problems of using a single item to capture change over time on this broad dimension of social liberalism as it seems likely that people were as, or more, socially liberal in the 1980s than they were in the 1960s, particularly with regard to issues of sexual morality. For example, Tilley (2005) shows that from 1974 to 1997 people in Britain tended to become more socially liberal with regard to equal opportunities (for women and ethnic minorities), the availability of abortion, and censorship.

Appendix to Chapter 4

Table A4.1. Measurement of independent variables used in models

	1963–2015 period	1974–2015 period
Occupational class	Old middle class; New middle class; Junior middle class; Personal service; Own account workers; Foremen; Working class.	As 1963–2015.
Education	Degree; Some higher education; A Level; Post-minimum school education; Left school at school leaving age.	Degree; Teacher or nursing qualification; A Level or equivalent; O Level or equivalent; CSE or equivalent; Apprenticeship or secretarial training; No qualifications.
Housing	Council housing or housing association; Private rental or other; Owner-occupier.	Council housing or housing association; Private rental; Outright owner; Owner with mortgage; Other.
Region	Scotland; Wales; North, Midlands and East; South West; London and South East.	Scotland; Wales; North East; North West; Yorkshire; East Midlands; West Midlands; South West; East; London; South East.
Race	Non-white; White.	Black; Asian—Indian sub-continent; Asian—Chinese; Mixed or other; White.
Employment sector	Not available.	Private sector; Public or charity sector.
Sex	Men; Women.	As 1963–2015.
Age group	18–29; 30–39; 40–49; 50–59; 60–69; 70+.	As 1963–2015.
Religion	Anglican; Presbyterian; Methodist; Baptist; Other non-conformist; Catholic; Other Christian; Non-Christian; No religion.	As 1963–2015.
Trade union membership	Current member of trade union or staff association; not member.	As 1963–2015.
Agricultural employment	Employed in agriculture; not in agriculture.	As 1963–2015.

Note: Occupational class is not available for the 2010 BES. Education is not available for the 1983 and 1984 BSA. Housing tenure is not available in the 2001 BES. The fuller race measure is not available for the two 1974 BESs. Public sector employment is not available in the October 1974 and 1979 BESs or the 1983 BSA. Religion is not available for the February 1974 BES. Agricultural employment is not available for the 2010 BES.

Part II
Political Change

5

The 'Papers'

Chapters 2–4 have shown how class, whether measured by occupation or education, affects how people live their lives and how they view different political issues. Part II of the book focuses on how the political world creates structures within which class is, or is not, linked to party choices. Chapter 6 looks at what politicians say, where they come from, and what policies they offer voters. But there is another important way in which structure is imposed on people's choices. This is via the information that voters consume about politics: information about where people are located in society, how those locations map on to political parties, whether class conflict is real and, if so, whether it is the basis of party conflict. This information comes primarily from the mass media and this chapter is an attempt to evaluate how the media tells the story of class in Britain and how that has changed. We show that newspapers have moved from a post-war portrayal of the working class as 'the people' with class stratification simply part of the scenery, to the newspapers of today that rarely mention class, stratification, or conflict. The structuring of the political world through the class-tinted lenses that newspapers used to provide no longer exists.

We focus on the British press in this chapter, and when one thinks of British newspapers, one does not think of subtlety or neutrality. Indeed a robustly partisan press has been a feature of British society since the early nineteenth century. Dickens' account of Eatanswill in *The Pickwick Papers* is perhaps the most eloquent description of how press and politics intertwine: 'it was essentially and indispensably necessary that each of these powerful parties should have its chosen organ and representative: and, accordingly, there were two newspapers in the town—the Eatanswill Gazette and the Eatanswill Independent; the former advocating Blue principles, and the latter conducted on ground decidedly Buff' (Dickens 1837, p.166). Of course 'Buff' and 'Blue' newspapers are common to many countries, but Britain is also remarkable in having such a small number of national newspapers that, until recently, were read by such a high proportion of the population. In the 1960s, three quarters of adults regularly read a daily national newspaper, and as recently as 2003 over half of people were still regular readers. This is high by international standards. Writing in the 1960s, Butler and Stokes (1969, p.282) note that in 1964 newspapers 'reached over 80 per cent of households—a higher proportion than in any other country' and that 'Britain has a smaller total of independent morning newspapers than any comparable nation'. As we will see the first of these generalizations is no longer true: newspaper circulation has been rapidly falling for the last twenty years. But newspapers still remain few in number and national in type. Moreover, the degree of partisan affiliation is unusual. The *Daily Telegraph*, the *Daily Mail*, and the *Daily Express* (apart from 2015) have endorsed the Conservatives in every single post-war election. On the other side, the *Daily Mirror* has endorsed Labour in every one of those elections. The *Guardian* has also remained manifestly left-wing over the last fifty years, mainly endorsing the Liberals or Labour depending on the election (Butler and Butler 2000; see Wring and Deacon (2010) or Thomas (1998) for detailed accounts of recent press partisanship). Some newspapers do switch. The *Sun* (and in its earlier incarnation as the *Herald*) supported Labour until the mid-1970s when it switched to the Conservatives; then at the 1997 election it declared itself to be 'backing Blair'.[1] Regardless of these switches (and in fact the *Sun* switched back again in 2010 to the Conservatives) newspapers do not feel constrained by their past in lavishing praise on the party that they currently support. Using data from the British Election Studies and British Social Attitudes surveys, Figure 5.1 shows the percentage of readers of the main newspapers that support the Conservatives over time.[2]

Knowing what newspaper people read is a good guide to their party support. *Guardian* readers rarely vote Conservative, while *Telegraph* readers almost always do. Well over half of *Mail* readers support the Conservatives, yet fewer than a fifth of *Mirror* readers do. These are, with the exception of the *Sun*, very long-standing relationships between partisans and partisan newspapers.

These extreme, or at least peculiar, aspects of the British press mean that we may well expect certain types of media effects to operate on readers more or less strongly. Typically, when we think of how the media affects people's views, we think of both priming and persuasion. Priming, or agenda setting, is the way in which a media source focuses on some issues at the expense of others. Persuasion, by contrast, is the way in which newspapers influence people, typically by framing issues in certain ways. Naturally these overlap. After all, the *Mirror* rarely mentions good economic news if the Conservatives are in government. What matters is the overall impact of these effects, which is arguably to reinforce people's partisan opinions.[3] Certainly the first serious attempts to analyse the effects of the mass media in the US, in the decades following the Second World War, claimed that this reinforcement effect was dominant (Lazarsfeld et al. 1948; Berelson et al. 1954; Klapper 1960; Campbell

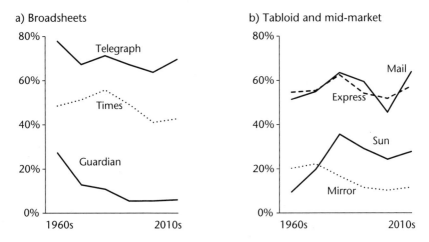

Figure 5.1. Proportion of readership supporting the Conservatives

Note: The figures here show the proportion of people who support the Conservatives by regular newspaper readership. The left-hand graph shows values for broadsheet newspapers; the right-hand graph shows values for tabloid and mid-market newspapers. Regular readership is taken as a positive response to the questions 'do you normally read any daily morning newspaper at least three times a week?'or 'do you read a morning newspaper regularly?'.

Source: British Election Studies 1963–2010; British Social Attitudes Surveys 1983–2015.

et al. 1960). This view was largely shared by Butler and Stokes (1969) writing about 1960s Britain and more recent work has also advocated the reinforcement model (Ansolabehere and Iyengar 1995; Finkel 1993; Newton 2006) or an 'enlightening of preferences' during election campaigns by the media that reinforces people's opinions (Gelman and King 1993; Andersen et al. 2005).

Nonetheless, there is continuing debate about the degree to which the media changes people's opinions. This is largely due to two major difficulties with establishing media effects. First, it is hard to know whether people change their opinions because of their newspaper, or change their newspaper because of their opinions. Both result in people having the same view as their newspaper, but only the former means that the media persuades people. Second, it is difficult to know whether readers follow their newspaper's views, or whether the papers follow their readers. Again, it is only the former that implies that the media have persuasive power.[4]

These are difficult problems to overcome. It means that much of the literature wants to answer the question: 'are the mass media politically powerful, in the sense that they have an effect of their own on political attitudes and behavior, or is their role a minimal one, restricted to reflecting or reinforcing attitudes?' (Newton 1991, p.51). We do not. We are not interested in whether newspapers directly persuade people to switch parties, or indeed to adopt new policy stances. We are interested in how newspapers, as a medium, portray a particular aspect of society, class, and its relationship to politics. Part of this is inevitably about partisan reinforcement, or even persuasion, but it is, more importantly, about how people's broader views of politics and society are subtly shaped by the messages that they see on a daily basis.

Who Reads What?

Different newspapers cheer on different parties and are also read by different kinds of people. Importantly from our point of view, different newspapers are read by people with varying levels of education and different sorts of occupation. These differences are very persistent over time. This is most obvious if we divide the main newspapers into three categories: broadsheet (the *Times*, the *Telegraph*, the *Guardian*, and the *Independent*), mid-market (the *Mail* and *Express*), and tabloid (the *Sun*, the *Mirror*, and the *Star*). We stick with the three stereotypical groups discussed in Chapter 4 to illustrate these differences: the intelligentsia (people with a new middle class job and high education), the bourgeoisie (people with an old middle class job and medium education), and the proletariat (people with working class jobs and low education). Using combined BES and BSA data back to 1963, Figure 5.2 shows how readership of these three types of newspaper are shaped by occupational class and education over time. These numbers come from statistical models that hold constant a number of other factors that affect readership, most notably age and sex.[5]

What Figure 5.2 illustrates is both the way readership has changed, and perhaps more importantly how readership is a persistent product of education and occupation. If you are in the intelligentsia then you either read a broadsheet or nothing. Almost no one in this group reads a tabloid and very few read the *Express* or *Mail*. Before the 2000s over half this group read a broadsheet newspaper. The proletariat group looks equally distinctive. Before 2000 around half or more of people in this group read a tabloid and almost none read a broadsheet. There has been a notable change, however, since the turn of the century. Readership of tabloids by the working class has almost halved and readership of broadsheets by the intelligentsia has more than halved.

Classes have become more similar in terms of readership, not because newspapers are drawing a more diverse readership, but rather because fewer people are reading a newspaper. In 2015 only 31 per cent of people regularly read a national newspaper. In 1964 it was over 80 per cent.[6] Figure 5.3 shows how aggregate newspaper readership has changed over time. Interestingly, here we see much bigger falls in tabloid readership and much smaller falls in broadsheet readership. Why? Because the people who generally read tabloids (people with lower levels of education and in working class jobs) have declined in number,

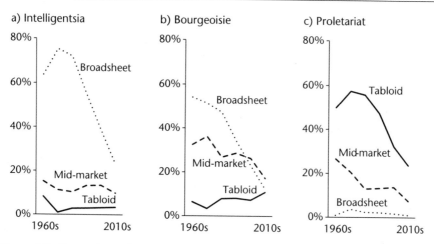

Figure 5.2. Proportion of people in different groups reading different types of newspapers

Note: The figures here show predicted probabilities from multinomial logit regression models using pooled data by decade that predict type of newspaper read. Newspapers are grouped into broadsheets (*Times, Telegraph, Guardian,* and *Independent*); mid-market (*Express* and *Mail*), and tabloid (*Mirror, Sun,* and *Star*). The left-hand graph shows results for the intelligentsia (high education and a new middle-class occupation); the middle graph shows results for the bourgeoisie (medium education and an old middle class occupation); the right-hand graph shows results for the proletariat (low education and working class occupation). As well as occupational class and education, these models include controls for sex, age, and region. Regular readership is taken as a positive response to the questions 'do you normally read any daily morning newspaper at least three times a week?'or 'do you read a morning newspaper regularly?'.

Source: British Election Studies 1963–2010; British Social Attitudes Surveys 1983–2015.

whereas there has been a growth in the number of people (the more educated and those in professional jobs) who generally read broadsheets.

What Figure 5.3 shows is therefore not just the decline of tabloid readership but the decline of tabloid readers. This has implications for how we should interpret Figure 5.2. At first glance, it might appear that there has been some decrease in the class differences in newspaper readership. But that is not really the case. People in the proletariat group are consistently about twenty times more likely to read a tabloid than a broadsheet regardless of the year. Equally, the intelligentsia are about eight times more likely to read a broadsheet than a tabloid in the 2010s, exactly the same ratio as we see in the 1960s. Class differences in press consumption stay constant. It is consumption of the mass press that has fallen.[7]

What the Papers Say

The fact that partisan class-based newspapers are less widely read is important and we will return to it later. Equally important is what those papers say to their readers about social class. We want to know how papers talk about class

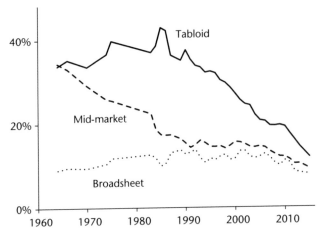

Figure 5.3. Proportion of people reading different types of newspapers

Note: The figures here show the proportion of people regularly reading a newspaper (two period moving average). Regular readership is taken as a positive response to the questions 'do you normally read any daily morning newspaper at least three times a week?'or 'do you read a morning newspaper regularly?'. Newspapers are grouped into broadsheets (*Times, Telegraph, Guardian,* and *Independent*); mid-market (*Express* and *Mail*), and tabloid (*Mirror, Sun,* and *Star*).

Source: British Election Studies 1963–2010; British Social Attitudes Surveys 1983–2015.

and how, if at all, they relate class to politics. Moreover, we want to know how this is shaped by the nature of the readership and how this has changed over time. These are not straightforward questions. And perhaps this is why there has been so little investigation of how the media reinforce social cleavages via their presentation of class politics. The way we answer them is twofold: quantitative and qualitative. The former approach involves coding editorials from three newspapers during every election campaign since 1945 for mentions of class and class politics. The latter involves grouping these editorials over time to allow us to talk about the narratives that underpin discussion of class. These narratives vary not just by time but by newspaper.

Which newspapers? We look at three that broadly represent three of the main occupational groups that we consistently examined in previous chapters: the *Mirror*, a Labour-supporting tabloid with a largely working class readership; the *Guardian*, a Liberal/Labour-supporting broadsheet with a largely new middle class readership; and the *Times*, a Conservative/Liberal-supporting broadsheet with one of the highest old middle class readerships.[8] In some ways, this is not an ideal spread of the newspaper market. We include no mid-market paper and no tabloid on the right. Nonetheless, the choice of these three newspapers allows us to look at newspapers with relatively consistent, and different, readership class bases, relatively consistent partisan stances, and newspapers that are not in vertiginous decline (such as the *Express*).

But which stories? We look here at editorials during the month-long formal election campaigns.[9] We pick editorials because we want to analyse the 'voice' of the newspaper. This allows us to hone in on what kind of readers are talked about in editorials and how politics and class structures are discussed with reference to those readers. We pick election campaigns for the practical reason of making the exercise more manageable, but also because this is a period in which we should expect linkages to be made between class groups and politics.

By looking at the papers four weeks before the election, and on the election day itself, we have twenty-five days of newspapers for each campaign. We do not analyse the Sunday newspapers, which are historically distinct from the dailies. With nineteen elections since the war, that means that there are 475 possible editorials to look at from each newspaper. In practice, there are fewer editorials than this, as newspapers were not printed on some days and not every paper contained an editorial[10], meaning that we have a total of 1,292 editorials to analyse: 390 from the *Mirror*, 456 from the *Guardian*, and 446 from the *Times*. Not all editorials have domestic political content either. In fact, about 8 per cent of the editorials, relatively evenly spread across the three newspapers, do not mention domestic politics. This reduces our sample further to 1,190 editorials: 348 in the *Mirror*, 435 in the *Guardian*, and 407 in the *Times*. It is these near 1,200 editorials that we analyse here.

How do we measure whether editorials talk about class? We separate out three main ideas. First, we are interested in whether there is any discussion of social class. Is there recognition of class divisions, and is there talk of people as working or middle class? Second, we are interested in class conflict. Do editorials talk about the classes as in conflict with one another? Third, we want to know how politics and class intersect and specifically whether particular classes are associated with particular parties.

These three areas allow us to see quantitatively how discussion of class in different newspapers has changed over time in different ways. In this section we will use the combined dataset of all the editorials from all three newspapers, since this allows us to assess change over time most accurately. Later in this chapter we will discuss in more detail how different newspapers portray class. Here we are more interested in describing the broader media milieu that exists at different points in time.

We start this description with class stratification. Are class differences an accepted part of the world that the newspapers are describing? The simplest possible measure here is to look at how many mentions of class there are in editorials over the period. We make no distinctions here about the way in which class is mentioned, or which class is mentioned, simply that it forms part of the editorial discussion in that newspaper on that day. Figure 5.4 shows exactly this.

Here we present the percentage of editorials for all newspapers combined that mention class stratification, class conflict, or either the middle or working class.[11] As we might expect, there is some overlap here: editorials that talk about class stratification or conflict also tend to mention specific classes.[12] What Figure 5.4 reveals is both the sheer number of mentions of class, especially before the 1980s, but also the clear change that has happened. Around a quarter of all editorials mention class in some form or another, but this has decreased substantially over time. Before 1997 over a third of editorials mention class, but barely 15 per cent mention it between 1997 and 2015. While newspapers still talk about class, they talk about it far less than they did fifty years ago.

Figure 5.5 gives more detail on this shift, showing how mentions of class stratification have changed and how mentions of the different class groups have changed. The former is about an acceptance of class divisions that structure society. Before 1992 over a fifth of all editorials mention this. To put it another way, someone reading a paper every day would come across editorial discussion of this idea at least once a week. From 1997 this falls to fewer than 10 per cent. During the last five election campaigns someone would need to read every editorial for over a fortnight before class division reared its head.

Even more illuminating is specific mention of the different classes. The working class was regularly mentioned as a group for the twenty years after the war Second World War: a third of all editorials specifically mentioned the working class during the 1955 election campaign. This fell in the mid-1960s, and then fell again in the late 1980s and it has since remained at a fairly low

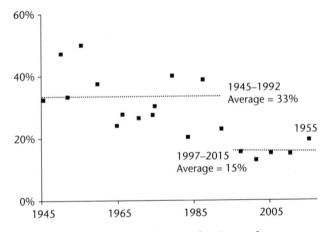

Figure 5.4. Proportion of editorials mentioning class in any form

Note: The figure here shows the proportion of editorials that mention social class in any form for the month before each general election.

Source: 1945–2015 coded newspaper editorials (Mirror, Times, and Guardian). N = 1190.

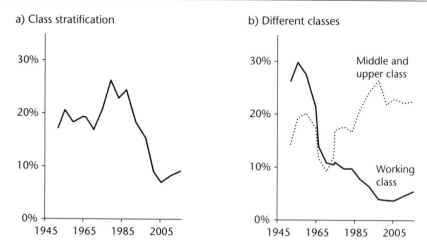

Figure 5.5. Proportion of editorials mentioning class in specific ways

Note: The left-hand graph here shows the proportion of editorials that mention class stratification for the month before each general election (three period moving average). The right-hand graph shows the proportion of editorials that mention different social classes directly for the month before each general election (three period moving average).

Source: 1945–2015 coded newspaper editorials (*Mirror*, *Times*, and *Guardian*). N = 1190.

level. At the last five elections, fewer than one in twenty editorials mentioned the working class. Discussion of the middle and upper classes[13] has followed an opposite trend. Fewer than 15 per cent of editorials mention them before the 1970s, but almost a quarter of editorials contain a reference to the middle or upper classes after the mid-1980s. Until the 1970s newspapers talked more about the working class than other classes. After the 1980s newspapers talked more about the other classes than they did the working class.

The nature of newspaper discussion about class has changed. Fewer editorials mention class stratification and the working class. The precise timing of these changes is more difficult to assess, but the direction of change is clear. What about class conflict? Figure 5.6 shows how mentions of class conflict and also broader discussion of equality and 'fairness' have changed over time.[14] There is a rather different pattern here. Rather than decline, we see a rise and fall. Conflictual class relations are rarely discussed in the earliest period, a time when class stratification was nonetheless regularly talked about, but become more salient during the 1960s, until dramatically falling again in 1992 to near zero levels by the 2000s. There is a similar, though more pronounced, pattern for the discussion of equality and fairness. Here we see a steady increase from 1945 onwards, sharply peaking during the two 1974 elections in which a third of editorials mention fairness, and then gradually falling to very low levels by the 2000s.

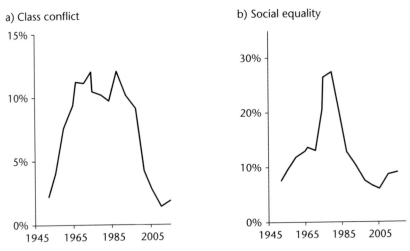

a) Class conflict   b) Social equality

Figure 5.6. Proportion of editorials mentioning class conflict and social equality

Note: The left-hand graph here shows the proportion of editorials that mention class conflict for the month before each general election (three period moving average). The right-hand graph shows the proportion of editorials that mention social equality or inequality for the month before each general election (three period moving average).

Source: 1945–2015 coded newspaper editorials (*Mirror, Times,* and *Guardian*). N = 1190.

The changing way in which class features in newspapers fits with what we might expect given the changing class structure of the country. The working class features less and the middle class more as the former declines in number and the latter increases in number. Equally, the reality of class stratification features less heavily as the people who lose out from that stratification are less numerically dominant in society. At the same time, class conflict and 'fairness' are less serious issues when most people are working class (and political parties are catering for that) in the 1950s, but both become more important as the numbers of people in the middle and working class groups become more evenly balanced. As the working class then shrinks further from the 1990s onwards, these issues recede again from editorial notice.[15]

Yet there is some evidence that this trend has reversed a little in recent years. In particular, the coverage of the 2015 election campaign was more focused on issues of class than it had been for over twenty years. It is notable that this is particularly the case for the newspaper which caters for working class readers. The *Times* and the *Guardian* had practically identical coverage of class in 2015 as they did in 2010 and 2005, but the *Mirror* mentioned class in one form or another in nearly 30 per cent of editorials in 2015, compared to only a few per cent in 2010 and 2005. These small reversals should not overshadow the broader trend, however. The landscape of information about social class has changed as the numbers of people in those classes changed.

There is a final mechanism that shapes how we see class. That is how the parties talk about class. After all, the media is often reporting on what parties say and do, especially during election campaigns. Although we will investigate this in much more detail in Chapter 6, which focuses on how party policy, party rhetoric, and party personnel have changed, and how this has affected public opinion about parties, it is useful to see the way in which the parties are portrayed by the media. This is particularly true when thinking about the election campaign period. Is it the case that the newspapers talk about parties in class terms? The short answer is yes, but not very much.

Table 5.1 shows the numbers of direct associations between class groups for three grouped time periods: the working class consensus period from 1945 to 1970, the breakdown of that working class consensus from 1974 to 1992, and the middle class consensus period from 1997 onwards. Only 2 per cent of editorials directly link a political party with a social class.[16] It is nonetheless telling how even these small numbers break down over time. About one editorial per campaign before 1992 either talked about Labour as the party of the working class or the Conservatives as the party of the middle class. This was particularly the case in the *Mirror* which articulated party politics in class terms at around double the rate of the two broadsheets. In the five campaigns from 1997 onwards, there are but three mentions of class and party in any newspaper, and two of those actually associate Labour with the middle class, not the working class.

Class and party are rarely linked explicitly in newspaper editorials, but when they are, the pattern appears driven by the party changes that we discuss in Chapter 6. We find the same kind of pattern when we look at how specific

Table 5.1. Proportion of editorials directly associating social class with specific parties or specific policies

	Working class consensus (1945–1970)	Breakdown of consensus (1974–1992)	Middle class consensus (1997–2015)
Parties and class			
Labour and working class	2.2%	1.6%	–
Labour and middle class	–	–	0.6%
Conservatives and middle class	0.7%	1.6%	0.3%
Policy and class			
Welfare policy	1.1%	1.3%	0.3%
Employment policy	1.3%	0.5%	–
Other policy	1.5%	0.3%	–
Total	3.9%	2.2%	0.3%

Note: The numbers here show the proportion of editorials that link a) political parties and classes and b) party policies and classes for the month before each general election from 1945 to 2015.

Source: 1945–2015 coded newspaper editorials (*Mirror*, *Times*, and *Guardian*). N = 1190.

policies are linked to class. Table 5.1 also shows when class is invoked in discussion of policy. We divide this into three areas: welfare policy, employment policy, and other areas of policy (which include the NHS and education). Again, there is discussion of class and policy, albeit at low levels, before 1997; afterwards there is essentially none.

We can take three important points away from this discussion. First, class forms a regular, but declining, part of editorial discussion in newspapers. The reality of class stratification, and the existence of classes, is a common feature of editorials in the 1950s. It is much less common by the 2000s. That decline is even more striking when we look at how often the working class is mentioned. Conversely, as the working class is talked about less, the middle class garners more attention. The second point is that editorials rarely talked about class and social conflict in the 1940s and 1950s, or from the 1990s onwards. It is the intervening period (the late 1960s, 1970s, and 1980s) in which we see editors deploying conflict as a motif. Finally, while it is rare for newspapers to directly associate policy and parties with classes at any point, they almost never associate classes with parties or policies today. Newspapers may have reinforced a view of Labour as a working class party with working class policies, and the Conservatives as a middle class party with middle class policies, from the war up to the 1990s, but they no longer do so.

This analysis is helpful, but partial. It ignores any detail of the narrative and framing that newspapers use when talking about class and it ignores differences between the newspapers. We know that different newspapers are read by different classes and different party supporters; how does this affect the way in which editors shape their editorials?

The Framing of Class

In this next part of the chapter we provide a more in-depth analysis of the newspaper editorials, focusing on themes that emerge during particular election campaigns for particular newspapers. What we are interested in here is not the number of mentions of class, but the specific narrative that editorials use when talking about class. How do the newspapers frame issues around class, and how does this vary over time? We argue here that there are three distinct periods which map on to different types of class narratives from all three newspapers. These are the same time periods that we used above to look at how parties and classes are associated in the newspapers. First, we have the working class consensus between 1945 and 1970 in which the working class was clearly the majority group in society; then the breakdown of that dominance after 1970 and up to 1992, which meant an intensification of class conflict as the middle class became the majority group; and finally a middle class consensus era from 1997 onwards in which the middle class was the dominant group. Obviously, the framing of class issues differs somewhat from newspaper to newspaper, and especially between the broadsheet and tabloid press, but interestingly these three periods see a similar set of frames used by each newspaper, albeit coloured by their readership and partisan view. We thus organize this section around these three time periods.

Working Class Consensus (1945–1970)

The most important facet of coverage up to 1970, which is especially obvious in the 1945 and the 1950s elections, is the way in which class is simply part of the background. Class stratification is a fact of life, and the average person is part of the working class. This latter point is especially obvious in the *Mirror*. The editorials in the *Mirror* are quite clearly addressing a relatively homogenous working class group that is treated as synonymous with most people in Britain. We repeatedly see references to 'the people of Britain' and social policies that benefit working class people are labelled as ensuring 'a better life for the men, women and children of this country' (24 May 1955). This is explicitly related to politics as well, 'the tradition of the Labour party is forward with the people. All the people' (5 May 1959). Similarly, the *Mirror* asks on the day of the 1970 election:

> Who stands for us? For all of us, the people of this great island. Not just . . . for the Fortunate Few, born to great privilege . . . It is Labour, the party led by gifted men and women who came from Us. (18 June 1970)

The *Mirror* is speaking to the working class, when the working class made up the majority of society. This is combined with a partisan appeal, in that Labour is portrayed as the party of 'the many' not the few, but it is 'the many' that is prominent, not the party political nature of these statements. Moreover, when politics is framed around class conflict, which is rare, the conflict is between the upper class, 'the few', and the working class, 'the many', as in the 1970 editorial above: those 'born to great privilege' are in opposition to everyone else. In both 1955 and 1964 there was extensive coverage of the public-school-educated Conservative cabinet with the headline in 1964 of 'Etonians of the world unite! You have nothing to lose but your privileges!' (12 October 1964) and when invoking the 'image of the Tory party, 1966' Alec Douglas-Home is described as the 'maestro of the grouse moors' (22 June 1966). For the *Mirror*, society is its readership, which is the working class. Any class conflict is between this working class and the upper class (or 'big industrialists' or 'Tory bankers'). Equally, strikes tend to be presented as the fault of a minority of irresponsible 'strikers', not 'workers'. This is nicely shown in its verdict on Ray Gunter (then Minister of Labour and former head of a railway workers union) calling him a:

> moderate with a fierce patriotism which is largely based on his faith in the virtues of the working class. So when unofficial strikers have behaved cruelly, stupidly or short-sightedly he feels they have betrayed the rest. (16 March 1966)

We see that same theme in the *Guardian* and the *Times*, albeit refracted through the lens of a very different readership, both in class and party terms. While both share a middle class readership, they differ in terms of party support during this era. The *Times*, apart from in 1945, endorsed the Conservatives or the Conservatives/Liberals, whereas the *Guardian* editorials were much more supportive of Labour during this period.[17] Regardless of these differences, both the *Guardian* and the *Times* talk at some length about the working class in editorials and recognize class stratification frequently. On the latter there is regular mention of 'all classes' with regard to almost every imaginable activity: from nutrition (*Times*, 25 June 1945) to education (*Times*, 22 June 1945), welfare services (*Times*, 28 April 1955) to the declining morals of the young (*Times*, 1 October 1959), productivity (*Times*, 10 March 1966) to the theatre (*Times*, 26 March 1966), and so on. On the former, both papers also talk a lot about specific policies that will benefit the working class and also, particularly in the *Times*, what issues motivate working class voters. In 1950 the *Times* has a detailed, and very neutral, discussion of working class jobs and how pay rates are motivating strike activity (26 January 1950). This is followed a fortnight later with an equally detailed discussion about working class housing and how subsidies are 'grossly maladjusted' (17 February 1950). Similar stories can be seen in the *Guardian* throughout this period as well. For example, in 1945 it is argued that the 'first need of the people . . . will be for houses to let at working-class rents' (22 June 1945) and in 1950, regarding unofficial strikes, the editorial talks of being 'brought into touch with working-class currents of opinion' (22 February 1950). Overall there is constant recognition of those who do jobs 'requiring heavy physical effort under rough or unpleasant working conditions' (*Times*, 02 May 1955) and how policies are, and to some extent should be, aimed at them.

Of course, neither the *Times* nor the *Guardian* are actually read by many of the 'workers' that they commonly talk about. This is perhaps best shown by the slightly snobbish tone that is sometimes adopted: the *Times* in 1959 talks, with no hint of irony, about 'cheaper beer for the workers' (16 September 1959) and often adopts a rather patrician tone when discussing differences between workers. The *Times* is also quite clearly addressing a readership within the upper middle class. One of the 1955 editorials bemoans the woe of 'sending children off to [boarding] school'[18] and there are regular references to the arcana of proctors and punting that would only be known to Oxbridge graduates. Perhaps more importantly, the two broadsheets also diverge from the *Mirror* in their slightly different discussion of class and politics.

Part of this difference is emphasis. The *Mirror* regularly mentions landlords and monopolies and their negative effect on 'ordinary people', yet this sort of issue is only sporadically covered in the *Times* and the *Guardian*. Similarly strikes, industrial disputes, and inflation, which more negatively affect the middle class, get more coverage in the broadsheets. The type of story does differ somewhat. The other difference is in the efficacy of class politics. Although it is rare for editorials to directly link classes with parties, there is recognition that the class system does feature in electoral competition to some extent. For example, in 1950, the *Guardian* remarks that:

> The chief difference [between the parties] is that either a Conservative or a Liberal government would be inclined to let a slightly larger share of the national cake go to the middle classes. (17 February 1950)

This is combined to some extent with suggestions that Labour should move away from class politics. The *Guardian* in 1951 calls 'for Labour to rid itself of its appeal to class instincts' (25 October 1951) and the *Times* in 1959 describes Labour as the 'party of jealousy; of a stubborn adherence to the class war . . . of a pathetic belief that the few can be made to pay for the many' (7 October 1959). The underlying premise of much of this type of discussion is that class politics benefits the dominant group of the working class and harms the middle class readers of *Times* and *Guardian* editorials. This is probably most apparent in discussion of trade unions. The *Mirror* talks of 'strikers' disrupting industry, whereas both the *Guardian* and the *Times* talk of 'workers' disrupting production. For the *Guardian* in 1955: 'the engine drivers who are threatening to deprive the public of trains next Saturday are not a group of downtrodden men: they are doing the oppressing' (21 May 1955). Commenting on the same proposed strike, the *Times* comments that 'for some groups of workers, readiness to strike has become a habit' (11 May 1955).

These differences are less notable than are the similarities, however. During the 1950s and 1960s, regardless of readership, class is a constant feature of the way in which newspapers talk about the world. The idea of a stratified society based around social classes is a regular explicit, and implicit, part of the language used to describe politics. It is also the working class and their needs and wants that are most frequently discussed, often not as in conflict with the middle classes, but simply as the group that politics should serve, and to which political parties should appeal. Clearly this is moderated to some extent by the type of readers that leader writers are writing for, and the middle class newspapers are more willing to accept that working class and middle class demands are different, but the basic story remains the same. This is not true once we enter the 1970s.

Breakdown of Consensus (1974–1992)

By the middle of the 1970s there is a clear recognition within the editorials of class conflict. Indeed, this can already be seen in 1970. The working and middle classes are seen as on different sides of a debate about unions, inequality, and welfare. Just as the demographics of class numbers shift, and as the nature of competition between the parties shifts, so does media coverage. This is true of all the newspapers, but is, unsurprisingly, most commonly seen in the middle class broadsheet papers. Both the *Guardian* and the *Times* comment directly on class conflict. Before the first 1974 election the *Times* says that it is undeniable that 'there are now social tensions more acute than existed ten years ago. There are tensions between the classes' (12 February 1974) and similarly in the *Guardian* it is argued that 'the country could quickly find itself in a class war' (27 February 1974) and that we 'must face the probability of a political, social and economic struggle which will make us poorer, more bitter towards each other, and with the growing inter-class tolerance of the post-war years sadly eroded' (5 February 1974). While 1974 is clearly exceptional in some ways (a snap election following the incumbent Conservative government's ongoing dispute with the miners), it is more typical than one might think of election coverage over the 1970s and 1980s. Both the broadsheets, and to a lesser extent the *Mirror*, focus much more on class conflict and how policy affects the working and middle classes differently. During the second 1974 election campaign, the *Guardian* lays out this division quite clearly:

> Ask most managerial or professional men today and they will say that they are worse off than a year ago. Taxation is biting deeper, money buys less, salaries and fees have risen less than proportionately, while mortgages and interest payments have gone up. Ask most wage earners and they will give the same answer. Wages have risen, but food and clothes and housing costs and getting to work have all gone up too. Both groups feel worse off. (23 September 1974)

The editorial then goes on to evaluate which of these groups has lost more (the former in the *Guardian*'s opinion, albeit from a much higher base). There is also a more explicit link made between party politics and opposing working and middle class interests. The *Mirror* expands its definition of the 'the few' to encompass a much wider swathe of the middle class. In 1979 the *Mirror* says that the Conservative manifesto 'is thick with predictable prejudice. Help for private medicine and fee-paying schools. The biggest tax cuts for the better-off' (12 April 1979) and in 1987 similarly accuses Margaret Thatcher of caring about:

private medicine, private schooling and private privilege. She doesn't care about the majority of the British people who will not be voting for her. She doesn't care about the National Health Service because she never uses it. She doesn't care about a shortage of school books because her children never went to a State school. She doesn't care about council tenants because she has never lived in a council house. (27 May 1987)

This is not the newspaper of the working class railing against the '1 per cent', but against a much wider section of the middle classes.[19] This theme of middle versus working class interests is quite starkly brought out in the some of the broadsheet editorials. Again this is most notable in the 1970s, where the *Guardian* leads in 1974 with 'Mr Heath has a party base which does not encourage him to favour manual workers at the expense of the well to do and of the middle classes generally' (13 February 1974). A few months later, during the October 1974 campaign, the *Guardian* claims that 'for the electorate, as before, the choice is one that often starts from sectional interests, whether as workers or as property owners' (18 September 1974). This type of discussion continues, although at a lower ebb, through the 1980s. For example, the *Times* in 1987 talking about privatization of Rolls-Royce argues that:

Part ownership of the company for which one works forges a still closer link between the fortunes of capital and labour. A class-based party like Labour is muddled about the desirability of strengthening that link. (2 June 1987)

Even so, by the end of the 1980s the class–party link is increasingly seen as historical rather than current. The eve of the election editorial in the *Times* a week later talks about changes between classes and parties over the last 200 years:

Peel realised that Conservatism's future lay not with the landed interest but with the newly enfranchised, early 19th century middle class. Disraeli realised it lay with the late 19th century, newly enfranchised working class. Mrs Thatcher realised that it lay with the late 20th century 'classless' class of skilled workers who had long been enfranchised in terms of the vote in elections but who were trying to enfranchise themselves economically. What is the evidence?...the Labour politicians' terror—in this campaign—of appearing to be the party of high taxation, the unions, and nationalization. (11 June 1987)

And by 1992 the *Times* is talking about the 'traditional purpose of Labour...to advance the interests of the great unions once concentrated in [the manufacturing] sector' (24 March 1992). This move to emphasizing class as a historical rather than current division is accompanied by decreasing attention to the working class and an increasing attention to groups not identified as 'workers', but as the 'poor' or the 'disadvantaged'. Before 1974 'the poor'[20] were mentioned in fewer than 7 per cent of editorials. Between 1974 and 1992 this ran at nearly triple the rate: 20 per cent of editorials. By 1992 Labour is less of a party of the working class than 'a party which exists to care for the poor' (*Mirror*, 17 March 1992). There are still ideological differences between the parties that map on to class divisions, but these are slowly changing. As the *Times* puts it a week before the 1992 election:

> Next week's general election is widely regarded as devoid of ideological choice. The Tories, having unceremoniously dropped the author of Thatcherism in 1990, smartly move towards the centre. The Labour party, smarting from wounds inflicted on it in three defeats, has performed a similar shift . . . The Labour leadership remains . . . the party of organised labour and of collective action: of the aspirations of a planned public sector and its multifarious beneficiaries. One of Mr Kinnock's achievements has been dramatically to expand the range of those with an interest in a Labour victory, from blue and white collar workers to the great professions, to doctors, to clergymen, academics, teachers, scientists, artists. (4 April 1992)

Already by 1992 the writing is on the wall. The working class is no longer a significant interest group that newspapers write about and class politics is slowly changing. By 1997 both of these processes, at least as viewed through the lens of Britain's newspapers, are complete.

Middle Class Consensus (1997–2015)

From 1997 onwards the working class as a group almost completely disappears from newspaper editorials, as do the ideas of class stratification and class politics. The only editorial in the *Mirror* that uses the word 'class' between 1997 and 2015 refers to Tony Blair's choice of underwear.[21] Moreover, the middle class is now the default class group against which policies are judged; the middle class is now representative of society as a whole.

During the 1997 campaign there is a degree of reflection on what was. In 1997 the *Guardian* suggests that 'the two sides of industry have declared a truce in the class war' (21 April 1997) and that Britain 'had already ceased to be the industrial society divided along traditional class lines which moulded the two party system' (30 April 1997). This can be seen towards the end of the period as well. As with many mentions of the working class over this period, it is seen as a group that is no longer relevant, with retiring Labour MPs referred to as 'old hands still in tune with Labour's working class origins' (*Guardian*, 12 April 2010). By 2015 both direct mentions of the working class in the broadsheets refer to them as a type of 'problem group'. The *Times* talks about the foundation of a think tank as a 'search for solutions to the challenges facing the working class' (2 May 2015) and the *Guardian* notes that 'working-class voters . . . will have been a large part of the third of the electorate who didn't vote in 2010' (16 April 2015). The latter point is a theme we return to in Chapter 8.

Most direct references to class and politics over this period refer to the way in which class politics has vanished and how the parties have converged. In 2015 the *Guardian* notes that 'parties long since stopped representing one half of the electorate or the other' (16 April 2015), and there is much coverage of how Labour is now a middle class party.[22] Unsurprisingly, these feature heavily in the paper with a left-leaning middle class readership: the *Guardian*. In 2001 it leads with this:

> Labour is harvesting some stunning endorsements from deep inside what were once the Conservatives' sociological heartlands. Tony Blair's lead over William Hague among professional and middle-class 'AB' voters is running at 42%, the Observer/ICM poll reported on Sunday...Labour has worked long and hard to earn such levels of support among the groups which once spurned the party's appeals with contempt and loathing. (14 May 2001)

This can also be seen in the 2010 campaign. Gillian Duffy, described as a 'bigoted woman' by Gordon Brown after she raised the issue of immigration when he was on the campaign trail in Rochdale, is for the *Guardian* 'Labour family, part of the hereditary working class' (29 April 2010). Yet this is someone whose views Labour now apparently spurns. Again the working class is only mentioned in order to say that their views are not held by Labour. In a slightly different way editorials in other newspapers, especially the *Mirror* before 2015, emphasize how Labour is now a classless party. Talking about Alex Ferguson's support of Labour in 2010, the *Mirror* argues that 'Labour represents working people, whether on low wages or the high income of the ex-toolmaker turned football manager' (28 April 2010). Given that Ferguson earned around £4 million a year in 2010, Labour presumably represented pretty much everybody bar the Queen. More generally, there is widespread acceptance that there is a new consensus, and this consensus is on the right. The *Guardian* bemoans the fact that no 'party in the 2001 election advocates redistribution from the rich to the poor, a rise in the top rate of income tax' (16 May 2001). Yet it is also more positive that, on the flip side, 'the business vote—historically and histrionically anti-Labour—is now split' (2 May 2005). And the *Times* points out in 2005 that:

> For all of the furious charges traded by Tony Blair and Michael Howard, in practice British politics has been witnessing a quiet conceptual convergence...There is also a broader, if not universal, understanding that these openings and opportunities are rooted in individual choices and responsibilities and, generally, not the result of delegating authority to the government. (3 May 2005)

Class does not completely disappear, of course. For example, the *Mirror* in 2010 runs an almost identical story about David Cameron's schooling at Eton as it did about Anthony Eden, complete with picture of him in Eton uniform in 1955.[23] More starkly, class does rear its head again in 2015. In the broadsheets this is in the mildest manner. The *Guardian* talks a little more about inequality and how the parties will address it, arguing that 'While most Tories shrug at that yawning gap between rich and poor, Labour will at least strive to slow and even reverse the three-decade march towards an obscenely unequal society' (1 May 2015). On the opposite side of the partisan fence, the *Times* agrees with Cameron that the Conservatives are 'the party of "of the small businesses, the techies, the rooftilers, the retailers, the plumbers and the builders"' (28 April 2015). Nonetheless 2015 does not mark a watershed moment for class politics, as seen from the pages of the broadsheets. The *Guardian* might ask the question, 'who is refighting the class war now?', with reference to Conservative proposals for union strike ballot legislation, but it asks it after pointing out the 'fiscal rectitude' of Labour and the reinvention of the Conservatives as the 'free-spending party of the workers' (15 April 2015).

The *Mirror* in 2015 is somewhat different. A leader at the beginning of the campaign argues that:

> The Conservatives have devoted five years to short-changing working people . . . Working people and Britain can do better than Cameron's Tories, a leader and a party who live in a different world to the rest of us. Most Tory candidates are a different breed—a breed that never cared about working people for five years. (15 April 2015)

This pattern continues to some extent through the month before the election, with exhortations that the 'economy is working for the very wealthy minority at the expense of the majority . . . Earnings and wealth need to be shared more fairly. A privileged few should not be receiving vast sums they could never feasibly spend' (29 April 2015). This is discussion of class conflict, albeit of the few versus the many, and this is spelt out in partisan terms. The Conservatives are 'not interested in workers struggling to earn higher wages' (2 May 2015) and Labour will set 'about creating an economy and politics which work for us all instead of that privileged minority' (6 May 2015). The day before the election, the *Mirror* states that 'Labour is a party of the people. It understands our lives and comes up with answers' (6 May 2015).

Part of this change in rhetoric is probably due to a strongly Labour partisan newspaper reacting to an incumbent Conservative government, but there is perhaps another message here. By 2015 the mainly working class readership of the *Mirror* are likely to feel that the incumbent government is further away from them than any government has ever been. As the lodestone of British politics moved to the right, it is the working class that are left behind and the *Mirror* is perhaps representing this. At the same time, the *Mirror* is still mentioning class less than it was in the 1980s, and much less than before that. It might be representing working class dissatisfaction with politics, but it is doing so through the partisan lens that is has always used. Overall, and even with the slight exception of 2015, class is simply much less visible after 1992 than it was previously. Few editorials talk about class, few refer to the working class, and few refer to conflict between class groups.

Conclusions

What does this all add up to? There are three important points to make. First, there have been dramatic changes in how newspapers portray class in society over time. The working class was the class that editorials were concerned with. Now it is the middle class. This reflects the change in society from being one numerically dominated by the working class to one with an increasingly large educated middle class. As those numbers changed, so did the nature of class conflict and how it was portrayed by the press. Conflict between the classes was not really mentioned in the 1950s, but by the 1970s and 1980s it formed a core part of many editorials. As the working class shrank further, so did editorials about conflict between the working and middle class. Perhaps most noticeably, the very idea of class stratification, which was part and parcel of journalism in the 1950s, now rarely makes an appearance. These changes are about quantity of coverage, but also about how stories are framed. Gone is the rhetoric about 'all classes'; gone is the talk of the 'working man' and how particular policies will benefit him; gone is the background acceptance of class differences.

Second, the way in which class is linked to party, and policy, has also changed. While direct links between policy, party, and class were never that great, they are now almost completely absent. When editorials mention class and politics today, it is mainly to note how the links between parties and classes are no more. The cues that newspapers gave to voters in terms of class politics are no longer as clear as they once were. The associations of Labour with the working class and the Conservatives with the middle class that were made before 1997 in every newspaper largely stop after this point.

Third, while what newspapers say is clearly important, so is the nature of their readership. The British newspaper market remains highly segregated by social class, and by partisanship. Few middle class Conservatives read the *Mirror* and few working class Labour voters read the *Times*. These patterns of partisan and class association have remained unchanged, but the numbers of people reading a newspaper has plummeted. When 80 per cent of people read a paper in the 1950s and 1960s, class and party identities were constantly reinforced by newspapers. Less than a third of people now read a newspaper, so these reinforcement pressures consequently affect far fewer people. It is not just that the material within newspapers has changed but that newspapers have less of an impact on the electorate than they did.[24]

The timing of these changes is also important. Discussion of class, and class politics, stops in 1997. Newspaper readership starts falling substantially during the middle of the 1990s. As we see in Chapter 6, the first of these changes coincides with changes within the political parties. Parties stop talking about class, and stop having class-based policies, which means newspapers no longer talk about class either. This is magnified by the coincidence of a declining newspaper market, largely due to new technology, which no longer reinforces class and partisan identities as it used to. We know that media messages that are consistent with party messages are more likely to shift the attitudes of partisans (Carey and Burton 2004). The disappearance of both media and party messages regarding class and party seems highly likely to disrupt voter views of class-based parties.

Notes

1. The precursor to the *Sun*, the *Daily Herald*, was effectively owned by the Trade Union Congress and was the most leftist mass newspaper after the war. After being re-launched as the *Sun* in 1964 it was taken over by Rupert Murdoch in 1969 and remained broadly on the left until the 1979 election when it endorsed the Conservatives. The impact of its switch back to Labour in 1997 has been a source of much debate. Whether the existing readership changed partisanship due to the editorial change, whether Conservative partisans stopped reading and Labour partisans started reading the *Sun*, or whether the editorial line simply switched after the readers switched, is very difficult to test. Editorial endorsements by the *Sun* have been argued to have had little effect (Curtice and Semetko 1994; Curtice 1997; Norris et al. 1999) and relatively large effects (Ladd and Lenz 2009; Newton and Brynin 2001) in shifting existing reader opinions. Interestingly, Rupert Murdoch himself said at the Leveson inquiry in April 2012 that claims that it was the 'Sun wot won it' in 1992 by influencing readers were 'wrong in fact—we don't have that sort of power' (*Daily Telegraph*, 25 April 2012).

2. This shows the proportion of people supporting the Conservatives of those who support one of the three major parties. These figures as a proportion of all people would look very similar, but with a small decline in Conservative support over time for all readers. This is due to the increasing number of people supporting smaller parties and the growth in the number of people who do not support any party (which has increased from under 10 per cent in the 1960s to over 20 per cent in the 2010s). Non-partisans are, perhaps unsurprisingly, over-represented in the groups of people who do not read a daily newspaper: a group which has grown substantially.

3. There may be a further effect of reinforcement at election time, which is to increase turnout. Brynin and Newton (2003, p.72) argue that 'those whose partisan views

are reinforced by their paper are more likely to vote'. These are relatively small effects, but show how reinforcing and cross-pressuring messages from newspapers can alter behaviour.

4. In principle, experimental work can overcome these problems (see, for example, Ansolabehere and Iyengar 1995; Iyengar and Kinder 1987; Norris et al. 1999). The problem here is external validity. While we might find persuasion and agenda-setting when people read newspaper articles in a psychology lab, can we assume that this happens outside the lab? Some of the best work in this area has used natural experiments. These typically involve looking at the effects of an outside event, like a printing strike or a change of newspaper partisan affiliation, on people's reactions in the real world. A good example, in the British context, is Ladd and Lenz (2009) who use panel data that follows the same people over time to argue that changing newspaper endorsements in Britain in the 1990s affected party choices.

5. These are multinomial logit regression models run separately for each decade of survey data. As well as education and class, also included in these models are sex, age group, and region. The probabilities reported here are thus for a woman living in the South East of England who is in her fifties.

6. The question asked in the BSA in every year since 1983 is, 'do you normally read any daily morning newspaper at least three times a week?'. This is slightly different to the question on the BES surveys which tend to ask a variant of 'do you read a morning newspaper regularly?'.

7. There is a separate question about whether this change is primarily generational, or a decline that has affected everyone. Curtice and Mair (2008, p.166) suggest that it is a combination of the two: 'newspapers have failed to keep older readers who were once loyal to them. But at the same time they have apparently found it more difficult to recruit and retain younger readers.'

8. In some ways the *Telegraph* might be thought to be a more obvious representative of the old middle class, but in fact a higher proportion of the *Times* readership is drawn from this group in both the 1960s and 2010s.

9. We also include a small number of election 'guides' typically printed on the day of the election that contain explicit endorsements of candidates.

10. Most notably the *Times* was not printed from 1 December 1978 until 12 November 1979 due to industrial action, meaning that we do not have any coverage of the 1979 election from the *Times*. Equally the *Mirror* did not consistently contain editorials before the 1980s, meaning that slightly more than 15 per cent of our *Mirror* sample does not have an editorial.

11. We include here some synonyms for class terms. For the working class we include words that concentrate on occupational class status such as 'workers', 'labour', or 'wage-earning class'. We do not include mentions of 'the poor', 'low earners', 'the needy', and 'slum dwellers': terms which focus on people with low incomes, but not a class group. For the middle class, we include 'the bourgeoisie', 'the privileged', 'the better off', and the 'well-to-do'. While these terms conflate income and occupation to some extent, the most common usage by far is 'middle class'.

12. While many of the editorials that mention specific classes also mention the class structure or class conflict, many do not. Three quarters of articles that talk about

the class structure or mention social class do not specifically mention the 'working class' or 'middle class', and over half do not mention any synonyms for working or middle class such as 'workers' or 'labour'.

13. The upper class group includes references to the upper class, the rich, landowners and 'capital'. About half the references are to the middle class and half to the upper class.

14. The second of these means editorials that, in the main, discuss fairness and social justice or directly issues of equality. We also include mentions of egalitarianism and inequality.

15. We see a similar pattern over time for discussion of trade unions. Mentions of unions peak in the 1970s (in February 1974 nearly two thirds of editorials mention trade unions) and then fall to very low levels from 1992 onwards. This decline is particularly notable for the *Mirror*, the working class newspaper, which does not mention unions once in an election campaign after 1987. This is unsurprising given that unions from the 1990s onwards became increasingly dominated by middle class public sector employees as discussed in Chapter 4.

16. Some editorials also identify parties as being against particular groups. This is most prominent in the *Mirror* portraying the Conservatives as against the working class. There are three of these editorials in the post-war consensus period, two in the 1974–1992 period, and another three after 1992. All but one are in the *Mirror*.

17. This is not to say that the *Guardian* endorses Labour in every election. In fact, the *Guardian* endorsed the Liberals in 1945 and 1950, and the Liberals/Conservatives in 1951 and 1955. Nonetheless, the editorial stance, in line with its readership, is systematically less supportive of the Conservatives than the *Times*.

18. In the same year the *Times* also describes 'unfair pressure on one group: large families with independent school fees' (4 May 1955). Needless to say, this is a group in which many of its readers are likely to find themselves.

19. According to the British Election Study in 1987 over a third of parents had used, or were thinking of using, a private school for their children and/or held private medical insurance. Equally, by 1987 only 23 per cent of people rented a house from a local authority or housing association.

20. Here we include mentions of 'the poor', 'the needy', 'slum dwellers', the 'less well off', and 'low earners'. The vast majority of references are to the first, and the pattern over time is the same if we just look at mentions of the poor.

21. His Calvin Klein underpants get the *Mirror* seal of approval as they 'ooze class and statesmanship. And modernity. And success. If anything personified cool Britannia, it's Tony Blair's pants' (6 June 2001).

22. There is occasional discussion of how this has meant that the parties have sometimes traded their historic positions as well. For example, the *Guardian* in 2015 notes that 'David Cameron launched the Conservatives' general election manifesto today in the same spirit of light-fingered transvestism. Twenty-four hours after Ed Miliband had wrapped himself in Labour's newfound fiscal rectitude, Mr Cameron came down the election catwalk sporting a Tory new look as the free-spending party of the workers' (15 April 2015).

23. In general, and in all periods, the *Mirror* focuses much more on the class background of politicians than the *Times* and the *Guardian*. This might be seen as a response to the bigger differences between politicians and the *Mirror* readership than between the broadsheets and MPs, although equally this could be seen as simply due to a classic tabloid focus on 'personality' rather than 'politics'.

24. One offsetting factor here might be the degree to which parties are distinct from one another. For example, Newton and Brynin (2001, p.282) argue that 'voters are more likely to follow their newspaper's lead when there is less to choose between the parties'.

6

The Parties

The media contribute their own perspective on politics and class, but they also provide a channel for communication between parties and voters. In this chapter we examine exactly what parties offer voters in terms of policy, group appeals, and descriptive representation. Our focus is on the two main political parties that have held genuine power throughout the post-war era: Labour and the Conservatives. Most countries have parties of the left and right, but Britain is arguably unusual in the political focus on class by these two parties. Is that now simply history? Our answer is yes, and the impact of these political changes on the relationship between voters and parties is fundamental to the message of this book.

In this chapter we focus on different key sources of political messages. First, we look at the manifestos that parties produce before each election. This involves coding the two main party manifestos for every election campaign since 1945. Manifestos are substantive: they elaborate the core policy and programmatic statements to which governing parties are often, if not always, held. Very few people actually read them, but they are extensively distributed and commented on by the media. The manifestos give us a way to examine both the positioning of parties and their appeals to particular groups. We particularly focus on the degree to which parties present distinctive left or right wing policy platforms in their manifestos. As noted by various scholars: 'the basic logic of party competition in Britain remains similar to that which held in the 1950s: in policy terms at least, it is . . . a predominantly left-right dimension' (Webb 2004, p.39; see also among many others, Laver and Budge 1992; Clark 2012). Equally, as we saw in Chapter 4, classes differ in the degree to which they express preferences for such left- versus right-wing policies. Parties are therefore representing the differing preferences of middle and working class people by offering distinctive policies. If the parties do not differ in the left–right choices they offer, this link between classes and parties will not be present. We argue that over time the parties have converged and, more specifically, the Labour party has become less left-wing and more like the Conservatives.

But political representation is not just about policies; it is also about the way that parties see their political role as representatives of social groups. As well as policy differentiation, therefore, we are also interested in references to types of voters. Our expectation is that over time parties will refer less to classes and more often to other social groups. We look at this with the manifesto data, but we also examine the party leaders' speeches. Leader's speeches are key platforms for party identity building, both positively about the leader's own party and negatively with respect to labelling the opposition. This form of communication is essentially about rhetoric rather than policy proposals, and is likely to be particularly useful for looking at which social groups are appealed to. We code party leaders' speeches at the annual party conferences for every year since 1945 and see how references to class, and classes, have changed, and whether other groups have taken their place.

Finally, we look at how the social composition of MPs within each party has changed over time, and most importantly whether voters have paid attention to anything that the parties have done. We show that voters have noticed these changes, both in terms of policy, and also in their views of the parties as class parties. Ultimately, our argument is that the signals, in terms of policy, rhetoric and personnel, from politicians to voters have changed and that voters have recognized these changes.

Party Policy

The post-war story of British politics and policy is thought to be well known. Labour's landslide electoral victory in May 1945 produced a raft of policies on health care, welfare, and public ownership that laid the fundamentals of what became known as the post-war consensus. The acceptance of many of these policies by the Conservatives, combined with an initial commitment in its 1947 Industrial Charter not to reverse them, ensured their continuation as the fundamentals of British public policy until the 1970s. The end of the post-war 'boom' in the wake of the 1973 oil crisis signalled the departure from this consensus. Ensuing strikes, three-day weeks, years of high inflation, and the intervention of the IMF laid bare underlying differences between the parties and ultimately led to Thatcherism. The emergence of 'Blairism' moving Labour to the right in response has likewise been well documented: the dropping of the traditional version of Clause IV of Labour's constitution in 1995 and the simple fact that Labour's manifestos have not contained the word 'socialism' since 1992.

Of course, this oversimplifies the movements of the two parties. Although most interpretations of political developments have been carried out by contemporary historians with rich descriptive studies of parties and their strategies, we turn here to quantitative measures of where parties stand on economic left–right issues. We analyse the party manifestos using coded policy content collected by the Manifesto Project on Political Representation (MARPOR) (Budge et al. 2001; Klingemann et al. 2006; Volkens et al. 2015). Sentences in the manifestos are grouped into fifty-six themes and policy areas, as shown in Appendix Table A6.1. Sentences are then divided by the total number of sentences in the manifesto to standardize for their varying lengths. Finally, the manifestos are coded into left-versus right-wing positions. Although MARPOR has developed a simple additive measure which sums and subtracts percentages of sentences referring to policies (RiLe), we use a more sophisticated economic left–right scale developed by Prosser (2014). This uses some of the same building blocks as the RiLe, but is more focused on economic

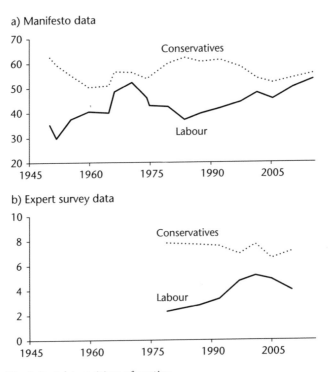

Figure 6.1. The left–right position of parties

Note: The figures here show the positions of the two main parties on left–right policy scales; higher scores indicate more right wing positions. The left-hand graph shows positions using manifesto data (two period moving average) and a procedure presented in Prosser (2014). The right-hand graph shows expert ratings of parties on 0–10 scales.

Source: Manifesto Project on Political Representation 1945–2015; Castles and Mair 1984; Laver and Hunt 1992; Ray 1999; Steenbergen and Marks 2007; Hooghe et al. 2010.

left–right positions and avoids some of the methodological weaknesses associated with RiLe. More detailed information on how the manifestos were coded using this procedure is presented in the appendix to this chapter.

The left-hand graph in Figure 6.1 shows the extent to which Labour and the Conservative manifestos emphasize left- or right-wing policy positions from 1945 until the present day. The absolute positions of parties on a left–right spectrum cannot be ascertained using these coding procedures, but their relative positions can be. We can see the size of the policy difference between the parties and how they move relative to one another. During the immediate post-war era there is a marked gap between the parties. Indeed it takes until the late 1960s for the Conservatives to converge with Labour. The policy gap then almost immediately emerges again during the 1970s. This perhaps fits better with more revisionist accounts of the post-war consensus that claim that any consensus was more myth than reality (Pimlott 1992). In fact, some argue that clear continuities can be observed in major areas such as economic policy, union relations, and welfare for the first fifteen years after the war (Kavanagh and Morris 1994). We would tend to agree with this. While the two parties did converge on policy after the war, this was not until the late 1960s and it was for a relatively limited period of time.

Yet there is another period of convergence. The policy divisions between the parties also collapsed during the 1990s, but this time did not re-appear. The most striking shift in Labour's position took place under Tony Blair between 1992 and 2001.[1] This was explicitly stated in their 1997 manifesto: 'We aim to put behind us the bitter political struggles of left and right that have torn our country apart for too many decades. Many of these conflicts have no relevance whatsoever to the modern world—public versus private, bosses versus workers, middle class versus working class. It is time for this country to move on and move forward.'

This dramatic shift is also shown in another source of information on policy convergence between the two main parties. This is a set of 'expert surveys' conducted over the period 1982–2010. These surveys are undertaken within the community of academics who study British politics. They are asked to score parties on a wide range of policy scales. These answers can then be used to give an assessment of party positions on the left–right dimension.[2] In the right-hand graph of Figure 6.1, we present estimates of the Labour and Conservative Parties' general left–right positions from the expert surveys that cover the elections during this period. Again we see a particularly pronounced policy convergence in British politics during the 1990s. There is a sharp tightening of the gap between Labour and the Conservatives at the time of the 1997 election. The move by Labour to a more centrist position, combined with a general re-branding of its image, appears to have been a one-step change. There has been some evidence of divergence since, but it is far less pronounced.

Group Appeals

Party positions are not the same as group appeals. Manifestos and expert surveys indicate that a more ideologically neutral policy programme has been adopted by both main parties. But this is an indirect indicator of different parties' concern with class groups. A more direct indicator is whether manifestos still refer to classes. While manifestos very rarely refer to class politics directly, they do talk about particular groups. To examine the use of class appeals, we code the use of terms that can be reasonably thought as representing the working class. We also consider references to groups—the unemployed, the poor, and unions—who are likely to be linked in some way with the working class, as well as alternative, class-neutral groups like 'families'. We code the manifestos using computer-based coding procedures (Lexicoder).[3] We were also able to obtain hand-coded analyses of the original full party manifestos for all elections between 1974 and 2005, the period of most marked change, from Mads Thau. He maps out which parties best represent which constituents in terms of the claims made about their interests (Thau 2016).

Figure 6.2 shows direct mentions of the working class in the manifestos using both methods. The graph on the left is the computer-coded data; the graph on the right is the hand-coded data. Both show very similar patterns. Over time, Labour's manifesto references to workers clearly decline. This

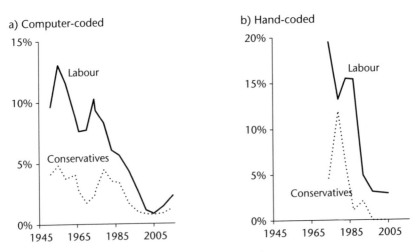

Figure 6.2. References to 'the working class' in manifestos

Note: The left-hand graph here shows the percentage of group references that refer to the working class in all Labour and Conservative Party manifestos (three period moving average). These are coded directly from the manifesto text using a computer-based coding procedure (Lexicoder). The right-hand graph shows the percentage of group references to the working class coded from the original manifesto documents 1974–2005 by Thau (2016).

Source: Manifesto Project on Political Representation 1945–2015.

change is most dramatic during the elections between 1987 and 2001. For the hand-coded data, the percentage of Labour class appeals referring to the working class falls from an average of just over 15 per cent in the 1970s and 1980s, to just 3 per cent from 1997 onwards. These sorts of references are generally less noticeable for the Conservatives, which is perhaps unsurprising, though they too used to refer to workers rather more than they do nowadays. Nonetheless, the main point is that Labour used to appeal regularly to the working class and it has stopped doing so to such a degree that there is now essentially no difference between the two parties.

Figure 6.3 shows how references to trade unions and the unemployed follow a pattern that matches the political saliency of the issues. High rates of union militancy and high rates of unemployment tend to mean that the parties talk about them more. The declining prominence of unions following the Thatcher government's reforms is reflected in the manifestos of both parties from the 1980s onwards. Union appeals peaked at the beginning of the 1980s for Labour, but fell after then. Although the Conservatives mentioned unions quite frequently in the immediate post-war period, the peak in the early 1980s is also quite pronounced. References to the unemployed increase for both parties during the period of high unemployment in the 1980s and early 1990s and then subside. Moreover, we can see the origins of a different perspective on the unemployed from the 1997 Labour manifesto which asserted that: 'we will get

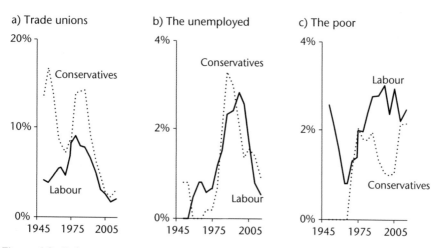

Figure 6.3. References to unions, the unemployed, and the poor in manifestos

Note: The left-hand graph here shows the percentage of group references that refer to unions in all Labour and Conservative Party manifestos (three period moving average). The middle graph shows the percentage that refer to the unemployed (three period moving average). The right-hand graph shows the percentage that refer to the poor (three period moving average). These are coded directly from the manifesto text using a computer-based coding procedure (Lexicoder).

Source: Manifesto Project on Political Representation 1945–2015.

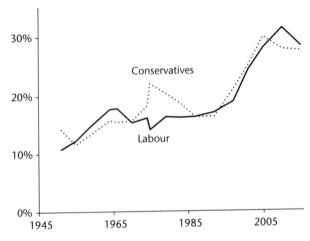

Figure 6.4. References to families in manifestos

Note: The figure here shows the percentage of group references that refer to families in all Labour and Conservative Party manifestos (three period moving average). These are coded directly from the manifesto text using a computer-based coding procedure (Lexicoder).

Source: Manifesto Project on Political Representation 1945–2015.

the unemployed from welfare to work' and we will 'stop the growth of an "underclass" in Britain'. The idea of the unemployed as an 'underclass' contrasts with previous manifestos which tended to blame the economy for unemployment.[4] References to the 'poor' display volatility in the earlier years but then reach a stable, but low, level from which there is no decline.

But if class appeals have withered, who or what have taken their place? If we want to see where parties nowadays focus their references and their appeals, we need to turn to 'class-neutral' notions of family and parenthood. As Figure 6.4 demonstrates, references to families increase dramatically for both parties.

References to families are not only of a much larger magnitude generally, they nowadays constitute approximately 30 per cent of all references for both parties. Even at their peak in the late 1950s, no more than 13 per cent of appeals by Labour, and far fewer by the Conservatives, concerned the working class in any form. Moreover, this is a dramatic and swift change, taking place almost entirely after 1997. Families are the inclusive reference group for the political parties today. The rapid rise of the family as the key political focal point can be illustrated by examining every mention in party manifestos of the now fashionable reference to 'working families'. We can see how it starts with the Conservatives who refer to 'working families' in their 1992 manifesto, followed by similar references in 1997 ('we are shifting power and wealth back to working families') and 2001 ('Labour have increased taxes on hard-working families'), before it was picked up by Labour in 2005 with 'a plan to improve the lives of hard-working families'. From then on both parties deployed this usefully class-neutral and socially positive construct, especially in 2015. Compare: 'We want a better deal—and low bills—for hard-working families' (Conservatives) versus 'we will reform the energy market so that it delivers fairer prices and a better deal for working families' (Labour).

In short, we find a striking decline in appeals to workers and a striking rise in references to general notions of family. Much of this transition in emphasis took place from the 1990s onwards.

Party Rhetoric

But what of rhetoric? Leaders' speeches are perhaps a better way of assessing group appeals. To examine leaders' speeches we use the same coding proced- ure as we used for the manifestos. As we shall see, they tell pretty much the same story, with one interesting exception that fits well with their function as a partisan, in-group versus out-group, rallying-call. This exception is the tendency for speeches to refer occasionally to class envy, division, and conflict explicitly. Always, however, this is for rhetorical purposes and even then is used very sparingly. Direct mentions of social class are so rare (fewer than sixty mentions in both parties' leaders' speeches over almost seventy years) that plotting quantitative figures makes little sense. We can get a clearer idea of this use of class by reading the speeches. When we do, we find some surprises. The leaders who most clearly assert the language of class are Blair for Labour and Churchill for the Conservatives.

For Churchill, this is true in opposition: 'The driving force of Socialism is class hatred and envy' (1949); and government: 'our opponents have another theme on which they greatly count—I mean class warfare and the exploit- ation of jealousy and envy' (1953). Labour's promotion of class warfare and class envy was a theme echoed more sporadically by later Conservative leaders such as Macmillan: 'Our aim is to harmonize different and conflicting inter- ests, not to set them against each other with the strident accents of the class war' (1960). And also Thatcher: 'Class warfare is immoral, a poisonous relic of the past' (1978) and 'Labour relish class division. They depend on it. It's the root of all Socialism' (1984). John Major briefly reiterated the idea: 'It's a matter of breaking down the false and futile divisions, based on class and envy, that have been around for generations. Labour fosters those divisions' (1991). However, the use of class as rhetoric by Conservative leaders seemed to have faded from then on. New Labour's leadership had effectively removed the power of class war rhetoric.[5]

References to class by Labour leaders are similarly rare. During the 1950s, class is not present at all, as speeches while in opposition focused primarily on foreign policy. Wilson did use the class warfare theme negatively to label the opposition: 'Let us leave to them their vision of Britain, the Britain they seek to restore, a class-ridden Britain, a Britain of privilege, of social privilege, of educational privilege, a Britain based on the right of that privileged class to lord it over all the rest of Britain's citizens whom we represent' (1966). But it is actually Blair who used the rhetoric of class most clearly. Like a Churchill in reverse, he used references to class divisions as a way of explicitly or implicitly denigrating the Conservatives: 'We are proud of our history, but its weight hangs heavy upon us. Why? Because for far too long it has left us defining ourselves as a nation, not by what unites us, but by what divides us: a class system, unequal and antiquated' (1994). His aim in contrast was to 'create a model twenty-first-century nation, based not on privilege, class, or background, but on the equal worth of all. The class war is over. But the struggle for true equality has only just begun...it is us, the new radicals, the Labour party modernized, that must undertake this historic mission. To liberate Britain from the old class divisions, old structures, old prejudices' (1999).

We might say that Conservative class war rhetoric was pronounced in the post-war era, returned intermittently in the conflictual 1970s and 1980s, and then faded once Blair had rendered Labour harder to criticize on that front. Labour's rhetorical use of class is like a mirror image of the Conservatives: class division is bad (them), openness and classlessness is good (us). Ironically, this class rhetoric was most forcefully invoked just as Labour decisively shifted away from the working class. It was then dropped again: Ed Miliband made no reference to class in any of his speeches.

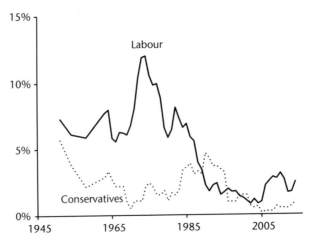

Figure 6.5. References to 'the working class' in speeches by party leaders

Note: The figure here shows the percentage of group references that refer to the working class in leaders' party conference speeches (six period moving average). These are coded directly from the full transcripts using both manual and computer-based coding procedures (Lexicoder).

Source: British Political Speech Archive 1945–2014.

These direct mentions of class politics aside, there are substantial similarities between the content of speeches and manifestos in terms of group references. Figure 6.5 shows references to workers as a proportion of all group references. As with the manifestos, we code the party leaders' speeches using computer based coding procedures. See the Appendix for details.

The figure is far denser than the same figures for the manifestos because of the far larger number of leaders' speeches. Apart from the added detail, however, this is a very similar picture to that seen with the manifestos. Conservative leaders rarely mention the working class, although the spirit of 'big working class' Britain can occasionally be seen in the immediate post war period. For example, in his 1950 speech Churchill encouraged constituencies to select 'active Trade Unionists and others representing the views of our brothers and sisters in the working classes of the nation'. Labour leaders emphasize the working class much more often, but from the late 1980s onwards the working class as a group largely disappears from view. Kinnock started to de-emphasize the working class and Blair finished that process. In fact, references to the working class by Blair declined to levels similar to those found in the party speeches of Conservative leaders.

If we look at references to unions, the unemployed, and the poor in Figure 6.6, we see the same pattern observed in the manifestos: both union and unemployment references spike sharply upwards during the 1970s and the 1980s respectively, but then fall back to insignificance. These changes clearly reflect the levels and urgency of unemployment (and union conflict) as an

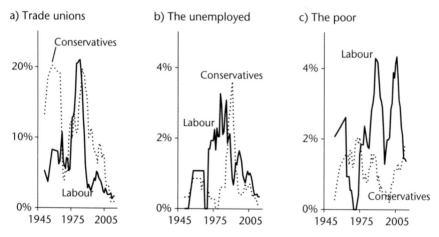

Figure 6.6. References to unions, the unemployed, and the poor in speeches by party leaders

Note: The left-hand graph here shows the percentage of group references that refer to trade unions in leaders' party conference speeches (six period moving average). The middle graph shows the percentage of all speech units that refer to the unemployed (six period moving average). The right-hand graph shows the percentage of all speech units that refer to the poor (six period moving average).

Source: British Political Speech Archive 1945–2014.

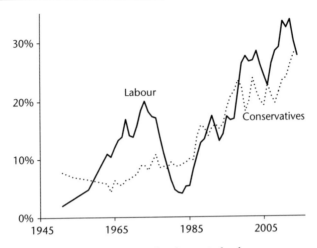

Figure 6.7. References to families in speeches by party leaders

Note: The figure here shows the percentage of group references that refer to families in leaders' party conference speeches (six period moving average).

Source: British Political Speech Archive 1945–2014.

issue. Unlike those groups, and just as in the manifestos, references to the poor did not decline in the 1990s. They persisted without being a major feature of contemporary speeches (a few percent of group references at most). As with the manifestos, however, the really marked trend is in a much greater emphasis on families. As Figure 6.7 shows, both parties' leaders increasingly refer to families, parents, and children.

In summary, the working class no longer features very noticeably in the vocabulary of our parties and politicians. It appears that politicians have moved from appealing to the working class, when formulating and discussing policy or programmes, to the catch-all politics of the Blair era and beyond. Modern reference groups are mainly neutral, such as the now familiar 'hard-working families'. Of course, this is a way to avoid supporting or opposing any particular social group.

Party Personnel

Signals can be sent by the things politicians and parties say and do, but they can also be sent by the background of politicians themselves. The social similarity between a social group and their representatives has become known as descriptive representation (Pitkin 1967). In principle a man can share the concerns and values of a woman, a middle class person those of a working class person, and a white person those of a non-white person, but there is likely to be a connection between socially similar representatives and their voters with respect to shared values and experiences. Political scientists have argued that 'demographic facts provide a low-information shortcut to estimating a candidate's policy preferences... characteristics such as a candidate's race, ethnicity, religion, gender, and local ties are important cues because the voter observes the relationship between these traits and real-life behavior as part of his daily experience' (Popkin 1991, p.63). So, whatever leaders proclaim publicly, voters might think it likely that their social character will dispose them to 'look after their own'. In short, social dissimilarity from politicians is expected to reduce the expected benefit of voting for them (Cutler 2002).

Consistent with these arguments, there is a body of empirical research, mainly in the USA, which finds that people prefer candidates or leaders who are the same race or gender.[6] Oliver Heath also argues that in Britain lower numbers of working class Labour MPs have depressed Labour voting among working class voters, reducing class voting (Heath 2015) and increasing abstention among the working class (Heath 2016). When Campbell and Cowley (2014) conducted a survey experiment on how people reacted to hypothetical candidates with differing levels of wealth, they found that working class people were indeed more negative about wealthy candidates, particularly with respect to a candidate's perceived 'approachability'.[7]

At the highest echelons of politics we can easily see that descriptive representation by class is not the case. Over half of the 2015 Conservative cabinet was privately educated.[8] For Labour, politicians from working class backgrounds traditionally played prominent roles: think of Ernest Bevin and Aneurin Bevan in the post-war years. This has changed over time, however. Whereas half of the 1945 Labour cabinet had previously held working class jobs, when Labour entered office in 1997 there was just one cabinet minister who previously had a working class occupation (John Prescott).

If the social make up of parties matters, then it is clearly important to examine what has happened to descriptive representation by class over the long-term. Fortunately, we can analyse how the social composition of the Labour and Conservative parties has changed over the last half century or so. Figure 6.8 shows the percentage of Labour and Conservative MPs who held working class jobs before being elected. We have data on this back to the 1959 election.[9]

By far the most noticeable feature of the figure is the very gradual nature of the decline of working class Labour MPs between 1959 and 1992—a fall, yes, but of barely more than 10 per cent over more than thirty years. The number then fell this much again in the space of just one electoral cycle between 1992 and 1997. Labour's 1997 landslide brought a raft of new MPs into Parliament and these MPs were middle class. The media attention at the time may have been on 'Blair's babes' in recognition of the number of women now in the Parliamentary Labour Party, but the dramatic increase was really in the proportion of people who had held middle class jobs.

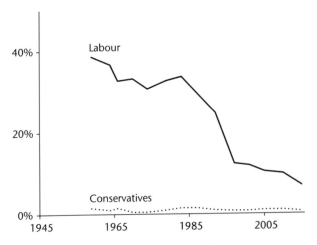

Figure 6.8. MPs who previously had working class jobs

Note: The figure here shows the proportion of MPs who previously had a working class job before entering Parliament. These are jobs that fall within our foremen and working class categories.

Source: Datacube collated by the EurElite network (Best and Cotta 2000; Cotta and Best 2007). Updated with figures taken from the British General Election book series published after each election.

Trade unions were historically an important route of access into Labour politics by the working class. To examine more detailed information about MPs we can use evidence from the Parliamentary Candidates UK Dataset.[10] This shows that while around 10 per cent of Labour MPs were previously union officials from the 1950s to the 1980s, by 2015 only 1 per cent of Labour MPs had worked for a trade union. The opposite story is the case for university education. Among Labour MPs in 1959 only 41 per cent had a university education, compared with around 80 per cent by 2010. As Figure 6.9 shows, the gap between Labour and Conservative MPs in university education has now been completely closed. In fact, it had closed by the 1990s. Since then both parties have increased their proportion of university-educated MPs in parallel.

These changes should not be taken to indicate that politics has been taken over by a socially exclusive elite, however. If we look at more fine-grained information on where MPs went to school and university as shown in Figure 6.10, we see that the two main parties have converged. Conservative MPs have become noticeably less likely to have attended a private school, and Labour MPs have changed little in this respect. Similarly, Conservative MPs have become less likely to have attended Oxford or Cambridge, while Labour MPs have become more likely to have done so. Interestingly, therefore, as Labour MPs have become more professionalized, the social composition of the Conservatives has become less exclusive and more similar to that of the Labour party. In terms of educational exclusivity in particular, the two parties have become more alike.

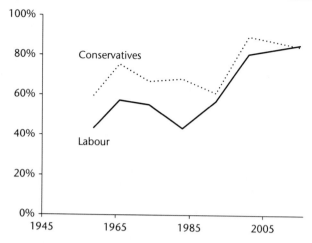

Figure 6.9. MPs who went to university

Note: The figure here shows the proportion of MPs who have a university first degree or higher degree.

Source: Parliamentary Candidates UK Dataset.

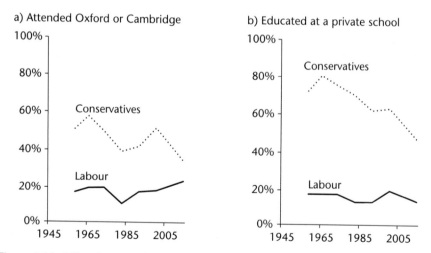

Figure 6.10. MPs who attended Oxbridge or a private school

Note: The left-hand graph here shows the proportion of MPs who went to the universities of Oxford or Cambridge. The right-hand graph shows the proportion of MPs who were educated at a private school.

Source: Parliamentary Candidates UK Dataset.

Former Conservative Chancellor, and Home Secretary, Kenneth Clarke recently described his memories of the Commons when he was first elected in 1970 as 'old landed gentry with rolling estates' on one side and 'retired trade union regional secretaries and 30-odd miners' on the other (*Independent*, 28 July 2014). This does not fit the reality today. We now see a preponderance of MPs who reach politics via university and jobs in the professions and management. The influx of women MPs has reduced the discrepancy between parties and their voters descriptively, but there has been a growing discrepancy between Labour and its working class supporters. This trend in part reflects the shrinking of the traditional working class as a recruitment base, but it is also because party recruitment procedures are very different now than in the mid-twentieth century (Norris and Lovenduski 1995). The contemporary trend is for politicians to enter politics through working as political interns or members of lobby groups. In 2015 18 per cent of MPs had moved into parliament from other directly political jobs and another 12 per cent had come from a different elected office (van Heerde-Hudson and Campbell 2015). This means that an increasing number of MPs spend their entire adult lives in politics or on its fringes.

Has Anyone Noticed?

The evidence of party change is pretty clear-cut, but the perception of such signals by ordinary voters cannot be assumed. After all, politics is for most people 'a side-show in the circus of life' (Key 1966). Did voters notice any of the changes to the parties over the last fifty years? To assess changes in voters' perceptions of party platforms on left–right issues, we examine their perceptions of party polarization. We do this using a question in the BES since 1964, and the BSA since 1997, that asks people: 'Considering everything the Conservative and Labour parties stand for, would you say there is a great deal of difference between the parties, some difference, or not much difference?'[11]

Although there is no explicit reference to economic left–right policy in this question, it seems reasonable to assume that voters are largely reacting to this dominant axis of political competition. As can be seen from Figure 6.11, the proportions of people who perceive a 'great deal' of difference between the parties in each election and the difference between the Labour and Conservative parties in left–right manifesto positions are connected. In particular, we see the impact of the brief convergence in the late 1960s/early 1970s and the sharp, and lasting, convergence that occurred between the 1987 and 1997 elections when Labour moved to its much more centrist position and rebranded itself as New Labour.

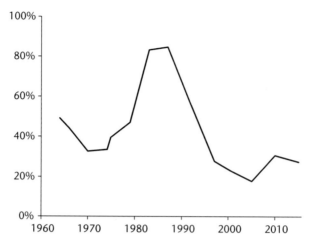

Figure 6.11. Perceived differences between the parties

Note: The figure here shows the percentage of people who believe there is a 'great deal of difference' between the Conservative and Labour parties at each election from 1964 to 2015.

Source: British Election Studies 1964–2015; British Social Attitudes Surveys 1997–2015.

If the parties are perceived to have converged in recent years, have the voters' perceptions of the degree to which they represent the working and middle classes changed accordingly? Both our analysis of the changes in group references and the decline in the number of working class Labour MPs might suggest that Labour is now more likely to be seen by the electorate as representing the interests of the middle class. We can test this using some questions on class representation by the main political parties that were introduced in the 1987 BES. These ask people how closely they think that the two main parties look after the interests of middle class and working class people. People can answer from 'not at all closely' to 'very closely'. We use these questions to create a measure of whether people think the parties look after working class people better than middle class people or vice versa. To construct this scale we scored the response categories as 1 (not at all closely) to 4 (very closely) and subtracted responses to the middle class question from those to the working class question. This gives a scale that runs from −3 to 3 for each party. As very few people have scores of +3 or −3, we combine −2 and −3 and +2 and +3 responses. A positive score means that people think that a party looks after the working class better than the middle class. Negative scores mean that people think a party looks after the middle class better than the working class.

Figure 6.12 shows how these perceptions have changed since 1987. We can see that by 1997 Labour's connection with the interests of the working class had dropped dramatically. The policy of reaching out across class boundaries had worked in the eyes of the electorate. Indeed it had worked so well that by

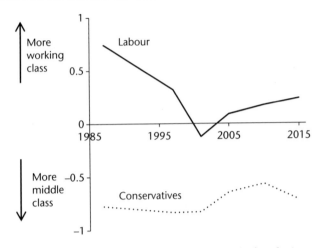

Figure 6.12. Perceptions of the extent to which parties look after the interests of classes

Note: The figure here shows people's perceptions of which classes the parties represent. A positive score means that people believe a party looks after the working class better than the middle class; a negative score means that people think a party looks after the middle class better than the working class.

Source: British Election Studies 1987–2015.

2001 the middle class was actually thought to be better represented by Labour than was the working class.[12] The changes in perceptions of the party after the Blair years blur this picture a little, but there has been no return to anywhere near the former level of perceived association between party and class. Perceptions of the Conservatives are much more stable over time. They are consistently seen as more likely to represent the interests of the middle class than the working class.

We can also take an even longer-term perspective on perceptions of working class representation by the parties. Although we do not have an identical question from the 1960s to the ones used above, in the 1964 BES people were asked to choose whether Labour 'is a working class or middle class party'. This question was repeated in the 2015 BES. In 1964 90 per cent said that the Conservatives were a middle class party and 85 per cent of people said that Labour was a working class party. In 2015 88 per cent still said that the Conservatives were a middle class party, but only 38 per cent said that Labour was a working class party. In fact, in 2015 more people thought that Labour was middle class (48 per cent) than working class.[13] Like the USA, Britain's party system is now dominated not by two class parties, but by two middle class parties.

It seems likely that the perception of the parties as class parties is shaped by several factors. One of these is the degree to which group rhetoric features in speeches, but another is what the party looks like in terms of elites. If MPs appear indistinguishable from one another in terms of class background, then voters are likely to make a much weaker connection between parties and class groups. As mentioned earlier, Heath (2015) makes exactly this argument. Thus some of the class-party perceptions that we look at here may be driven by a number of 'objective' factors about the parties. The specific role of descriptive representation can be looked at more closely, however. The 1966 BES survey asked respondents about their local MPs and specifically whether they 'would say that he/she is upper class, middle class, or working class?'. We repeated this question after the 2015 election. Of course, both surveys cover only a fraction of the constituencies and so we cannot say anything about general perceptions of MPs. What we can do is link people's responses to characteristics of their actual MP, as well as linking those MP's characteristics to their general view of the parties.

What would we expect? There are two possibilities. The first is that people today make a weaker link between their MP's occupational background and their class, and they also make a weaker link between their MP's class and their general perceptions of the party. The second is that these processes have remained the same; it is simply that the background of MPs has changed. It appears that the second of these fits better with the evidence. It is the parties that have changed, not the way in which people form political opinions.

Table 6.1 shows predicted probabilities from a multinomial multilevel logit regression model that predicts the class to which people think their MP belongs for the 1966 and 2015 surveys. Respondents are also asked, beforehand, to identify the party of their MP and we just look at people who can correctly identify their MP's party.[14] We use both the party of the MP and two key social characteristics of the MP: their educational background and their occupational social class measured by their previous job.[15] Both of

Table 6.1. The proportion of people who think their MP is working class by party and social background of MP

		1966	2015
Conservative MP	*Elite background*	0%	4%
	Working class background	1%	24%
Labour MP	*Elite background*	5%	19%
	Working class background	44%	63%

Note: The numbers here are predicted probabilities from multilevel multinomial logit models that predict whether people think their MP is working class (as opposed to upper or middle class). These models include measures of the local MP's party affiliation and educational/occupational characteristics and are only run for people who know the party of their MP. Two types of constituency are displayed, split by party. The first are constituencies with an 'elite MP': elite MPs previously had managerial jobs and attended Oxford or Cambridge. The second are constituencies with a 'working class MP': working class MPs previously had manual jobs and did not attend university. The models that we use here are multilevel and thus account for the fact that people are clustered by constituency. In 1966 we have data on 68 constituencies with 618 individual voter responses spread across those constituencies. In 2015 we have data on 261 constituencies and 1,387 individual voters.

Source: British Election Studies 1966 and 2015.

these factors are strong predictors of how people perceive the class of their MP. Table 6.1 shows the predicted probability of someone placing their MP into different classes for two types of MP by party. The first MP type is someone who was formerly a manager and went to Oxbridge (an MP from the 'elite'). The second MP type is someone who previously had a working class job and had not been to university (a working class MP).

In 1966 44 per cent of people with a Labour MP who previously had a working class job and had not been to university thought that he (and all the Labour constituencies included in the 1966 survey had male MPs) was working class compared to only 5 per cent of people with a Labour MP from a managerial background with a degree from Oxbridge. As the figure shows, that difference is almost exactly the same in 2015. The MP's occupational and educational background is clearly telling people something about that MP's social class, and this has not really changed over time. Indeed, if anything, people appear to make stronger connections in 2015 between the characteristics of their MP and their social class. The alleged increased concentration on candidates in British elections and the increased levels of constituency work that MPs undertake (Norton 1994) may have strengthened the ability of voters to make these judgements. Nonetheless, the bigger picture is one of stasis.

We can also link the characteristics of MPs more directly to the perceptions of parties. Part of the reason that people think that Labour is less representative of the working class may be due to the changing nature of descriptive representation. If so, then we should find that people with working class Labour MPs are more likely to view Labour as a working class party. This also appears to be the case. Figure 6.13 shows the results of models run with the 1966 and 2015 data predicting whether people think Labour is very or somewhat working class for people who were in a constituency with a Labour MP.[16] Again we use the MP's former occupation and educational background as predictors of these perceptions.

Figure 6.13 shows the differences between people who had a Labour MP who was formerly a manager and went to Oxbridge (an MP from the elite) versus a MP who previously had a working class job and had not been to university (a working class MP). These differences are both large and constant. In 1966 nearly 70 per cent of people with a working class Labour MP saw Labour as a working class party compared to fewer than 40 per cent of people with an elite Labour MP. By 2015 both these figures had dropped, due partly of course to the changes that we have already discussed in this chapter, but the gap remains. Nearly 40 per cent of people with a working class Labour MP in 2015 still thought that Labour was a working class party, compared with only 15 per cent of those with an elite Labour MP.

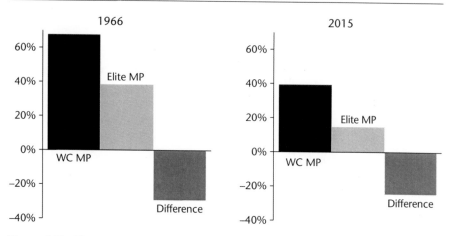

Figure 6.13. The proportion of people in Labour constituencies who agree that Labour is somewhat/very working class given the social characteristics of their MP

Note: These figures show predicted probabilities from multilevel logit models that predict whether people agree that Labour is a somewhat or very working class party. The models include measures of the local MP's educational and occupational characteristics and are only run for people who live in a Labour constituency. The darker bar in both graphs shows people in constituencies with a 'working class MP': working class MPs previously had manual jobs and did not attend university. The lighter bar in both graphs shows people in constituencies with an 'elite MP': elite MPs previously had managerial jobs and attended Oxford or Cambridge. The models that we use here are multilevel and account for the fact that people are clustered by constituency. In 1966 we have data on 43 constituencies with 453 individual voter responses spread across those constituencies. In 2015 we have data on 161 constituencies and 762 individual voters.

Source: British Election Studies 1966 and 2015.

This helps us to understand how perceptions of Labour have changed. Sixty-five per cent of people, in all constituencies, thought that Labour was a very or somewhat working class party in 1966 (a further 11 per cent said it was slightly working class). By 2015 just 23 per cent said that it was very or fairly working class (with a further 15 per cent saying it was slightly working class). At least part of the explanation for that change is that the direct cues that sitting Labour MPs give to constituents have altered. Using the figures above, if half of Labour MPs had remained working class as was the case fifty years ago, that decline would have shrunk by about a third (for at least those people in Labour constituencies and plausibly beyond). Descriptive representation does not explain everything as Heath (2015) alleges, but it is an important part of the story.

Conclusions

In Chapter 5 we argued that media discussion of class appeared to fall into three broad periods. There was a period of consensus around a dominant working class, a breakdown of that consensus over the 1970s and 1980s and then a new consensus from the 1990s onwards in which the middle class was dominant. In this chapter we see some echoes of that pattern of change in at least policy. While we should not exaggerate the degree of policy consensus that existed for the first twenty-five years after the war, there were points at which the major parties held relatively similar economic positions. This was driven by parties trying to appeal to the ordinary working man or woman. They had to do so if they were going to win elections. As noted in Chapter 1, the emergence of the welfare state, the extension of the public sector and the adoption of a Keynesian approach to minimizing unemployment were all implemented in the name of the working class. These policy differences widened during the 1970s and 1980s, and then converged in the 1990s onwards with the emergence of a new consensus.

Policy differentiation along left–right lines is only one form of interest representation, however. Parties can signal interest representation through direct references or appeals to relevant groups, via both policy and rhetoric. We have seen that references to the working class were particularly pronounced by Labour in the post-war era, but started to fall dramatically in both manifestos and leaders' speeches from the late 1980s onwards. Political appeals to the working class have now effectively disappeared from the lexicon of party politics. Just as discussion of class and class politics by the newspapers more or less stops by 1997, so do appeals to the working class by the political parties.

This picture is repeated when we look at party elites. Since the 1990s recruitment has been dominated on both sides by middle class people who are highly educated. The route from a working class job into politics, often through trade union activism, has effectively disappeared, and almost identical proportions of MPs in both parties now have a university background.

We have seen the two parties growing more alike: in policy, in class appeal, and in their patterns of recruitment by education and social class. Importantly, these different types of changes coincided most strongly during the 1990s. The earlier, and rather brief, period of convergence in the 1960s only applied to policy positions, not to the class-related appeals, rhetoric, and the personnel of the parties. Growing cross-party uniformity across a broad range of indicators only arrived in the early 1990s. Significantly, the electorate has in turn noticed these changes.

As a result of these combined transformations, there is now little connection between policy, party, and class in mainstream British politics. The disappearance of class from both media and party messages leaves few class-based cues for voters. In Chapters 7 and 8 we explore the consequences of this change for how people choose to vote.

Notes

1. There are of course numerous commentaries examining the Blair effect and New Labour's transformation which also qualitatively indicate this change (King 1997; Seyd 1997; Seldon 2007; Fielding 2003).

2. Rehm and Reilly (2010) provide details of most of the expert surveys used here (but also see Castles and Mair 1984; Laver and Hunt 1992; Steenbergen and Marks 2007; Hooghe et al. 2010; Bakker et al. 2015). Unfortunately, this approach for measuring party positions did not start until 1982 so cannot be used to measure positions before the 1979 election.

3. For example, for workers the coding dictionary is composed of three terms: 'worker', 'miner', and 'working class'. The Lexicoder coding system also includes preceding words, so 'ordinary workers' and 'factory workers' are both coded as 'workers'. For 'the poor' the stem is just 'poor' (so 'poor', 'the poorest', 'poor people', etc.). See the Appendix for more details of the coding system.

4. In 1966, for example, Labour proclaimed that 'The level of economic activity in the community must be sufficient to provide jobs for all'. The idea of 'jobs for all' was a dominant theme of many Labour manifestos before the 1990s.

5. In 1999 William Hague was moved to claim: ' "The class war is over", says Tony Blair. Tell that to thousands of vindictive, mean-spirited, class-obsessed Labour party activists' But notice that his reference is not to the Parliamentary Labour Party, but Labour activists.

6. On the gender of candidates see: Tolleson Rinehart (1992); Huddy and Terkildsen (1993); Bendyna and Lake (1994); Huddy (1994); Cook (1994); Plutzer and Zipp (1996); Dolan (1998); Campbell et al. (2010); Childs and Webb (2010). On the race of candidates see: Tate (1993); Terkildsen (1993); Sigelman et al. (1995).

7. We do not address here the question of whether parliamentarians' own class backgrounds matter for policy. The most significant research on this has been done by Carnes (2012) in the US. He shows that, all things being equal, legislators from working class occupational backgrounds have more left-wing economic preferences.

8. Although the incoming 2015 cabinet was still noticeably less socially exclusive than it was in the 1950s. Ten of Eden's fourteen ministers were related to aristocratic families, thirty-five out of eighty-five of Macmillan's government were relatives following his marriage to a Duke's daughter, and half of Douglas-Home's cabinet were Etonians (Nordlinger 1967: 41).

9. These data are taken from those collected by the datacube project (Best and Cotta 2000; Cotta and Best 2007) with additional information presented in the British General Election books published after each election. Similar figures up until 2010 are presented in Heath (2015).

10. For more information see http://www.parliamentarycandidates.org.

11. This question changes very slightly over time. Before 1974 the first option is a 'good' rather than a 'great' deal of difference, and before 1979 the wording is 'Considering everything the parties stand for, would you say there is a great deal of difference between them, some difference, or not much difference?'.

12. An interesting contrast is with the degree to which people think that Labour represents the interests of 'black and Asian people'. The proportion of the

population who believed this increased to 90 per cent during the first decade of this century before falling back to just under 80 per cent in 2015; still an extremely high level. There appears to be a trade-off in the extent to which the party represents the working class versus how closely it represents ethnic minorities: when one goes up the other goes down. This may relate to the party's endorsement of diversity and affirmative action policies at the perceived expense of groups such as the working class (Barry 2001, pp.11–12) with, according to some, Labour having 'learned to love identity and ignore inequality' (Michaels 2006).

13. Gavin (1996) shows that people's answers to open-ended questions about why they voted for Labour were just as focused on class in 1987 as they were in the 1960s, suggesting that this change in perceptions did not happen before the 1987–2015 data shown in Figure 6.12.

14. The proportions of people who are able to do this are not completely comparable between the 1966 and 2015 surveys because of question-wording effects regarding 'don't knows', question-ordering effects (whether people were asked the name of their MP first), and to some extent timing effects. In the 1966 survey, which took place directly after the election, 90 per cent could accurately identify their MP's party. For 2015, for which the fieldwork continued for almost six months after the election, these rates are lower: 60 per cent of people in England and Wales accurately named their MP's party. The 2015 SNP landslide reduced this accuracy rate to 22 per cent in Scotland, with many people not realizing that their previous Labour MP was no longer in place. However, because the question on MPs' social class in the 1960s was preceded by a filter question ('Have you heard anything about your MP?') we actually end with similar rates of response to class questions for both surveys. For example, in 1966 90 per cent of people knew the party of their MP, but only 50 per cent of them had 'heard anything' about their MP and therefore 45 per cent of people assessed their MP's social class (with 8 per cent saying 'don't know'). In 2015 56 per cent of people correctly identified their MP's party, but all of them gave a response to the question about their MP's social class (with 32 per cent saying 'don't know'). This means that overall we end up with about 40 per cent of respondents in both 1966 and 2015 giving an upper, middle, or working class designation to their MP.

15. Education is categorized into three groups: no degree, non-Oxbridge degree, and Oxbridge degree. This divides the 1966 MPs roughly into three. The occupational class groupings are not exactly the same as the one we have used before for voters, but are similar, apart from more differentiation within the middle class and less differentiation within the working class. This gives us five groups: managers; employers including farmers; professionals; intermediate ancillary and supervisory workers and any junior non-manual workers; working class which includes personal service workers and foremen/technicians. MPs previously in the armed forces are coded as managers. The models that we use here are multilevel and thus account for the fact that people are clustered by constituency. In 1966 we have data on 68 constituencies (with 616 individual voter responses spread across those constituencies). In 2015 we have data on 261 constituencies and 1,387 individual voters.

16. This question is the same as the seven category question discussed earlier which asks people, 'how middle class or working class are the main political parties?' and allows them to answer from 'very middle class' to 'very working class'.

Appendix to Chapter 6

Further Information on the Coding of Party Manifestos and Leaders' Speeches

Manifestos

The text of the manifestos came from http://www.politicsresources.net/area/uk/man.htm and the manifestos were also cross-checked manually. Numerous manifesto components are included in the manifesto left–right scale. These are shown in Table A6.1.

Responses for each of these categories are then coded to create a uni-dimensional left–right scale. The scale was derived by an inductive process that begins from a 'naïve' starting scale (based on earlier scales). The scale is then constructed using Lowe et al.'s (2011) logit scaling technique, using the formula:

$$\theta^L = log \frac{R + 0.5}{L + 0.5}$$

where R is the total number of quasi-sentences in the manifesto components on the 'right' of the scale and L is the total number of quasi-sentences in the manifesto

Table A6.1. Manifesto components included in the left–right scale

Left		Right	
105	Military: Negative	109	Internationalism: Negative
106	Peace	401	Free Enterprise: Positive
107	Internationalism: Positive	407	Protectionism: Negative
202	Democracy	414	Economic Orthodoxy: Positive
301	Decentralization	505	Welfare State Limitation: Positive
303	Governmental and Administrative Efficiency	507	Education Limitation: Positive
403	Market Regulation: Positive	601	National Way of Life: Positive
408	Economic Goals	603	Traditional Morality: Positive
411	Technology and Infrastructure	608	Multiculturalism: Negative
412	Controlled Economy: Positive	702	Labour Groups: Negative
413	Nationalization: Positive		
416	Anti-Growth Economy		
501	Environmental Protection		
502	Culture		
503	Social Justice		
504	Welfare State Expansion: Positive		
506	Education Expansion: Positive		
602	National Way of Life: Negative		
604	Traditional Morality: Negative		
701	Labour Groups: Positive		
705	Underprivileged Minority Groups		
706	Non-economic Demographic Groups		

components on the 'left'. The logit scaling method combines the advantages of both additive and ratio-scaling methods for manifesto data, while avoiding the problem of polarization found in ratio scales. It also has an additional benefit of a diminishing impact of repeated emphasis and it therefore mirrors natural language usage. For ease of interpretation the scale is rescaled as follows:[1]

$$Rescaled\ dimension = (Scale\ position - Scale\ mean + 7) \times \frac{100}{14}$$

The robustness of this interpretation was checked using the hand-coded policy estimations of these party manifestos provided by Ian Budge, Judith Bara, and colleagues in the Comparative Manifesto Project (Budge et al. 2001; Volkens et al. 2015). These authors also provide an estimate of party positions on a left–right scale—what they refer to as RiLe.[2] As can be seen from Figure A6.1, the pattern identified by the RiLe scale mirrors those identified by our own coding procedures.

RiLe converges more quickly in the 1950s and there is a greater spike of polarization in 1974. It does not converge completely in the 1990s but the parties get very close in 1997 and remain so. On the whole it confirms the validity of the procedure used here. For more information on this scale, see Prosser (2014). Prosser's coding is preferred to RiLe, not just on the basis of face validity but because Prosser's scales make fewer assumptions about what categories 'should' go on the left or right. To give one example that changes sides, RiLe has 'Freedom and Human Rights' on the right-hand side (presumably because classical liberal parties will talk about individual freedoms) but left parties actually talk much more about things that get coded in that category (which is unsurprising). In the RiLe scale talking about human rights makes a party more right-wing; in Prosser's scale it makes a party more left-wing. Estimates of the reliability of Prosser's left–right scale, using the method that the authors of the RiLe scale themselves propose, find that it is more reliable than RiLe (McDonald and Budge 2014).

Leaders' Speech Sources

The group references in the leaders' speeches are coded using the same dictionary developed for the manifestos. The speeches are taken from the 'British Political Speech Archive' (http://www.britishpoliticalspeech.org/speech-archive.htm) collated by Alan Finlayson and Judi Atkins (2015). Finlayson and Atkins kindly sent us the Churchill speeches, which are not posted on the website. Although there are Labour speeches from 1945 to 1951, there are no Labour leader's speeches from 1952 to 1964 in the archive. This was because there was no 'leader speech' at those Labour party

---

[1] The logit scale does not have a natural midpoint or endpoint and so the mean of each scale is subtracted from the scale (which gives a midpoint and mean of 50 once rescaled). In practice, the endpoint of each scale approaches ±7, suggesting the rescaling formula used here.

[2] There have been recent debates about the reliability and validity of the CMP measures of party positions and the RiLe left–right scale (Laver and Garry 2000; Armstrong and Bakker 2006; Benoit and Laver 2007; Bakker and Hobolt 2013).

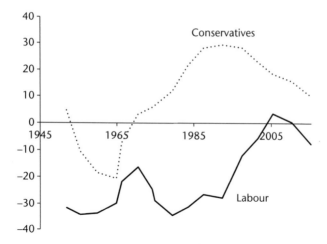

Figure A6.1. The comparative manifesto project estimate of left–right party positions (RiLe)

Note: The figures here show the positions of the two main parties on the RiLe left–right policy scale (three period moving average); higher scores indicate more right-wing positions.

Source: Manifesto Project on Political Representation 1945–2015.

conferences. However, between 1952 and 1964 the leader almost always spoke in various debates and was unsurprisingly given a prominent place. For those years we obtained the Labour party records held in the Bodleian Library and scanned each of the speeches. These were then turned into OCR files. This yielded several extra speeches (1954, 1958, 1963, and 1964).

Coding Procedure for Group Appeals in Manifestos and Leaders' Speeches

Coding up the group references was a multi-step process. The first stage was conducted on a subset of the full corpus, using the speeches from the party conference before each general election.

1) Each speech transcript was read and any reference to a group was coded as a group reference.
2) A group classification scheme was developed inductively.
3) Using the manual group coding, a dictionary of words identifying groups was constructed.

The second stage was conducted on the full corpus.

1) Using the dictionary constructed in stage 4, the full corpus was coded using Lexicoder 2.0 (http://www.lexicoder.com/).

2) The fact that some group speeches were coded both manually and by Lexicoder means we obtained an estimate of how reliable the auto-coding is. For the thirty-four speeches that are double-coded, the average correlation between the coding for all categories is an exceptionally high 0.91. But it is actually substantially higher for the ones we are interested in (e.g. workers = 0.98, families = 0.99). The average is brought down by some groups that we are less interested in (e.g. farmers = 0.66 and the elderly = 0.65).

Part III
Consequences

7

Class Politics Is Dead

The day before the 1964 election, the then leader of the Labour party Harold Wilson went to see Hughie Greene, the then Director General of the BBC. On his mind, unsurprisingly, was the upcoming general election. More surprisingly, also on his mind was the sitcom 'Steptoe and Son'. Greene said that Wilson 'had been very much upset because the BBC had planned the beginning of a series of repeats of a very popular light enter-tainment programme, "Steptoe and Son", on the evening of polling day. He thought that would keep away particularly Labour supporters from the polls'. Working class people voted Labour and working class people watched 'Steptoe and Son'. Indeed Wilson's comments on this are almost a parody; he claimed that having 'Steptoe and Son' on at 9 p.m. meant that people would not get to the polling station. That for 'a lot of our people—my people, working in Liverpool, long journey out, perhaps then a high tea and so on, it was getting late, especially if they wanted to have a pint first'.[1]

If anything sums up post-war assumptions about class and electoral behav-iour, it is this anecdote. Class was at the centre of British politics in 1964. In this chapter, and in Chapter 8, we explore the consequences of the political changes described in Chapters 5 and 6 for class and voting. In this chapter we show that class is no longer at the centre of politics, and that class has become a marginal force within mainstream politics. We concentrate on not just the way the link between class and party choice has changed but also the reasons for this change. We show that there is little evidence of class divisions in party support narrowing before the 1990s. During the 1990s, however, there was a striking dealignment between classes and parties. The reasons for this are mixed, but clearly relate to the changes we have described in Chapters 5 and 6: changes in party policy and rhetoric, changes to politicians, and changes to the media environment. The decline of mainstream class politics is a consequence of the decline of mainstream class parties.

The Decline of Class Voting?

There is of course nothing novel about suggesting that class has declined as a political force. Any article or book on British political history will at some point refer to this as a simple statement of fact. For example, Clarke et al., in *Political Choice in Britain*, conclude that 'at the end of the twentieth century class had come to play a very limited role in determining the voting preferences of the British electorate' (2004, p.50). In fact, tales of this decline date back to some of the first books and articles to look at how class shaped vote choices in Britain. By the time Butler and Stokes published the second edition of their study of the 1960s elections in 1974, they were already talking of the 'weakening of the class alignment' (Butler and Stokes 1974, p.208) and others argued that Butler and Stokes' data, particularly the study after the 1970 election, showed that class voting was waning (Books and Reynolds 1975). This was followed in the early 1980s by an important book authored by the new team in charge of the BES arguing that 'class voting is on the decline and has already reached modest levels' (Sarlvik and Crewe 1983, p.91). Franklin (1985), Robertson (1984), and Rose and McAllister (1986) made similar points in three other influential books of the period. It seemed at the time that there was no doubt class voting was, if not dead, at least dying, that the 'old class-equals-party model of politics is no more' (Rose and McAllister 1986, p.1).

This consensus led to a 'revisionist' challenge which emphasized stability rather than change, and it was this perspective that dominated debate during the late 1980s and 1990s. Anthony Heath and colleagues consistently argued that the death of class voting had been exaggerated and coined the expression 'trendless fluctuation' to describe levels of class voting up to the mid 1980s (Heath et al. 1985, p.35; see also Weakliem 1989). They pointed to problems with data and measurement in previous work, arguing that 1964 (the first BES) showed an unusually high level of class voting and was therefore an unhelpful baseline against which to measure change and that the common manual/non-manual distinction was an overly crude way of capturing class. Much of the initial critical response to Heath et al. (1985, 1991, 1994) was focused on measurement (Dunleavy 1987; Crewe 1986), but whether the measures were problematic or not was largely seen as a moot point a decade or two later. Why? Because by then, a new consensus had emerged around the fact that class voting by the end of the 1990s and certainly by the 2000s was definitely lower than it had been at some rather vaguely specified point in the past.[2] Yet, while the decline of class voting in Britain is now widely accepted, and as we will proceed to show, well evidenced, the pattern of change and the reasons for that change remain much less clear.[3]

Most accounts of decline are shaped by the idea that classes are more similar; that there has been a 'loosening' of social structures (Butler and Kavanagh 1984, p.8), an attenuation of 'bonds linking voters to politically relevant class groups' (Dalton 2008, p.157) or a 'weakening of class stratification, especially as shown in distinct class differentiated life-styles' (Clark and Lipset 1991, p.408). These arguments reverberate all the way back to the 1950s. After the 1959 Conservative election victory, there were predictions of Labour's inevitable decline due to the 'the growing homogeneity of styles of life of workers and middle classes, and the continuing prosperity of Britain' (Alford 1964, p.127) or the fact that the 'old working class ethos is being eroded by prosperity and the increasing fluidity of society' (Abrams and Rose 1960, p.106).

The basic assumption was that classes, and particularly the working class, had lost their social cohesion and distinctiveness. Of course, this is not what we have seen in previous chapters. Neither the objective realities of class, nor the political attitudes that these objective realities produce, have changed greatly. This does not, therefore, seem like a promising explanation for change. Rather, we argue here, as we have previously argued (Evans and Tilley 2012a, 2012b, 2013), that it is political change which produces class voting change. This perspective emphasizes the 'top down' structuring of cleavages by the actions of political parties, in Przeworski's words: 'individual voting behaviour is an effect of the activities of political parties' (1985, pp.100–1). Robertson (1984, p.225) ends his book by noting that changes to class voting in Britain are essentially 'changes inside the clay round which the mould fits. The clay is what it always has been, and modifications to the Conservative and Labour parties ought to suffice them as moulders for a long time to come'. Less poetically, if parties look very different, then classes vote differently; if parties look very similar, then classes vote similarly. As we will see, the pattern of change strongly supports this view.

Before focusing too much on the 'whys', we need to establish the 'what'. What has changed and when did it change?

Labour and the Conservatives

Assessing whether, and more importantly when, the link between class and vote choice changed is not quite as straightforward as it might seem. We need consistent measures of class over long periods of time, consistent measures of party choice over long periods of time, and long-running survey series that allow us to track change. Unfortunately, no single survey series spans the period since the Second World War in Britain. We therefore use data from three different overlapping sources in this chapter: Gallup surveys from 1945 to 1968, BES surveys from 1964 to 2015, and BSA surveys from 1983 to 2015. We have discussed the BES and BSA data previously; suffice to say that for the post-election BES surveys we use vote choice at the election, but since the BSA surveys are yearly, we use a broader measure of party choice. This uses three questions, as below, to identify which party someone supports.

'Generally speaking, do you think of yourself as a supporter of any one political party?'

[IF NO] 'Do you think of yourself as a little closer to one political party than to others?'

[IF NO] 'If there were a general election tomorrow, which political party do you think you would be most likely to support?'

The Gallup surveys allow us to track class voting back to the 1940s, as we can use three surveys from 1945 and 1946 as well as a run of nearly annual surveys from 1955 to 1968. The measure of occupational class is extremely similar to the one that we have used previously with the BSA and BES data: it is based on occupation and self-employment status and allows us to effectively distinguish at least four groups: new middle class professional workers, old middle class managers and employers, the junior middle class of clerical non-manual workers, and manual workers.[4] We use recalled vote choice in election years and vote intention otherwise ('How would you vote if there were a general election tomorrow?').[5] In this chapter we focus on the three main parties, although all vote percentages are proportions of people questioned so include non-voters and voters for smaller parties. In Chapter 8 we look at both non-voters and the emergence of class voting for minor parties, most notably UKIP since 2010 and the SNP in 2015 in Scotland. Here we are interested in how class matters for picking one of the three main parties and how this has changed.

Figures 7.1 and 7.2 show changes in vote share for Labour and the Conservatives by the four main occupational class groups: the old middle class, the new middle class, the junior middle class, and the working class. The Gallup and BSA graphs present moving averages as the samples are yearly and rather small. The BES graph shows the raw percentages. There are three very important points to make. The first is about the lack of change, particularly for the Conservative vote. It is easy to assume from some of the literature that occupational class has everything to tell us about party choices in the past, and nothing to tell us about people's party choices today. That is incorrect. There were always working class Conservatives and middle class Labour supporters: Eden and Macmillan's election victories in 1955 and 1959 were due to

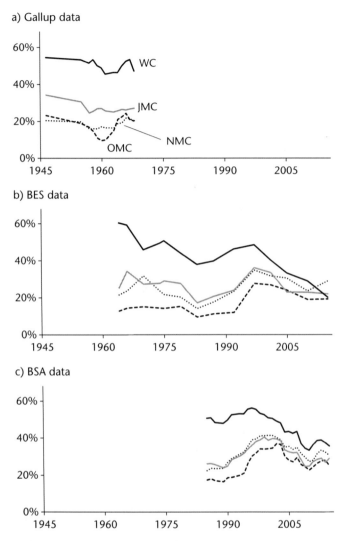

a) Gallup data

b) BES data

c) BSA data

Figure 7.1. Labour support by occupational class

Note: The figures here show the proportion of people who support the Labour party as a percentage of the electorate. The top graph shows vote intentions from Gallup data (three period moving average); the middle graph shows vote choices from BES data; the bottom graph shows party support from BSA data (three period moving average). Four occupational class groups are displayed: old middle class (OMC), new middle class (NMC), junior middle class (JMC), and working class (WC).

Source: Gallup 1945–1968; British Election Studies 1964–2015; British Social Attitudes Surveys 1983–2015.

more than a third of the working class supporting the Conservatives. Equally there is still a difference in Conservative vote share between the old middle class and the working class in 2015: 25 per cent for the BES data and 29 per cent for the BSA data. This should not surprise us given the results from earlier

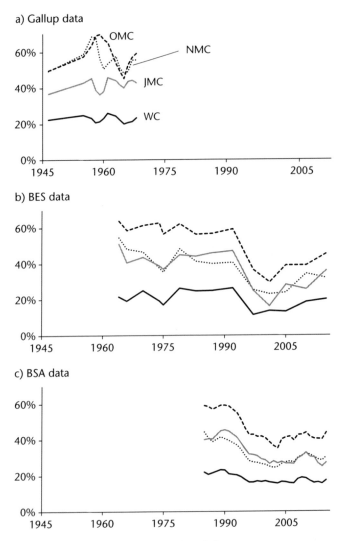

a) Gallup data

b) BES data

c) BSA data

Figure 7.2. Conservative support by occupational class

Note: The figures here show the proportion of people who support the Conservative party as a percentage of the electorate. The top graph shows vote intentions from Gallup data (three period moving average); the middle graph shows vote choices from BES data; and the bottom graph shows party support from BSA data (three period moving average). Four occupational class groups are displayed: old middle class (OMC), new middle class (NMC), junior middle class (JMC), and working class (WC).

Source: Gallup 1945–1968; British Election Studies 1964–2015; British Social Attitudes Surveys 1983–2015.

chapters. As Chapter 4 showed, people's policy preferences are driven by class in the same way today as they always have been. Chapters 5 and 6 showed that while parties are less obviously talking about class and less obviously different from one another, they are still somewhat different. Occupational class remains a useful predictor of vote choice in Britain and we should not forget this.

The second point is about the scale of change. Class may still predict vote choice, but it is much less important than it was. This is most obvious for the Labour vote. After the war, there was around a 30 percentage point gap between the old and new middle class groups and the working class in Labour support. From 1997 onwards that gap was more like 10 percentage points. The BES data shows that at the most recent election, that difference has completely disappeared. There can be no doubt that class voting has declined over the period that we are examining. This change is apparent for both major parties, but is much starker for Labour.

The third point is perhaps most important, and this is about the nature of change. What is fascinating is the way in which differences between the groups alter at particular points in time. Most notably the main change occurs in the mid-1990s, although for Labour 2015 also appears to be a critical election. The three middle class groups all sharply move towards the working class group in their preferences between 1995 and 2000. This contrasts with only slight changes in the gap between the three middle class groups over the entire period.[6] Figure 7.3 illustrates just how abrupt the change is by plotting the difference between the three middle class groups and the working class in their support for Labour. Here we combine

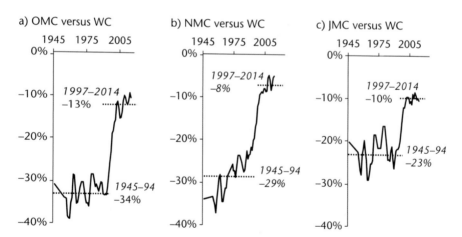

Figure 7.3. Differences in Labour support between working class and middle class groups

Note: The figures here show the difference between the proportions of middle and working class people who support the Labour party as a percentage of the electorate (three period moving average). The top-left graph compares the old middle class (OMC) to the working class (WC); the top-right graph compares the new middle class (NMC) to the working class; the bottom graph compares the junior middle class (JMC) to the working class.

Source: Gallup 1945–1967; British Election Studies 1964–1992; British Social Attitudes Surveys 1983–2014.

the Gallup, BES, and BSA data to give a continuous time series over the 1945–2014 period.[7]

The average difference in Labour support between the old middle class and the working class before 1994 is 34 per cent. There is fluctuation around this level, but it is essentially trendless. Similarly there is trendless fluctuation from 1997 to 2014, but at a much lower level of difference: just 13 per cent. There is an identical story for the junior middle class group: trendless fluctuation in class voting before 1994 and then trendless fluctuation in class voting, but at a much lower level, from 1997 to 2014. The pattern is slightly different for the new middle class group: there seems to be some shift towards Labour in the 1950s, although we should note the slightly different measure of 'professional' workers that Gallup uses in the 1945–68 period compared to the BES and BSA surveys that cover later time periods. Overall, the changes in the 1990s mainly involve the middle class groups. By moving towards Labour in the 1990s, they close the gap with the working class in Labour support.

There are also hints from Figures 7.1 and 7.2 that the 2015 election appeared to be another break point, at least for Labour. Table 7.1 shows people's reported votes by occupational class for 2015 from the BES and BSA data.[8] This is the first election since the war in which the working class voted for Labour at a lower rate than some of the middle class groups. The new middle class and junior middle class are now *more* likely to vote Labour than the working class, and the difference between the working class and the old middle class has narrowed considerably. This is largely driven by a sharp fall in working class support for Labour. In 2005 almost identical numbers of the new middle class (31 per cent in the BES and 28 per cent in the BSA) and junior middle class (23 per cent in the BES and 27 per cent in the BSA) supported Labour as in 2015. Yet the proportion of the working class supporting Labour

Table 7.1. Impact of occupational class on vote choice in 2015

	Labour	Conservative	Liberal	Other	No vote
BES data					
Old middle class	19%	46%	6%	11%	19%
New middle class	29%	32%	7%	13%	19%
Junior middle class	22%	36%	3%	12%	26%
Working class	20%	20%	4%	21%	35%
BSA data					
Old middle class	17%	44%	5%	11%	23%
New middle class	26%	30%	9%	14%	21%
Junior middle class	24%	30%	4%	12%	30%
Working class	25%	17%	3%	13%	42%

Note: The numbers here show the proportion of people who reported voting for each party in the 2015 general election.

Source: British Election Study 2015; British Social Attitudes Survey 2015.

has shrunk dramatically. In 2005 33 per cent of the working class BES sample and 37 per cent of the working class BSA sample reported voting Labour. In 2015 the equivalent figures in Table 7.1 are 20 per cent and 25 per cent.

In the rest of this chapter we focus on the changes before 2015 that affected class voting most obviously and most dramatically. As Chapter 8 shows, the changes to Labour support in 2015 were a mixture of defection to UKIP and the SNP as well as continued increases in non-voting among the working class that started in the late 1990s.

Drawing this all together, there is a relatively clear story to be told about the two main parties. Class voting was very high in the immediate post-war period. The middle classes were much less likely to vote Labour, and much more likely to vote Conservative, than the working class. This remained the case until the mid-1990s when there was an abrupt change which reduced class voting to much lower, although by no means zero, levels. Macmillan may have claimed that the 'class war is obsolete' after the 1959 election, but it was not until forty years later that things actually changed with Blair's declaration that the 'class war is over' to the Labour party conference in 1999. To start with, this change was largely due to the middle class groups becoming more likely to vote Labour, but after 2001 it has mainly been driven by the desertion of the working class from Labour. As Chapter 8 shows, the nail in the coffin of Labour class voting was hammered in at the 2015 election, which, unprecedentedly, saw lower proportions of the working class voting Labour than some of the middle class groups.

The Liberals

Britain over the last seventy years has not been a two-party system. As well as nationalist and minor parties, which we discuss in Chapter 8, there has been the constant presence of a third party in various incarnations: the Liberals from 1945 until 1981, the Alliance of the Liberals and the SDP from 1981 until 1988, and after 1988 the Liberal Democrats. Whatever the name, the third party has traditionally been seen as a more centrist, but still recognizably middle class, alternative to the Conservatives. While Sand-brook's characterization of the Liberals in the 1950s as 'the province of middle class eccentrics' (2006, p.94) is perhaps a little harsh, the image of the Liberals as a haven for the bearded and sandal-shod middle class has some basis in fact. Academic studies of voting behaviour have generally found a middle class basis to the Liberal vote since the 1960s (Robertson 1984; Heath et al. 1985, 1991; Russell and Fieldhouse 2005) especially

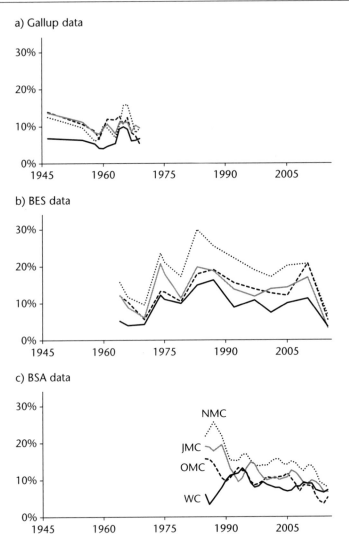

a) Gallup data

b) BES data

c) BSA data

Figure 7.4. Liberal support by occupational class

Note: The figures here show the proportion of people who support the Liberal party (and later incarnations) as a percentage of the electorate. The top graph shows vote intentions from Gallup data (three period moving average); the middle graph shows vote choices from BES data; the bottom graph shows party support from BSA data (three period moving average). Four occupational class groups are displayed: old middle class (OMC), new middle class (NMC), junior middle class (JMC), and working class (WC).

Source: Gallup 1945–1968; British Election Studies 1964–2015; British Social Attitudes Surveys 1983–2015.

for 'core' Liberal support (Alt et al. 1977). Figure 7.4, which tracks Liberal support over time by occupational class, supports this view. The three middle class groups are always more likely to vote for the Liberals than the working class. Moreover, rates of Liberal voting among the new middle class group are especially high, almost twice the rate of Liberal voting among the working class. One might argue that part of class politics in Britain is located not just in the competition for voters between the Conservatives and Labour, but also in the appeal of the third party.

The pattern of change in the link between class and party is rather different for the Liberals, however. We see, if anything, growth in the differences between the middle class groups and the working class over the 1960s and 1970s, and little evidence of the steep decline in class-based support in the 1990s that we saw for the Conservatives and Labour. The explanation for the lack of change for the Liberals is intimately tied to the explanation for the changes in support for the two main parties. Part of this story relates to the reasons why occupational class matters for vote choice. In Chapter 4 we discussed how people's occupation, but also their education, shapes their political views. In fact, much of the difference in Liberal support between the new middle class and working class groups is due to educational differences (see Franklin et al. 1992, pp.126–7, for an earlier discussion of this). Table 7.2 shows estimates from a multinomial logit regression model that allows us to look at the separate effects of education and occupation on party support for each decade from the 1960s onwards. Party choice is a five category variable: Conservative, Labour, Liberal, other party, and no party. We run these models using the BES and BSA data separately (the Gallup surveys do not ask about educational attainment). Similar predictions from these same models for Conservative and Labour support are in Appendix Tables A7.1 and A7.2.

As Table 7.2 shows, it is both education and occupation that account for differences in the Liberal vote. People with higher education are about 10 percentage points more likely to support the third party than are people who left school at fifteen or sixteen.[9] This illustrates a much broader point about the underlying processes that generate party support. Chapter 4 showed that occupational class is a good predictor of people's economic attitudes (whether they want redistribution, public ownership, and the like), but a much weaker predictor of social liberalism (whether they want the death penalty reintroduced and so forth), which is much more a function of education. This directly relates to people's party choices. As we will see shortly, the decision to vote Conservative or Labour is largely about people's positions on the economic left–right dimension. The decision to vote Liberal is largely about people's positions on the social liberal–conservative dimension. As we have discussed in previous chapters it is the two main party positions on left–right economic policy that shifted in the 1990s, just as class voting shifted in the 1990s. For us, it is party change that is a key part of understanding why we see class voting decline for the two main parties, just as the lack of party change is

Table 7.2. Impact of occupational class and education on Liberal support

a) BES data

Vote Liberal	1960s	1970s	1980s	1990s	2000s	2010s
Old middle class	10%	13%	18%	15%	10%	5%
New middle class	11%	23%	27%	18%	14%	4%
Junior middle class	10%	20%	20%	14%	14%	4%
Working class	5%	15%	18%	12%	10%	3%
New middle class – working class	7%	8%	9%	6%	4%	1%
High education (degree)	19%	28%	28%	21%	25%	7%
Medium education (A Level)	13%	21%	21%	15%	16%	5%
Low education (school leaving age)	9%	20%	19%	11%	14%	3%
High education – low education	9%	8%	8%	11%	11%	4%

b) BSA data

Support Liberals			1980s	1990s	2000s	2010s
Old middle class			15%	9%	10%	3%
New middle class			23%	12%	13%	4%
Junior middle class			21%	11%	12%	4%
Working class			18%	8%	10%	3%
New middle class – working class			5%	4%	3%	2%
High education (degree)			32%	15%	22%	8%
Medium education (A Level)			23%	12%	15%	6%
Low education (no qualifications)			19%	10%	11%	3%
High education – low education			14%	5%	11%	5%

Note: The numbers here are predicted probabilities from multinomial logit regression models using pooled data by decade that predict vote choice for the BES data and party support for the BSA data using occupational class, education, and year. The predicted occupational class probabilities are for someone in the medium education category and the predicted education probabilities are for someone in the junior middle class category. Year is set as close as possible to the middle of each decade (and the same year for both datasets).

Source: British Election Studies 1964–2015; British Social Attitudes Surveys 1986–2015.

key to understanding why class voting, or more accurately education voting, for the Liberals remains the same.

Explaining Change in Policy, and Therefore Class, Voting

In order to explain the changes that we saw in the 1990s we need to connect people's political views with their party choices. There are two important tests. The first is that when we account for people's policy views and their changing impact on party choice, we should eliminate much of the change in class voting over the 1990s when the parties radically altered their policy. The second is that people's policy stances, especially on economic issues, should have a much weaker effect on their party choices when the parties became more similar in terms of policy in the 1990s.

Figure 7.5 tests the first of these. Here we aim to assess whether holding constant economic ideology, but allowing its effect to vary over time weakens the relationship between class and vote and reduces any change in that relationship. Since class differences in ideology are relatively stable, if we account for ideology and the declining motivation for choosing parties due to ideology, we should eliminate changes in class voting. We focus here on the critical period of change: 1987–2010. The two left-hand graphs show Labour support using both the BES and BSA data between the mid 1980s and the 2010 election. These simply replicate what we saw in Figure 7.1 at the beginning of the chapter, and the steep decrease in class voting is very obvious for both data sets. The two graphs on the right-hand side are from regression models which hold constant people's views on the economic left–right scale that we used in Chapter 4.[10] The lines at the bottom of the figures show the differences between the middle classes and the working class, and illustrate quite clearly that much of the rapid change in class voting over the period that we see in the left-hand graphs is not present in the right-hand graphs. It is not only that most of the differences between classes in vote choice are due to differing values but also that the weaker effect of these values over time has decreased class voting. As we have found previously (Evans and Tilley 2012b), the changes in class voting are not eliminated, but they are substantially reduced. This is remarkable given that there are no variables other than occupational class and left–right values in the model.

The second test is to look at how well people's policy stances predict their vote choice. For our argument to hold, these views on left–right economic policy should have become less important as the parties become more similar in the 1990s. Using the same regression models as in Figure 7.5, Figure 7.6 shows the proportion of left-wing and right-wing people who we predict support Labour over time.[11] Both the BSA and BES data tell the same story. In the 1980s and early 1990s, while very few people on the right voted Labour, a large majority of people on the left crossed the box next to the Labour candidate. In 1987 the difference in Labour support between people on the left and right was enormous. This gap begins to decline from the mid-1990s and almost disappears during the 2000s. In 1992 the difference between people on the left and right was nearly 40 percentage points in the BES data; by 2001 this difference was only 3 percentage points. It is not surprising that class voting has declined, because the underlying basis of much class voting, economic policy voting, was in freefall over the 1990s, and by the 2000s had virtually disappeared.

These figures allow us to put together the different patterns of change from earlier chapters. Chapter 4 showed that people in different occupational classes had different positions on redistribution and other economic policy.

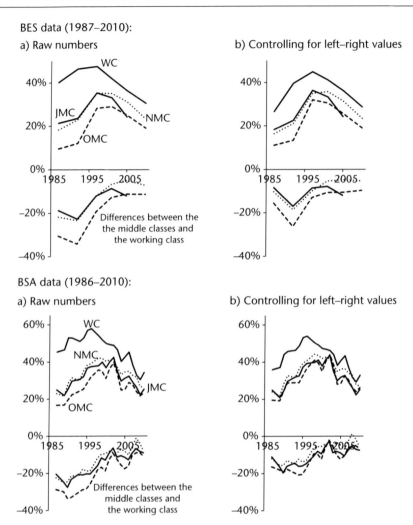

BES data (1987–2010):

a) Raw numbers

b) Controlling for left–right values

BSA data (1986–2010):

a) Raw numbers

b) Controlling for left–right values

Figure 7.5. Labour support by occupational class controlling for left–right values

Note: The figures here show predicted probabilities of Labour support from multinomial logit regression models that predict vote choice (BES) and party support (BSA, two period moving average) as a percentage of the electorate for each year separately. The left-hand graphs include occupational class as an independent variable; the right-hand graphs include a measure of economic left-right values as well as occupational class. Four occupational class groups are displayed: old middle class (OMC), new middle class (NMC), junior middle class (JMC), and the working class (WC).

Source: British Election Studies 1987–2010; British Social Attitudes Surveys 1986–2010.

These differences between classes are fairly constant over time, which is perhaps not surprising given that the objective differences between occupational groups discussed in Chapter 2 are also fairly constant. Chapter 6 showed a rather different pattern when it came to the political parties.

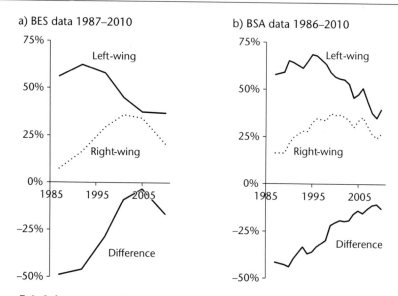

Figure 7.6. Labour support by economic left–right position

Note: The figures here show predicted probabilities of Labour support from multinomial logit regression models that predict support as a percentage of the electorate for each year separately. The dependent variable in the left-hand graph is vote choice. The dependent variable in the right-hand graph is party support (two period moving average). The models include occupational class and a measure of economic left–right values. Left-wing people are assumed to score one standard deviation below the mean score for the year and right-wing people one standard deviation above the mean score for the year.

Source: British Election Studies 1964–2010; British Social Attitudes Surveys 1986–2010.

Here there was change, especially in the 1990s when the two main parties converged in terms of policy. People's policy views have not changed, but the policy choices that parties offer have. This has meant that ideology, and the root of ideology—class, has become a weaker determinant of people's party choice. After all, if the parties all offer the same economic policies, why would someone's views on economic policy affect their vote?

All this makes the evolution of the Liberal vote an interesting contrast. Higher education, and to a lesser extent having a new middle class job, are relatively good predictors of a Liberal vote, as we saw earlier. Moreover, they are a fairly consistent predictor over time. There has been none of the rapid change in class voting that we see for the two main parties in the 1990s. There are two reasons for this. First, divisions among voters by social liberalism have remained relatively constant over time, but second, the Liberals have almost always offered a more socially liberal platform of policies than the two main parties. The expert survey data described in the previous chapter has measures of social liberalism that go back to 1999 and these show that the Liberals had

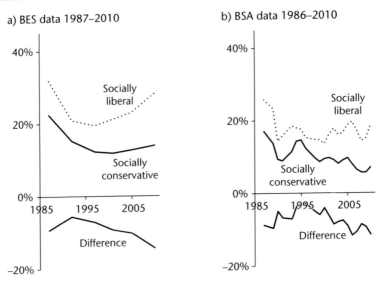

a) BES data 1987–2010   b) BSA data 1986–2010

Figure 7.7. Liberal support by social liberal–conservative position

Note: The figures here show predicted probabilities of Liberal support from multinomial logit regression models that predict support as a percentage of the electorate for each year separately. The dependent variable in the left-hand graph is vote choice. The dependent variable in the right-hand graph is party support (two period moving average). The models include a measure of economic left–right values and a measure of social conservative–liberal values. Socially conservative people are assumed to score one standard deviation below the mean score for the year and socially liberal people one standard deviation above the mean score for the year. Left–right values are held at their mean for each year.

Source: British Election Studies 1964–2010; British Social Attitudes Surveys 1986–2010.

more consistently socially liberal policies than both the Conservatives and Labour from 1999 to 2014.[12] In 2006 the Conservatives score 6 (on a 0–10 scale, where 10 is most socially conservative), Labour 4.7, and the Liberals just over 2.5.

The second of these factors means that we should expect that social liberalism remains a fairly consistent predictor over time of a Liberal vote. Figure 7.7 shows that this is the case. Since the Liberal party is always more socially liberal, more socially liberal voters are always more likely to support it.[13] Indeed, if anything, social liberalism appears to have become a little more important in explaining people's votes for the Liberals.

Beyond Policy Voting

People's ideology affects to their vote. Left-wing people are more likely than right-wing people to prefer Labour, just as socially liberal people are more likely than socially conservative people to prefer the Liberals. But this relationship is altered when the parties' policy offerings alter. When parties offer similar policies, then fewer people use their own policy preferences to choose between the parties. This process can explain much of the steep decline in class voting that we saw in the 1990s. It cannot explain it entirely, however. Figure 7.5 certainly showed that holding constant people's left-right values reduced the change in class voting, but it did not eliminate that change.

Why is this? Part of the reason relates back to the discussion in Chapter 6 about the parties themselves. While people choose parties on the grounds of policy, they also make choices because they feel that one party represents them, or their group, better than another. This is related to the policies that a party offers, but is not the same. Two parties might have very similar policies, but if one offers rhetoric that emphasizes that it is for the working class, has candidates from recognizably working class backgrounds, and both of those factors are emphasized by newspapers that everyone reads, then it seems likely that there will still be class voting. This hypothetical example is, of course, rather similar to the situation that we describe in Britain in the late 1960s. The parties briefly offered quite similar policies, but they were still clearly distinctive in terms of their appeal and this was strongly reflected by a mass partisan press stratified by class. A final part of our story then is how people's views of the parties as class parties have changed and ultimately how this has depressed class voting.

How can we test this part of our explanation? The key issue here is perceptions of the parties. Do people think that particular parties defend particular classes? Fortunately, and as discussed in the previous chapter, there is a question in the BES surveys since 1987 that asks people exactly this. For the two main parties survey respondents are asked first how well each party 'looks after working class people' and then how well each party 'looks after middle class people' on a four point scale. We focus here on perceptions of Labour since that is the party which has changed the most and use the same two questions discussed in Chapter 6 that measure the class basis of party image. Again, positive scores mean that people think Labour looks after the working class better than the middle class; negative scores mean that people think Labour looks after the middle class better than the working class. If Labour was seen as a purely working class party it would score 2; if a purely middle class party it would score −2. As shown in Chapter 6, Labour's image has changed dramatically over time. In 1987 the mean score was 0.74, about a standard deviation above zero. Most people in 1987 saw Labour as a party for the working class. In 2005 the mean score was 0.09 and in 2010 it was 0.17. By the 2000s people were almost as likely to see Labour as a middle class party as they were to see it as a working class party.

a) Controlling for left–right values

b) + Controlling for perceptions of Labour as a working class party

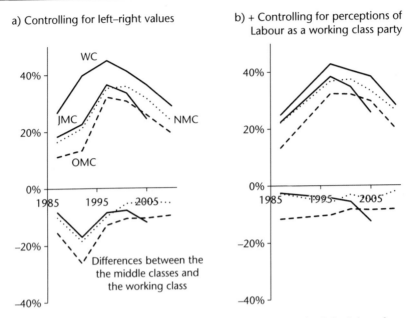

Figure 7.8. Labour support by occupational class controlling for left–right values and class perceptions of Labour

Note: The figures here show predicted probabilities of Labour support from multinomial logit regression models that predict support as a percentage of the electorate for each year separately. The lines below zero show the differences between the working class and the three middle class groups. The left-hand graph includes occupational class and economic left–right values as independent variables; the right-hand graph also includes a measure of whether people perceive Labour to be a more working class or middle class party. Four occupational class groups are displayed: old middle class (OMC), new middle class (NMC), junior middle class (JMC), and the working class (WC). Left–right values are held at their mean for each year and perceptions of Labour are set for every year at zero (i.e. as though people thought that Labour was equally good for the middle class as the working class).

Source: British Election Studies 1987–2010.

These changing perceptions affect how people vote. If we add these perceptions into a model of vote choice then we can see how perceptions of the parties as class parties are important. Figure 7.8 has two graphs. The left-hand one is simply a repeat of the graph in Figure 7.5 showing the occupational class differences in Labour vote choice, but holding constant people's left–right ideology. The right-hand graph shows support for Labour by occupational class from a model that holds not just left–right ideology constant but also our measure of people's perceptions of Labour as a working or middle class party.[14] We show our prediction of class voting for Labour if everyone had scored zero on our class-party perceptions scale in every year. That is, we are asking the counterfactual question: if Labour had always been viewed as an equally middle class and working class party, what levels of class voting would there have been in the 1980s and 1990s? The answer to that question is that levels of class voting would have been dramatically lower. In fact, we would have seen almost no change in class voting for Labour over the period. What is most striking about Figure 7.8 is that what remains of class dealignment over the period up to 2010 is essentially eliminated. The lines are now parallel for all occupational classes. The new middle class is almost identically likely to support Labour as the working class at all times when we simply account for left-right ideology and class perceptions of the parties. The old middle class is still slightly less likely to vote Labour than the working class, but crucially this difference is invariant over time. This is not because the relationship between perceptions of Labour as a class party and vote choice have changed (these are remarkably constant: people in working class occupations that see Labour as a working class party are always more likely to support Labour); rather it is because far fewer people see the parties as 'looking after' one class or the other.

Therefore, there are two processes here. First, parties adopted more similar policies, broadly speaking on the right, and that meant that people's own policy differences became less important in shaping their vote choices. Second, however, as parties became more similar, not just in terms of policy, but also personnel, rhetoric, and media coverage, they became less identified with particular classes. As fewer people recognized the parties as class parties, fewer people voted on that basis. Ultimately, this means that the decline in class voting in the 1990s in Britain was caused by parties. Parties became more similar, and therefore both ideology and the direct class appeal of parties mattered less to voters. This was likely exacerbated by the decline of mass class-based partisan newspapers. If we account for changes in party policy and class perceptions of the parties, we account for the class dealignment that we saw between 1992 and 2005.

What happened in 2015? After all, perceptions of Labour as a middle or working class party barely change between 2005 and 2015. We will deal with this in more detail in Chapter 8, but in essence new parties become viable options. UKIP in England and Wales and the SNP in Scotland attracted support from the working class. All the change before 2010 was about change to the main parties; all the change after 2010 is about new parties that offer policies that appeal differently to different groups.

Conclusions

Class voting has declined in Britain. If you knew someone's occupation, and to a lesser extent their education, in the 1950s, you had a very good chance of guessing how they would vote. Today those clues would be a lot less helpful. On that we can agree with almost all observers of British politics. Just as was claimed after the 2001 election, the 'relationship between class and vote has weakened appreciably over time' (Clarke et al. 2004, p.33). Where we disagree is in the pattern of change, when that weakening happened and the reasons behind it. Using the best possible data over the longest period of time we have shown that levels of class voting were largely static for half a century from the 1940s until the mid-1990s. There was then a dramatic weakening of the relationship between class and party over a short space of time. How does this fit with our findings from the earlier chapters on parties, politicians, and the media environment, and how well does it fit with the top down model that we advocated at the start of this chapter?

In the narrowest sense it does not fit. Parties had relatively similar policies in the 1960s when class voting was high and also had relatively similar policies in the 2000s and 2010s when class voting was low. This neglects three very important points. The first is that the narrowing of policy differences in the 1960s was more sudden and more temporary than is often thought. While the post-war consensus is often talked about, the actual economic policy differences between parties as measured by the manifesto data in the last chapter were relatively large for most of the fifty years after the war apart from the late 1960s. Policy differences between the two main parties immediately after the war were sizable, and the brief convergence at the 1966 and 1970 elections was reversed by 1974. Yet economic policy differences between the parties have been consistently small since 1997.

The second point is about perceptions relative to realities. The two main parties may have adopted relatively similar policies in the 1960s, albeit briefly, but that does not mean that voters' views of the parties as better or worse for particular classes changed. Perceptions of parties are not just about policy but about the people, the rhetoric, and the mediation of both via the press. None of these three factors changed until the 1990s. Parties can change policy, but if that does not affect people's perceptions of the parties, both in policy and class image terms, then it will not lead to changes in class voting.[15]

The final point is about the persistence of image. David Weakliem (2001) argues that people's views of the two US political parties as defenders of different occupational groups had barely shifted from the 1947 to 1990. This might seem surprising given the policy shifts of the Democrats, in particular, over that time period. He argues that, invoking Hout et al.'s (1993) idea of class as a psychological heuristic, 'people *expect* to see a party of the rich and party of the poor; even if parties try to go beyond the traditional categories of Left and Right, people will continue to put them in these roles' (Weakliem 2001, p.219). The point here is that these views of parties are stubbornly held and it takes a shock to change them. In Britain in the 1990s there was such a shock. Labour radically changed its nature in a short space of time and crucially made this very obvious to the electorate. The information that people received about politics changed both as a result of, and coincidentally to, this. The press, which was previously structured around class divisions, stopped talking about class and people also stopped reading the press.

Radical change all at once, in every form, changed people's views of the parties. It became clear that both were offering similar policies and Labour was a party for the middle class as much as it was a party for the working class. These changes in perceptions help explain the findings at the end of this chapter for the 1987–2010 period. Class voting has disappeared because economic left–right policy voting for the two main parties declined when the parties had recognizably similar policies, and because group-based voting declined when the parties no longer clearly represented classes. The 'top down' view of party shifts causing voters to change is correct, but with the proviso that those party shifts need to be very obvious to voters. While Labour and the Conservatives offered rather similar policies at the 1966 election, this convergence was short-lived and not accompanied by any other change in party image. It was thus only in the 1990s, the era of party policy and image change, that the hold that class voting had on the British electorate was finally overthrown.

The story does not end there, however. If one consequence of these changes is that working class voters deserted Labour, where have they gone? In Chapter 8 we show that the political changes of the 1990s and 2000s have led to many working class voters exiting the system and simply not voting. We also show that new viable and visible parties, the SNP and UKIP, have led to Labour losing even more of the working class vote at the 2015 election.

Notes

1. When Greene asked what he would prefer on television at that time, Wilson allegedly replied 'I suggest that you put on Oedipus Rex' (Cockerell 1988, p.107). All the quotations in the text come from interviews with Wilson and Greene that were made available by the BBC in 2015: http://www.bbc.co.uk/historyofthebbc/elections/invention-3.
2. For example, while Weakliem and Heath (1999) convincingly show that class voting at the 1992 election is much the same as it was in 1935, Heath's book after the 1997 election admits that class voting had finally declined in Britain (Heath et al. 2001).
3. Some argue that declines in class voting have happened in other developed countries (Dalton 2008; Clark 2001b; Nieuwbeerta 1996; Pakulski and Waters 1996a, 1996b; Franklin 1992), but others claim that there is no universal decline (Elff 2007, 2009) or even that in some cases, like the US, there have been increases in class voting over the last twenty years (Bartels 2008).

4. Inevitably there are minor differences. Foremen and supervisors cannot be separated from manual workers, and personal service workers cannot easily be separated from manual or non-manual workers. Housewives (in some cases even if in part-time work) are also not generally classified by husband's profession, so form a group which is simply excluded from our analysis. The latter problem means that we are likely to overestimate any class voting in the early period given that people's own occupations are generally stronger indicators of vote intention than their spouse's occupation.

5. People who said 'don't know' were asked their party 'inclination' from 1963 to 1968 and we have treated these answers as vote intentions.

6. The one exception to this is the move of the new middle class away from the Conservatives, and away from the old middle class, after the 1950s, and even this may well be an artefact of the slightly different Gallup measure of professional workers compared to the BES and BSA.

7. We use the Gallup data from 1945 to 1968, the BES data from 1964 to 1992, and the BSA data from 1983 to 2015. This allows for some overlap between the different surveys while maintaining consistency of measurement. In years with data from more than one source, we take the mean of the two data points.

8. This is not the broader measure of party choice for the BSA data, but a separate question asking people how they actually voted in 2015.

9. The impact of education on Labour and Conservative voting is more muted, and it has little effect on the occupational class differences (see Tables A7.1 and A7.2 in the Appendix to this chapter). For example, those with school leaving age education or higher education support Labour at relatively similar rates, and those with a medium level of education are about 5 per cent less likely to support Labour than those with a degree. The effect of holding constant education does not substantially change the magnitude of class differences in Labour or Conservative support, or the pattern of change. For example, holding constant education, there is around a 20 per cent gap between the new middle class and working class in Labour support in the 1980s, which reduces to around 5 per cent in the 2000s.

10. We use multinomial logit regression models which predict party choice, with survey year, class, left–right ideology and interactions between survey year and class and survey year and ideology. Party choice is a five category variable: Conservative, Labour, Liberal, other party, no party. For the BSA data the left–right scale is identical to that described in Chapter 4. To maintain consistency across the whole time period, the BES left–right scale is slightly different and uses three questions about whether there is 'one law for the rich and one law for the poor', whether 'ordinary people get a fair share of the wealth', and whether people think that 'there is no need for strong trade unions to protect employees' working conditions and wages'. As could be seen in Chapter 4, the average score on these kinds of scales remains similar over time, but we hold the values constant at each year's mean value.

11. Left-wing people are taken to have a score one standard deviation below the mean value for that year, and right-wing people are taken to have a score one standard deviation above the mean value for that year. The other variable in these models is class, which is held constant at the working class category.

12. This is the 'Gal-Tan' measure (see Bakker et al. 2015). Experts are asked where they would place the parties given that: ' "Libertarian" or "post-materialist" parties favor expanded personal freedoms, for example, access to abortion, active euthanasia, same-sex marriage, or greater democratic participation. "Traditional" or "authoritarian" parties often reject these ideas; they value order, tradition, and stability, and believe that the government should be a firm moral authority on social and cultural issues.'

13. These figures come from multinomial logistic regression models that predict party choice using left–right values, social conservative–liberal values, and survey year. The first two variables are all interacted with survey year in the models and are hence allowed to vary in impact from year to year. We use a slightly different version of the liberal–conservative scale described in Chapter 4. It uses only four of the five questions as the item about the morality of homosexuality is not present in some of the surveys. Socially liberal people are taken to be one standard deviation above the mean value for that year, and socially conservative people are taken to have a score one standard deviation below the mean value for that year. Left–right values are held constant at their mean value for that particular year.

14. This model takes the same form as previously, except with the addition of the scale score of which class the Labour party is 'for'. We interact the scale score with occupational class, since middle class people will prefer a party that represents middle class people and working class people will prefer a party that represents working class people. Both the direct and moderated effects of the scale are allowed to vary by year.

15. It is also possible that voters after the 1970s were more responsive to what parties said and did. Some argue that party choice became more instrumental and less an expression of partisan loyalty (Franklin 1984, 1985; Rose and McAllister 1986). If this did happen, and class-based responsiveness to parties' ideological signals was stronger by the 1980s, then this would further exaggerate the impact of the key changes made by Labour.

Appendix to Chapter 7

Table A7.1. Impact of occupational class and education on Labour support

a) BES data

Vote Labour	1960s	1970s	1980s	1990s	2000s	2010s
Old middle class	12%	11%	9%	22%	26%	18%
New middle class	22%	19%	15%	32%	35%	23%
Junior middle class	25%	22%	18%	31%	29%	22%
Working class	51%	39%	36%	46%	41%	25%
High education (degree)	16%	29%	22%	37%	22%	29%
Medium education (A Level)	19%	17%	17%	31%	24%	20%
Low education (school leaving age)	37%	33%	24%	40%	25%	20%

b) BSA data

Support Labour	1980s	1990s	2000s	2010s
Old middle class	11%	27%	30%	20%
New middle class	17%	36%	35%	25%
Junior middle class	18%	34%	33%	25%
Working class	36%	50%	43%	32%
High education (degree)	26%	43%	39%	32%
Medium education (A Level)	17%	34%	35%	27%
Low education (no qualifications)	26%	41%	40%	31%

Note: The numbers here are predicted probabilities from multinomial logit regression models using pooled data by decade that predict vote choice for the BES data and party support for the BSA data using occupational class, education, and year. The predicted occupational class probabilities are for someone in the medium education category and the predicted education probabilities are for someone in the junior middle class category. Year is set as close as possible to the middle of each decade (and the same year for both datasets).

Source: British Election Studies 1964–2015; British Social Attitudes Surveys 1986–2015.

Table A7.2. Impact of occupational class and education on Conservative support

a) BES data

Vote Conservative	1960s	1970s	1980s	1990s	2000s	2010s
Old middle class	64%	67%	63%	44%	47%	49%
New middle class	53%	48%	47%	30%	33%	40%
Junior middle class	50%	46%	50%	31%	33%	35%
Working class	27%	29%	31%	17%	20%	21%
High education (degree)	39%	30%	36%	19%	21%	27%
Medium education (A Level)	52%	48%	46%	28%	23%	33%
Low education (school leaving age)	36%	35%	42%	22%	20%	31%

b) BSA data

Support Conservatives	1980s	1990s	2000s	2010s
Old middle class	66%	46%	43%	51%
New middle class	50%	32%	31%	39%
Junior middle class	49%	33%	29%	36%
Working class	30%	17%	17%	21%
High education (degree)	30%	24%	20%	31%
Medium education (A Level)	51%	36%	27%	35%
Low education (no qualifications)	41%	31%	27%	35%

Note: The numbers here are predicted probabilities from multinomial logit regression models using pooled data by decade that predict vote choice for the BES data and party support for the BSA data using occupational class, education, and year. The predicted occupational class probabilities are for someone in the medium education category and the predicted education probabilities are for someone in the junior middle class category. Year is set as close as possible to the middle of each decade (and the same year for both datasets).

Source: British Election Studies 1964–2015; British Social Attitudes Surveys 1986–2015.

8

Long Live Class Politics

If people do not like the party that they used to vote for, what can they do? There are really three choices: vote for the opposing party, vote for a new party, or stop voting.[1] This chapter sets out how the decline of class voting for the two major parties, has led to a revival of class voting in terms of new parties, but most importantly in terms of abstention. As Labour, and to some extent the Conservatives, have left people with working class jobs and low levels of education behind, those same people have become disengaged from mainstream politics. We show here that the previously small gap between the classes in terms of turnout sharply increased during the 2000s, resulting in a voting population that has been systematically shorn of the working class. Class *voting* may have disappeared, but class *non-voting* is stronger than ever. This is a direct result of disillusionment with political parties that fail to represent people's views. The 2015 election also heralded a set of new party choices that have increased class voting. In Scotland the Scottish National Party (SNP) is now the most working class party after taking great swathes of former Labour voters in 2015. In England and Wales, the United Kingdom Independence Party (UKIP) is the new home of the working class, with voters deserting the mainstream to join the emergent radical right party. This chapter thus shows how both non-voting and new parties have signalled a resurgence of the importance of class in politics.

To Vote Or Not To Vote?

Rates of turnout in Britain until 1997 were relatively static. Some elections saw small increases, and some saw small decreases, but around 75 per cent of the electorate regularly turned out to vote. The 78 per cent turnout rate in 1992 was almost the same as the 79 per cent in 1959. Even 1997, which saw the lowest turnout since the war at 71 per cent, witnessed only slightly fewer voters than 1970 (with 72 per cent turnout). This changed quite dramatically

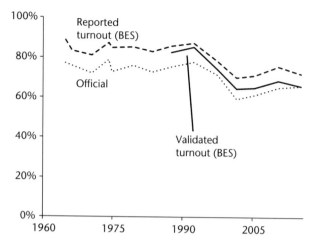

Figure 8.1. Turnout over time

Note: The figure here shows official turnout figures, reported turnout from the BES, and validated turnout from the BES.

Source: Electoral Commission; British Election Studies 1964–2015.

after 1997. The nadir was the 2001 general election when voter participation fell to 59 per cent. While turnout has crept back up since then, rates of voting are still substantially below where they stood in 1992. Figure 8.1 shows these changes (from 1964 to 2015) and also illustrates an important issue with measuring turnout. The dotted line shows official turnout rates as recorded by the Electoral Commission (this is the percentage of people who cast a ballot as a proportion of all registered voters). The dashed line is the reported rate of turnout in the British Election Surveys since 1964. This is systematically higher because a) the BES sample tends to favour the inclusion of voters rather than non-voters and b) people tend to exaggerate their involvement in politics. The thick line in between accounts for the second of these, as it shows validated turnout rates from the BES. These figures come from the BES as well, but show the actual turnout rates of people who were surveyed using checks of the official electoral record.[2] These validated turnout figures are only available from 1987 onwards, but are the data that we will use mainly in this chapter, not least because there is so little change in turnout between the 1960s and the 1980s.

Regardless of the exact measure, Figure 8.1 clearly depicts the sharp decline in turnout since 1992. The reasons for this dramatic change are often argued to be similar to the factors that underpinned the changes in class voting that we discussed in Chapter 7. Heath and Taylor (1999) focus on the lack of ideological distance between the main parties, and Heath (2007) argues that public perceptions of the main parties as indistinguishable were the main driver of lower turnout. The particular circumstances of the 2001 election are also potentially important since this was an election which was widely seen as a foregone conclusion and sparked little interest among the public (Johnston and Pattie 2003). Implicitly these kinds of explanations call upon ideas of the 'rational voter': someone who pays attention to their chances of being the pivotal voter who decides an election and weighs the expected benefits from one party or another winning against the costs of actually voting (Downs 1957; Aldrich 1993). This is one way of thinking about the decision to vote or not. We will largely duck the long-running debate about whether any voters really think like this, because it is not crucial for us to explain why fewer people in general vote today than did in 1992.[3] What we are interested in is whether certain types of people are less likely to vote today than they were twenty years ago. In fact, there are two other important explanations of the decision to vote that we should consider insofar as they relate to different types of people voting. One involves mobilization and psychological engagement: do people care about politics and care about the parties? The other concerns resources.

Mobilization can take many forms, but in essence the argument is that 'people participate in electoral politics because someone encourages or inspires them to take part' (Rosenstone and Hansen 1993, p.161). Related to this is the expressive power of voting: that turning out to vote is about expressing one's belonging to a particular partisan or social group (Brennan and Hamlin 1998; Hamlin and Jennings 2011). These explanations are rooted in ideas about how well parties relate to specific groups of voters and represent their interests. Of course, this all intersects with the process of parties becoming indistinguishable from one another. If Labour no longer looks like a working class party then it is less able to 'inspire' working class voters. As those same working class voters leave Labour, it makes sense that they will become non-voters if there are no more 'inspiring' options available. This model suggests that rising levels of class-based abstention may be due to the changing parties.

Yet some might argue we would expect lower turnout from certain social classes anyway. The resources model of participation holds that socio-economic resources have substantial effects on people's likelihood to vote. Implicitly, this model suggests that the costs of voting, and maybe also the benefits, are different for different types of people. In the US, it has long been recognized that class, income, and education influence participation (Verba and Nie 1972; Verba et al. 1978; Leighley and Nagler 1992a, 1992b; Verba et al. 1995; see Leighley and Nagler 2014 for an excellent overview). The argument runs that people in higher social classes, with more education and income, are more likely to vote because it is less costly for them to vote (especially in terms of acquiring political information). This is an explanation that lends itself to more static and constant class differences in non-voting, as in the US case (Leighley and Nagler 1992a, 2014).

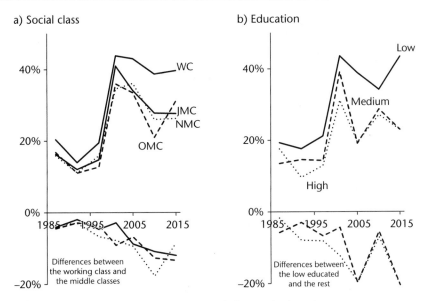

Figure 8.2. Non-voting rates by occupational class and education

Note: The figures here show predicted probabilities of non-voting from logit regression models that predict validated non-voting for each year separately. The left-hand graph disaggregates the results by social class; the right-hand graph disaggregates the results by education. As well as occupational class and education, these models include controls for trade union membership, gender, age, region, religion, and race. Four occupational class groups are displayed: old middle class (OMC), new middle class (NMC), junior middle class (JMC), and working class (WC). Three educational groups are displayed: people with degree-level education (high), people with A Level equivalent education (medium), and people who left school at the minimum school leaving age for their cohort (low). The predicted probabilities are for a white man with no religion in his forties, who has middling educational attainment/a junior middle class job, who lives in the south east of England, and is not a trade union member.

Source: British Election Studies 1987–2015.

Is it mobilization or resources that matters? In Britain, like the US, class has sometimes been shown to be associated with rates of turnout (Swaddle and Heath 1989; Pattie and Johnston 2001; Heath and Taylor 1999; Whiteley et al. 2001; Parry et al. 1992; Heath 2016). However, the differences in Britain have been generally rather small and before the 2000s often zero (Crewe et al. 1977a; Heath et al. 1991; Denver 1995; Pattie and Johnston 1998). Figure 8.2 shows the differences by occupational class and education in rates of non-voting. High numbers thus indicate that people are less likely to vote. As in Chapter 7, the lines below the x-axis are the differences between the three middle class groups and the working class, and the differences between those with a high or medium education compared to those with a low level of education. The numbers here are derived from regression models using the BES data with class, education, age, sex, region, religion, race, and trade union membership as independent variables predicting validated voter turnout.[4] As we look at validated votes only, we are limited to the 1987–2015 period. Nonetheless, the pattern is quite clear. From 1987 to 1992 there are only small differences between class and educational

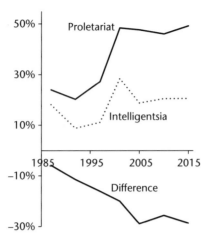

Figure 8.3. Non-voting rates by combined social group

Note: The figure here shows predicted probabilities of non-voting from logit regression models that predict non-voting for each year separately. As well as occupational class and education, these models include controls for trade union membership, gender, age, region, religion, and race. The predicted probabilities are for a white man with no religion in his forties, who lives in the south east of England and is not a trade union member. The two groups are low education and a working class occupation (proletariat) and high education and a new middle class occupation (intelligentsia).

Source: British Election Studies 1987–2015.

groups in rates of non-voting. The maximum difference between occupational or educational groups in these two elections is barely five percentage points. This reflects a long-standing pattern that is found in the 1960s and 1970s as well. Using non-validated measures of voting, the differences between the three middle class occupational groups and the working class in 1964 are between 2 and 6 per cent; in October 1974 they are between 1 and 5 per cent.

There are differences between the classes before the 1990s, but there is little real support for the resource model of turnout, because these differences are so small. More importantly, while resources have not changed, non-voting rates between the classes have dramatically altered. By the 1997 election we see the start of bigger gaps between the classes and by 2010 these have become large divides. To return to our class archetypes from Chapters 4 and 5, we predict that in 2015 someone in the bourgeoisie (old middle class job and medium education) has a 16 per cent chance of not voting and someone in the intelligentsia (new middle class job and high education) has a 13 per cent chance of not voting. Over 85 per cent of the middle class archetypes vote. Compare that to the proletariat (people with a working class job and low education), of whom we predict 52 per cent do not vote. Figure 8.3 displays the changes in non-voting over time for the intelligentsia and proletariat. From a position in the 1980s of almost equality between groups in turnout rates, we now see large

Table 8.1. How 1997 Labour voters voted in 2001 by occupational class

	Labour	Conservative or Liberal	Didn't vote
Old middle class	70%	15%	13%
New middle class	70%	16%	10%
Junior middle class	66%	14%	15%
Working class	67%	8%	23%

Note: This table shows the percentages of people who voted Labour in 1997 and how those same people voted in 2001. The total unweighted number of 1997 Labour voters in the sample is 947. Not shown are the percentage of people who voted for minor parties (3 per cent of the sample) or people in the personal service, own-account, foreman occupational class categories, or could not be coded (183 respondents).

Source: British Election Panel Study 1997–2001.

inequalities. Heath shows a similar pattern up to 2010, and argues that by 2010 'class is more important as a participatory cleavage than it is as an electoral cleavage' (Heath 2016, p.9). This change occurred precisely when parties and the media environment radically changed their nature and therefore suggests that it is not resources that matter, but party appeals.[5] As the set of parties available becomes less appealing to certain groups, those groups vote with their feet and stop participating. If it is not possible for me to express my identity or preferences because no parties represent that identity or preference, then why would I vote?

Using panel surveys which interview the same people repeatedly, we can show exactly this process at work in the 2000s. We take people who voted Labour in 1997 and then look at how those same people voted in 2001. Table 8.1 shows the proportion of 1997 Labour voters, by their occupational social class in 1997, who a) continue to support Labour in 2001, b) switch to another mainstream party, and c) stop voting. As the table shows, the proportion of voters who Labour retains in the different occupational class groups is fairly similar (around two thirds). What is quite different is the proportion of people who become non-voters over those four years. Only 10 per cent of the new middle class 1997 Labour voters do not vote in 2001. For the equivalent working class group, the figure is 23 per cent. Middle class voters may have tired of Labour between 1997 and 2001 at the same rate as the working class, but they had other party options that were appealing. Fifteen per cent of the three middle class groups switched to the Conservatives or Liberals. Only 8 per cent of the working class group did this.[6]

We also have panel data for the 2005–2010 period. Unlike the 1997–2001 election cycle which saw a large decrease in turnout, 2005–2010 saw a (small) increase in turnout. Nonetheless, the same pattern of the working classes deserting Labour to become non-voters can be seen. Table 8.2 shows that nearly 10 per cent of people in working class jobs[7] who voted Labour in

Table 8.2. How 2005 Labour voters voted in 2010 by occupational class

	Labour	Conservative or Liberal	Didn't vote
Old middle class	60%	30%	3%
New middle class	64%	34%	1%
Junior middle class	58%	27%	5%
Working class	62%	22%	9%

Note: This table shows the percentages of people who voted Labour in 2005 and how those same people voted in 2010. The total unweighted number of 2005 Labour voters in the sample is 666. Not shown are the percentage of people who voted for minor parties (6 per cent of the sample) or people who could not be placed in the four occupational class categories shown (166 respondents).

Source: British Election Panel Study 2005–2010.

2005 became non-voters in 2010, but fewer than 2 per cent of the old and new middle class groups who voted Labour in 2005 did not vote at the next election.

What does this tell us? Chapter 7 showed how the decline of class voting is partly a product of middle class people being more likely to support Labour. What we reveal here is that the disappearance of the class differential for Labour is also partly a product of working class people ceasing to vote altogether. This has produced the kind of class non-voting that has long been prevalent in the US, but until 20 years ago was barely noticeable in Britain. Just as the changes to the Labour party in the 1990s and 2000s attracted middle class voters, they put off working class voters. This is most obvious when we look at people who stopped voting and their attitudes towards Labour. The 1997–2001 BES panel study asks people whether they think Labour 'looks after working class people' in 2001. Figure 8.4 shows whether people who voted Labour in 1997 agree with this statement. We separate people by occupational class group and their eventual 2001 vote choice. Essentially everyone who stuck with Labour, regardless of their class, thought Labour looked after working class people. On average 93 per cent of the middle class groups and 95 per cent of the working class agreed. This figure is somewhat lower for middle class people who stopped voting in 2001 (82 per cent on average), but substantially lower for working class people who left Labour for the ranks of the non-voting in 2001. Nearly 40 per cent of working class voters who voted Labour in 1997, but stayed at home in 2001, thought Labour did not look after working class people.

There is no matching effect for middle class people in perceptions of whether Labour looks after the middle classes. Labour loyalists consistently think that Labour is a party that helps the middle class (94 per cent of people in middle class jobs and 89 per cent of people in working class jobs agree with this) and the figures among those who switch from Labour to abstention are very similar (91 per cent for the middle class occupational groups and 81 per cent for the working class occupational group). As the changes that we

a) Voted Labour in 2001

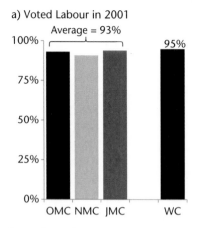

b) Did not vote in 2001

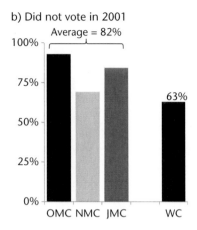

Figure 8.4. The proportion of people who voted Labour in 1997 and think that Labour 'looks after working class people' well in 2001 by occupational class and 2001 vote choice

Note: The figures here show the percentage of 1997 Labour voters who agreed that the Labour Party 'looks after working class people' in 2001. The left-hand graph gives results for those who voted Labour in 2001; the right-hand graph gives results for those who did not vote. The total unweighted number of 1997 Labour voters in the sample is 947. Not shown are people who voted for parties other than Labour (16 per cent of the sample) or people who could not be placed in the four occupational class categories shown (183 respondents). Four occupational class groups are displayed: old middle class (OMC), new middle class (NMC), junior middle class (JMC), and working class (WC).

Source: British Election Panel Study 1997–2001.

discussed in Chapters 5 and 6 occurred, working class Labour voters stopped seeing Labour as a suitable repository for their votes. Given that there were no more appetising choices on the table in terms of viable parties that either offered policies that were appealing to the working class or talked about representing the working class, the only option was to exit the system. This is what happened. The winning 'party' among working class voters today (whether measured by education or occupation) is none of the above.

If this was being written in 2010, we would leave it there, but the 2015 election saw further changes to vote choices. Why? Because there were now viable alternative options to the three main parties. The next part of this chapter therefore turns to how class voting continues to evolve with the emergence of new class-based parties.

Fruitcakes, Loons, and Nationalists

The 2015 election saw a small increase in turnout (from 65 per cent in 2010 to 66 per cent in 2015). The big story of the 2015 election, however, was the rise of non-mainstream parties. In Scotland, the SNP took 56 of the 59 seats available with over half of Scottish voters casting their vote for the nationalists. In England and Wales, UKIP increased their share of the vote by 10 percentage points, putting them in third place on nearly 15 per cent of the vote. Both of these changes have something to tell us about class voting in Britain and particularly the continued decline of Labour as a working class party. While the 1997–2010 period is characterized by working class voters leaving Labour to join the ranks of non-voters, the 2010–2015 electoral cycle is one in which working class voters that who stuck with one of the major parties departed to support the SNP in Scotland and UKIP in England and Wales.

The rise, fall, and rise again of the SNP makes for a fascinating political tale. Members of the party were 'generally regarded as cranks' (Kellas 1968, p.202) before the 1960s, with little electoral support and little organization. Mitchell et al. (2012, p.22) suggest that the party had only '200 members in the late 1950s' and until the 1964 general election the SNP only contested a handful of seats. Yet a series of local election successes and a by-election win in 1967 were a precursor to unprecedented electoral success in the two 1974 elections. It almost became the biggest party, by votes, in Scotland at the October 1974 election with over 30 per cent of Scottish votes cast for the nationalists, which was less than 6 per cent behind Labour. While many different reasons were given at the time for this success, some to do with the mainstream parties and their record in government, some to do with better SNP organization, and some to do with North Sea oil, much of that success evaporated fairly quickly (see Lynch (2002) for a full account). In fact, from 1979 to 2010 the SNP rarely got more than 20 per cent of the votes at Westminster elections. Nonetheless, from the 1970s onwards Scotland clearly had a four party system, with the Conservatives, the Liberals, and the SNP vying for second place behind a dominant Scottish Labour party. Who then was voting for the SNP?

One might be forgiven for thinking that the SNP has always attracted working class voters. In fact, the history of Scottish nationalism is not a history of working class activism. While Scottish nationalists might talk of working class Scotland, historically their votes have actually been drawn from all classes. Most literature emphasizes the way in which social cleavages[8] such as class fail to shape SNP support. Writing in the 1990s, Newman argues that the 'SNP was not dependent on one particular class for the votes it received' (Newman 1992, p.14) and that this was not surprising given that the 'SNP social and economic programme did not highlight class differences...the villain of SNP propaganda was not the upper class or the lower class but the centralized British state' (p.15). This is also what we find, at least until 2010.

Table 8.3 shows SNP vote share by occupational class from when the SNP first emerged as a political force in the 1970s. The number of Scottish respondents in the 1970s and 1980s surveys is small, so we combine the two 1974 and 1979 elections (at which the SNP did rather well, receiving 30 per cent of the

Table 8.3. SNP vote share by occupational class and education

	1970s	1980s	1992	1997	2001	2005	2010	2015
Old middle class	16%	11%	15%	18%	14%	22%	13%	32%
New middle class	28%	12%	23%	15%	13%	11%	16%	37%
Junior middle class	19%	7%	19%	16%	18%	13%	8%	34%
Average (middle class groups)	21%	10%	19%	17%	15%	15%	12%	34%
Working class	21%	7%	21%	16%	16%	16%	17%	42%
Middle class average - working class	0%	3%	−2%	1%	−1%	0%	−4%	−8%

Note: The numbers here are the proportions of people who voted for the SNP as a percentage of the Scottish electorate. The 1970s numbers are the average for the two 1974 elections and the 1979 election, the 1980s numbers are the average for the 1983 and 1987 elections.

Source: British Election Studies 1974–2015; British Social Attitudes Surveys 1997–2015.

Scottish share of the vote in the October 1974 election), and the 1983 and 1987 election surveys (at which the SNP did rather badly, receiving less than 10 per cent of the vote).[9] What the table shows is that differences by occupational class in SNP support are essentially zero before 2010, but are of modest importance in 2010 and 2015, with the working class being more likely to vote for the SNP than the middle class groups. These differences would be more striking if we looked at shares of the Scottish vote rather than shares of the Scottish electorate as the proportion of working class people not voting is much higher. In fact, nearly 60 per cent of working class voters voted for the SNP in 2015, compared to fewer than 45 per cent of voters in the three middle class groups.

Holding constant other factors does not affect this change; if anything it makes it more obvious. Figure 8.5 shows the predicted probability of SNP support by occupational class from logit models that hold constant education, age, religion, and other important factors.[10] The lines at the bottom show the differences between the three middle class groups and the working class. All show the increasing differences between the working class and the other groups after 2005. Ultimately, the SNP has gained votes among all classes in Scotland over the last ten years, but it disproportionately gained votes among the working class. This matches perceptions of the party. Unfortunately, we cannot track perceptions over time, but the 2015 BES asked whether people thought of the SNP as a working class or middle class party. Whereas 67 per cent of Scots thought it represented the working class, only 34 per cent thought it represented the middle class. Although SNP support has not historically been class-based, Scottish nationalists have traditionally 'emphasize[d] their concern with the working class community' (Brand et al. 1994, p.629).

At the same time, we should not exaggerate these changes. A revived post-referendum SNP meant that a new option was available to Scottish voters in 2015 and to some extent that option was more appealing to the working class

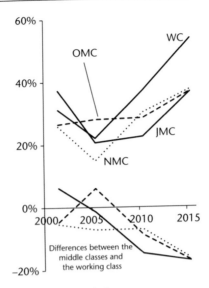

Figure 8.5. SNP support by occupational class

Note: The figure here shows predicted probabilities of SNP support in Scotland from multinomial logit regression models that predict vote choice as a percentage of the electorate for each year separately. As well as occupational class, these models include controls for education, trade union membership, gender, age, religion, and race. The predicted probabilities are for a white man with no religion in his forties, who has middling educational attainment and is not a trade union member. Four occupational class groups are displayed: old middle class (OMC), new middle class (NMC), junior middle class (JMC), and working class (WC).

Source: British Election Studies 2001–2015; British Social Attitudes Surveys 2001–2015.

than the middle classes. But the SNP relied on mostly middle class voters to make its electoral breakthrough. The perception that it is 'for the working class' is actually weakest among working class people (52 per cent of working class people see it as a working class party compared to nearly 80 per cent of the old and new middle classes). Nor was this breakthrough based on underlying attitudinal differences between the classes. There is no greater enthusiasm for Scottish independence among the working class than among the middle class. The 2015 BES shows that of people who voted in the referendum in 2014, 44 per cent of people with working class jobs claimed to have voted for an independent Scotland: exactly the same percentage as the overall Scottish sample.

Probably more important were perceptions of Labour. In 2015 only 34 per cent of working class Scots saw Labour as a party for the working class (and of those nearly two thirds said it was only 'slightly working class'). The rising tide of Scottish nationalism did affect working class voters more than middle class voters, but this was more due to changing perceptions of Labour than perceptions of the SNP. As Brand et al. (1994) pointed out in the 1990s, long before the SNP breakthrough of the twenty-first century, the SNP and Labour had similar policies and offered similar rhetoric. What has changed is the position in which the two parties find themselves. Twenty years ago Brand et al. (1994, p.629) said that 'the important cards are in Labour's hands' because it had 'much more media exposure than the Nationalists', 'a tradition of support among Scottish voters', and that the SNP had not built 'secure bases of local support', partially because it did not have a very happy record in local government. All those factors have changed. The Scottish Parliament has meant that the SNP has a strong base of support in Scotland and that 'traditions of support' have been tested. Equally, the independence referendum meant that the SNP built up a formidable campaigning organization and dominated media coverage. It is this shock to the system that generated realignment of class voting in Scotland. Nevertheless, we should not overstate this. The lines of party conflict have been redrawn to some extent, but there has certainly not been a complete redefinition of class politics in Scotland.

What of England and Wales? The story of UKIP south of the border is not the same as the SNP north of the border. The insurgent party here is newer and differs from the SNP in that its class appeal is more pronounced: UKIP has distinctive policy stances that more clearly and directly appeal to working class voters. This is not just about rejecting Labour, but also embracing UKIP.

In the run-up to the 2015 election it looked remarkably like David Cameron's dismissal of UKIP as 'fruitcakes, loonies and closet racists' a decade earlier (Ford and Goodwin 2014, p.71) would come back to haunt him. In the end, the British electoral system translated UKIP's four million votes into one seat. Moreover, while many of those four million voters were Conservative defectors, many were also Labour and Liberal defectors.[11] In fact, there was a substantial renewal of class voting in England and Wales in 2015 because it was working class voters who were predominantly drawn to UKIP. This is not a new point, nor is it specific to Britain. The links between class and radical right parties are well known both historically in Britain and comparatively on the continent.

Support for radical right parties, commonly defined as parties that oppose immigration and multi-culturalism, is low among new middle class and highly educated voters in almost all European countries (Arzheimer 2009; Oesch 2008; Ivarsflaten 2005, 2008; Lucassen and Lubbers 2012). Indeed, the academic consensus today is that core radical right support is located within the less educated working class and those voters are primarily mobilized by the issue of immigration (Mudde 2007; Rydgren 2008). This has traditionally been the case in Britain as well, although until recently parties on the extreme right have been relatively unpopular with everybody in Britain. This is partially because of the electoral system and partially because of these parties' association with fascism and some rather nefarious characters. The first past the post electoral system has not allowed parties to flourish and establish an electoral base (Norris 2005), and the lack of a radical right party with, what Ivarsflaten (2006) calls, a 'reputational shield' has meant that extremist parties on the right have been easy to tar as 'fascists' or 'Nazis'. While the National Front experienced some success in the mid 1970s, primarily driven by younger working class voters in inner cities (Harrop et al. 1980), this did not last.[12] More recently, the British National Party managed to mobilize a small percentage of voters over the immigration issue at European and local elections in the 2000s, with the BNP regularly getting over 10 per cent of the vote in local elections over the decade. The class basis of BNP support, like National Front support, was again working class and less educated men, albeit older rather than younger men (Ford and Goodwin 2010; Cutts et al. 2011). Ultimately the lack of national representation and links with violence and overt racism now appear to have put paid to the BNP as a longer-term project, however.

UKIP is of course a very different beast to the BNP and the National Front. Its policies around immigration are not racist, and it has another dominant policy issue of opposition to EU integration. Like other parties in Europe that started as anti-EU parties, before adopting an anti-immigration platform, UKIP has been largely protected from vote shedding accusations of racism. In the parlance of the literature it is a 'populist', not a 'neofascist' party like the BNP (Golder 2003; see Ford et al. (2012) about UKIP specifically). A recent influential book by Ford and Goodwin (2014) suggests that UKIP has thus become a party similar to many successful populist radical right parties on the continent. Part of that similarity is the mobilization of working class and less educated voters. Although Ford and Goodwin show links between occupational class, and more importantly education, and UKIP support, almost all their data comes from a period before UKIP's sustained success outside of European elections. Here we confirm to a large extent the predictions that they made three years ago about the role of social characteristics in predicting UKIP support.

Figure 8.6 shows the basic picture using yearly BSA data on party support by occupational class and education. The rise of UKIP is obvious. Also obvious is the growing occupational and educational differential in its support. These effects are not due to the slightly older nature of the UKIP electorate, nor its regional basis. Table 8.4 shows the effects of occupational class and education on UKIP party choice from models that hold constant the usual long list of other social characteristics. We split the data into two time periods: dormancy (2004–2013) and success (2013–2015). The first column shows pooled data from 2004–2012 for the BSA and the 2005–2010 elections for the BES. The second column shows pooled data from 2013–2015 for the BSA and the 2015 election for the BES.[13] UKIP support is generally very low in the dormant

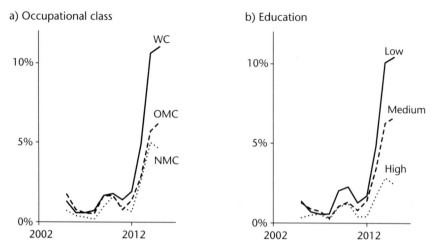

Figure 8.6. UKIP support by occupational class and education in England and Wales

Note: The figures here show the proportion of people who support UKIP as a percentage of the English and Welsh electorate. The left-hand graph disaggregates results by social class; the right-hand graph disaggregates results by education. Three occupational class groups are displayed: old middle class (OMC), new middle class (NMC), and the working class (WC). Three educational groups are displayed: people with degree-level education (high), people with A Level equivalent education (medium), and people who left school at the minimum school leaving age for their cohort (low).

Source: British Social Attitudes Surveys 2004–2015.

pre-2013 period, but it is interesting that there are very few consistent differences between classes and educational groups.

After 2012 both the BSA and BES data show that occupational class and education have a clear role to play in explaining UKIP support. The three middle class occupational groups and people with a degree are systematically less likely to support UKIP. The pattern for occupational class is a facsimile of Labour support of yesteryear. Is this class voting then? It is, but for different reasons than we saw previously. Labour class voting was based on left-wing policies appealing to left-wing (and therefore working class) voters. UKIP also offer policies that are particularly appealing to those in working class occupations. The difference is that these are not left-wing economic positions, but rather anti-immigration and anti-EU integration policies. While the policy area might be different, voter attitudes are nonetheless strongly shaped by class and education, particularly in the last decade. As discussed in Chapter 4, both economic and cultural factors drive people's attitudes towards the EU and immigration. Middle class, degree-educated people gain economically from EU integration and mass immigration, and people in working class jobs or without higher education lose (Anderson and Reichert 1995; Gabel and Palmer 1995; Hooghe and Marks 2004; McLaren 2015). Equally the

Table 8.4. UKIP support by occupational class in England and Wales

Support UKIP (BSA data)	2004–2012	2013–2015
Old middle class	2%	9%
New middle class	2%	10%
Junior middle class	3%	11%
Working class	2%	15%
New middle class – working class	0%	−5%
High education (degree)	2%	6%
Medium education (A Level)	3%	11%
Low education (school leaving age)	3%	14%
High education – low education	−1%	−8%

Vote UKIP (BES data)	2005 and 2010 elections	2015 election
Old middle class	1%	12%
New middle class	2%	14%
Junior middle class	2%	13%
Working class	2%	23%
New middle class – working class	0%	−9%
High education (degree)	2%	3%
Medium education (A Level)	0%	13%
Low education (school leaving age)	1%	12%
High education – low education	0%	−9%

Note: The numbers here are predicted probabilities of UKIP support in England and Wales from logit regression models. As well as occupational class and education, these models include controls for housing, trade union membership, gender, age, region, religion, and race. The models using BSA data also include controls for employment sector and agricultural employment. The predicted class probabilities are for a white man with no religion in his forties, who is a homeowner, has middling educational attainment, lives in the south east of England, is not a trade union member, and works in the private sector. The predicted education probabilities are for the same type of person in the junior middle class category.

Source: British Election Studies 2005–2015; British Social Attitudes Surveys 2004–2015.

cultural threat that integration and immigration pose to people is greatest among people who have the strongest group, cultural, and national identities. These people are typically working class and do not have degrees (McLaren 2002, 2015; McLaren and Johnson 2007; Garry and Tilley 2009; Sides and Citrin 2007).

This helps to explain the pattern of support by education. Degree-level education tends to make people different in their attitudes towards immigration and the EU, and it is this split that really matters for UKIP support. Whereas Labour traditionally drew support from highly educated people (because it was a little more socially liberal than the Conservatives) and also people with low levels of education (because of its left-wing economic policies), UKIP draws support from the 75 per cent of people without a degree relatively evenly.

It is perhaps not surprising then that if we hold attitudes towards immigration and EU integration constant, most of the differences between the educational and occupational groups disappear. Figure 8.7 shows predicted probabilities of UKIP support from models that do (on the right) and do not (on the left) control

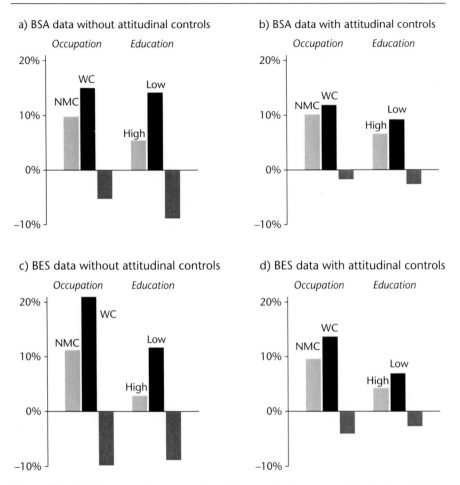

Figure 8.7. UKIP support by occupational class and education in England and Wales controlling for attitudes to immigration and the EU

Note: The figures here show predicted probabilities of UKIP support in England and Wales from logit regression models. The top two graphs are based on BSA data; the bottom two graphs are based on BES data. As well as occupational class and education, these models include controls for housing, trade union membership, gender, age, region, religion, race, and agricultural employment. The models using BSA data also include controls for public sector employment and year. Both figures on the right also include three attitudinal variables: attitudes towards immigration, attitudes towards the EU, and left-right values. The predicted class probabilities are for a white man with no religion in his forties, who is a homeowner, has middling educational attainment, lives in the south east of England, is not a trade union member, and works in the private sector. The predicted education probabilities are for the same type of person in the junior middle class category. All attitudes are held at their mean. Two occupational class groups are displayed: new middle class (NMC) and the working class (WC). Two educational groups are displayed: people with degree-level education (high) and people who left school at the minimum school leaving age for their cohort (low).

Source: British Election Study 2015; British Social Attitudes Surveys 2013–2015.

for these attitudes. For both the pooled 2013–2015 BSA data and the 2015 BES data, holding constant EU and immigration attitudes removes most of the differences between groups, despite having to use rather crude measures of both attitudes.[14] This makes sense. UKIP attracts voters who are most opposed to immigration and EU integration. For example, at the 2015 election 79 per cent of UKIP voters felt very strongly that immigration should be reduced compared to 38 per cent of the whole electorate (and only a quarter of Labour voters). Equally, 53 per cent of working class people very strongly agreed that there were too many immigrants compared to 26 per cent of the new middle class group. Put together these two facts—policy differences between classes and a party offering a distinctive set of policies which appeals to one class more than another—and you get a recipe for UKIP class voting.

Is this a new class politics? In 2013 Betz and Meret claimed that the 'the working class profile is valid for virtually all right-wing populist parties' (p.108), and it is clear that UKIP is no exception to that rule. But the basis of this class politics is rather different to the past. Rather than being based on economic issues of redistribution and public ownership, it is based on issues that, while linked to economic factors, are about cultural identities as well. It is also not a mobilizing form of class politics; the rise of UKIP does not appear to have ameliorated the class and education differences in turnout that we saw earlier in this chapter.

Conclusions

'Saturday Night and Sunday Morning' was a landmark novel of the 1950s, arguably one of the first authentic accounts of working class life. In the penultimate chapter, Arthur says of politicians: 'They shout at you from soapboxes: "Vote for me, and this and that", but it amounts to the same in the end whatever you vote for' (Sillitoe 1958, p.202). In 1958 Arthur was a rebel, an exception. Most working class people voted, and most voted Labour. In 2016 Arthur's view would be shared by most others, doing the actual, or modern equivalent of, sweating over a lathe. The new party of the working class is no party at all. This is not due to differing amounts of 'resources' that different people have. Resource models of turnout suggest education and wealth allow people to engage more with politics in various ways, resulting in higher rates of turnout for middle class educated people. This is not what we see in Britain. Working class people were almost as likely to vote in the 1960s, 1970s, and 1980s as the middle classes. There was no gap in turnout to explain. The gap only began to emerge in the 2000s. This is not because working class voters have suddenly realized they lack 'resources'; it is because of their lack of political choices. With no party committed to representing working class views, working class people choose not to vote.[15] Writing about the 1997 election Heath et al. (2001, p.155) argue that there were 'hints' of working class disillusionment with Labour already and speculate that Labour's changing nature would lead to 'a gradual rise in class non-voting'. That prediction has proved very accurate.

We started this chapter by presenting the options to voters who do not like their former party: vote for the opposition, vote for a new party, or do not vote. For most of the twenty-first century, the second of those options was not a real possibility and working class voters who no longer felt attached to the mainstream parties therefore chose option three: stay at home. At the last election, real choice opened up, and the calculus changed for working class voters. In Scotland, a revitalized SNP offered a real alternative to Labour which attracted all voters, but disproportionately appealed to working class voters. In England and Wales, UKIP became the party with, by a narrow margin, the highest percentage of the working class vote of any party. While there are similarities, there are also differences between the Scottish and English experiences. In Scotland, the SNP is offering policies that are either very similar to Labour or, like the issue of Scottish independence itself, do not strongly divide people by class. In that sense, increased class voting in Scotland is due mainly to the rejection of Labour as a working class party and the availability of a substitute that happened to be relatively popular. In England and Wales, voting for UKIP was not just a rejection of Labour, not least because much of their support came from former Conservative and Liberal voters, but was also an endorsement of UKIP policies that appeal directly to working class voters.

Is this a lasting change? We are writing this shortly before the 2016 EU referendum, and it seems likely that the results of this may determine the future electoral success of both the SNP and UKIP. It may have less effect on class differences in their support. It seems difficult to imagine that Scottish Labour will regain the title of the working class party and this means that working class voters will likely stay with the SNP or stop voting, depending on whether the SNP can sustain its universal appeal. The class basis of UKIP support is stronger because there are real policy issues that divide the classes and that divide UKIP from the other parties. Given the unpopularity of the EU and mass immigration among working class voters, plus the seeming inability of unwillingness of any other major party to articulate that unpopularity, the continuation of class divisions in UKIP support seems likely. Whether UKIP as a party can maintain its existence after the EU referendum, regardless of the result, while handicapped by the electoral system, is much more difficult to predict. What is more certain is that there will remain significant numbers of voters, many working class, providing a potential pool of support for any niche party advocating less immigration, less multi-culturalism, and greater national sovereignty.

Nonetheless, what is crucial in that last sentence is the word 'voters', because while UKIP may well continue to attract working class people to defect from other parties, the biggest change in class voting patterns is the new bloc of working class non-voters. And for all the excitement that SNP and UKIP success may have generated, it is this shift that is the most important. It means that not only are working class people less likely to be voters due to mainstream party changes but also that vote seeking parties have even less reason to put forward policies that might appeal to those non-voters. To echo Oliver Heath (2016, p.22) writing about turnout changes up to the 2010 election: 'the working class have not become incorporated within the political system, they have become marginalised from it.'

Notes

1. Or to quote Przeworski and Sprague (1986, p.61): 'the workers who would otherwise have voted for a Socialist party have three avenues open to them: they can vote for bourgeois parties; they can abstain from voting altogether, and in some countries, they can vote for other parties that appeal to them as workers.'

2. For example, in 1987, 3,104 people reported that they voted. After checking the electoral records, the BES team found that 158 of those 3,104 people did not actually vote. There were also a small number of people who reported not voting when they did. Of the 514 people who reported that they did not vote, 29 actually made it to the polling station according to the official records. It may be particularly important to use validated votes when looking at turnout differences between classes as there is evidence that middle class and highly educated people are more likely to over-report their turnout (Bernstein et al. 2001; Silver et al. 1986; although see Swaddle and Heath (1989) who find the opposite effect).

3. Although we can at least rule out institutional changes, and their consequent effect on costs and benefits, as being responsible for decreased voting rates. It has been argued that the lowering of the voting age to 18 before the 1970 election accounted for the low levels of turnout at that election (Heath and Taylor 1999; Franklin 2004). However, there have been no large institutional changes since the 1970s that could be expected to affect turnout. Indeed, if anything, the moves towards increased postal voting should have increased turnout rates.

4. We run a model separately for each election, thereby allowing all the independent variables to vary over time in their impact. Education is measured by qualification (seven categories), age is six age-groups, region consists of the eleven standard regions of Britain, religion is eight categories measuring religion and Christian denomination, race is five categories. These are as reported in Appendix 4.1A for the 1974–2015 time period. The most important of these control variables is age. Although there is much debate in the literature as to whether it is ageing that causes increased turnout (Glenn and Grimes 1968; Wolfinger and Rosenstone 1980; Plutzer 2002), or whether it is older generations of voters who are more likely to vote (Clarke et al. 2004; Franklin 2004; Bhatti et al. 2012), we make no claims one way or the other. By including age-groups and modelling turnout for each survey separately, we are explicitly making no assumptions about whether it is

really age or generation that matters. For the figures, we show predicted probabilities for a white man in his forties, living in the southeast of England, with no religion who is not a member of a trade union. The occupational class figure holds education constant at O Levels (or equivalent) and the education figure holds occupational class constant at the junior middle class category.

5. As Heath (2007, p.499) also points out, the resources model presents 'something of a paradox in relation to levels of turnout. Since the middle class are more likely to vote than the working class, and there are more middle class people in Britain today than there were previously, it would seem logical all other things being equal that turnout should be higher'. Equally, over time the electorate has also become more educated, yet we have seen decreasing political participation.

6. There is a similar pattern by educational attainment. Fewer than 10 per cent of 1997 Labour voters with a degree switch to non-voting in 2001, but 20 per cent of 1997 Labour voters with no qualifications become non-voters in 2001.

7. Unfortunately, the 2005–2010 panel has a rather limited measure of occupation and so these categories are broad approximations of the occupational class categories that we use elsewhere in this chapter and the rest of the book, which are based on the SEG. The 2005–2010 panel asks people to place themselves in a category (with eight options), which inevitably means that there is much less measurement precision. As one of the respondents themselves notes in an open-ended response to the occupational class question: 'your general options are frankly reductive.'

8. While most authors concentrate on class, as we do here, there were substantial political divisions within Scotland along religious lines as well: Catholics supported Labour and Presbyterians supported the Conservatives (Seawright and Curtice 1995; Seawright 2000; Tilley 2015). Some have argued that SNP support is somewhat weaker amongst Catholics (McLean 1970; Bennie et al. 1997), but this is disputed (Johns et al. 2010; Mitchell et al. 2012).

9. We combine the BES and BSA surveys for each election from 1997 onwards. Doing this means that we have over 500 respondents for each year/period: 536 respondents for the 1970s, 725 for the 1980s, 911 for 1992, 1,152 for 1997, 998 for 2001, 1,363 for 2005, 697 for 2010, and 531 for 2015.

10. We run a model separately for each election, thereby allowing all the independent variables to vary over time in their impact. Education is measured by qualification (seven categories), age is six age-groups, religion is eight categories measuring religion and Christian denomination, race is two categories. For the figures, we show predicted probabilities for a white man in his forties with no religion who is not a member of a trade union and has education equivalent to O Levels.

11. Interestingly, it appears that many of the Liberal and Conservative defectors to UKIP in 2015 were actually former Labour, and often working class, voters who had left Labour in 2005 to vote for other parties in 2010 (Evans and Mellon 2016a).

12. The National Front may have been partially derailed by the Conservative party adopting a somewhat tougher line on immigration: what Meguid (2005) would call an 'accommodative strategy' by a mainstream party. In January 1978 Thatcher gave a famous interview in which she sympathized with people who were 'afraid that this country might be rather swamped by people with a different culture'

(Cockerell 1988, p.239) and, as Sandbrook (2012, p.593) points out, Keith Joseph shortly afterwards sounded 'rather like a diluted Enoch Powell' when he said that 'there is a limit to the number of people from different cultures that this country can ignore' in a by-election speech.

13. We run a model separately for the two periods, thereby allowing all the independent variables (sex, age, religion, trade union membership, race, and housing tenure) to vary in their impact. We include sector of employment and agricultural employment for the models using BSA data. Education is measured by the five-category variable that combines qualification and school leaving age, age is six age-groups, region consists of the ten standard regions of Britain outside Scotland, religion is eight categories measuring religion and Christian denomination, and race is two categories. For the figures, we show predicted probabilities for a white man with no religion in his forties, who is a homeowner, has middling educational attainment, lives in the south east of England, is not a trade union member, and works in the private sector. The predicted education probabilities are for the same type of person in the junior middle class category.

14. For the BSA data we use a question that asks people what they think 'Britain's long-term policy should be' with options of 'leave the EU, stay in the EU and try to reduce the EU's powers, to leave things as they are, to stay in the EU and try to increase the EU's powers, or to work for the formation of a single European government' and two 0–10 scale questions which we combine which ask whether 'it is generally bad or good for Britain's economy that migrants come to Britain from other countries' and whether 'Britain's cultural life is generally undermined or enriched by migrants coming to live here from other countries'. For the BES data, we use a 1–5 scale question that asks whether people 'approve or disapprove of Britain's membership in the EU' and a question that asks whether people think 'too many immigrants have been let into this country'. We also include the general measure of economic left–right values in the models. In both cases it is not a strong predictor of UKIP support, but UKIP supporters are, on average, slightly more economically left-wing.

15. This mirrors patterns found elsewhere. For example, Hill and Leighley (1996) find that US states that have a more left-wing Democratic party are better able to mobilize working class voters, and Weakliem and Heath (1999) show that class non-voting in the US increases sharply after 1960 as the Democrats move away from the New Deal working class coalition of voters.

9

Conclusion

In the 1950 general election 'the party contest was not so much "wooing the middle class" as more intense competition for the working class' (Bonham 1954, p.35). The presence of a large working class shaped British party politics for much of the post-war period. As we have seen, this has fundamentally changed. Why has this happened? Class has not disappeared: objective inequalities among classes, class identities, and ideological divisions between classes are unchanged. Britain remains a class-divided society. It is the very fact that class divisions have remained so pronounced that has produced such important changes in the political parties. As the middle classes have expanded, the policies and images that parties present to voters have changed to accommodate this. Voters have noticed and reacted accordingly. In the preceding chapters we have mapped these processes in detail.

In Part I of the book, we showed that differences over time among groups based on occupational class and education are very static. In Chapter 2 we focused on evidence of continuing class-based inequalities in resources, opportunities, and risks. Whether it is income, unemployment, or health, there are still systematic differences among class groups. Indeed, in some respects these differences may have actually increased. Equally, perceptions of income inequality remain largely unchanged, although awareness of inequality is systematically less pronounced than the reality.

In Chapter 3 we documented the resilience of class identities and people's continued awareness of class. Changing class sizes and increased upward social mobility do not appear to have dramatically weakened class identity, although some people in middle class occupations are more likely to see themselves as working class today. Conceptions of broad class divisions are also persistent, as are perceptions of class barriers. The more day-to-day manifestations of class appear to show little sign of erosion as well. Most people appear aware of class and our data appear to indicate that everyday manifestations of class constraints, in terms of friendships for example, are still present.

This continued distinctiveness is also evident in people's social and political attitudes. In Chapter 4 we showed that ideological differences among social classes have remained constant across the entire half century or so that we examine. Persistent class divisions in resources, risks, opportunities, and educational attainment have fostered continuing differences in policy preferences by class. These differences have combined with the changing sizes of classes to produce a different average voter today than when Bonham was writing about the 1950 election. As levels of education and the numbers of people with middle class jobs have increased, the average voter's views have become more economically right-wing and more socially liberal. The working class and less educated are now further away from the average voter. The electorate is also more fractured than it was in 1950. Immediately after the war most people had left school at fourteen and most people had a working class job. Today there is no equivalent monolithic group that numerically dominates society.

The political elite have responded to these changes in class size by decoupling class and politics. This can be seen in a number of ways. In Chapter 5 we showed that while class, and especially the working class, was central to media coverage of politics sixty or seventy years ago, today class is rarely mentioned. It is particularly rare to find newspaper editorials that directly link parties and class. This is not surprising given the evidence of party change in Chapter 6. Here we saw three big changes to the main parties, especially Labour.

First, the policy stances of the parties converged during the 1990s towards a more right-wing set of policy positions. The two main parties now cover a far less extensive ideological range than was the case over most of the twentieth century. The second change was not about ideology, but other types of signals from parties to voters. We looked at how both manifestos and speeches referred to different groups. Labour's shift to being a party of the middle class under Tony Blair was as much about the party's social image as policy change. While Labour, and to a lesser extent the Conservatives, regularly referred to the working class in both speeches and policy documents in the past, today there is little recognition of class. Both parties have settled on more neutral terminology (their beloved 'hard-working families') rather than making explicit appeals to class groups. The third change concerns descriptive representation. More than ever politicians, and most notably Labour politicians, are drawn from a similar pool of highly educated, upper middle class people. All three of these changes have combined to affect voter perceptions of the parties. Chapter 6 showed that people today see the main parties as both offering similar policies and representing similar types of (middle class) people.

Chapters 7 and 8 showed the consequences of these changes. In Chapter 7 we demonstrated how the connection between class and party choice was static for most of the post-war period, until it dramatically weakened in the mid 1990s. This timing indicates that the decline of class voting resulted from the increasing shift to the centre by Labour and thus party convergence on both policy and image. Because of party change, left–right ideological positions, largely based on class, no longer predict vote choices with anywhere near the same strength as before. Equally, as perceptions of the parties as class parties disappeared, people were no longer able to match themselves to a party on the basis of group identity. As Chapter 7 showed, the combination of these two factors essentially accounts for all the change in class voting since the war.

There is a further consequence of Labour's shift to the political centre and their recasting as a party of the middle class. In Chapter 8 we explored how the evolution of Labour has allowed new parties to flourish, but also depressed voter turnout among certain groups. Both UKIP and, to a lesser extent, the SNP in Scotland are examples of class-based parties. UKIP draws much of its support from working class people. In that sense, class voting is alive and well. Nonetheless, the major change is not really this re-emergence of class voting, but the emergence of class non-voting. Chapter 8 showed that differences by class in turnout rates through most of the post-war period were negligible. This changed in the 2000s because of a lack of political choice. As Labour's policies moved to the right and its image became more middle class, working class people have increasingly chosen not to vote.

What does this tell us about electoral politics? Ultimately our findings illustrate the critical role of top down processes in accounting for major electoral changes. Class differences in voting and non-voting depend upon the choices offered to voters, as well as the presence of class differences. The political choice thesis argues that when party signals to voters are indistinct, the differences between the party choices of social groups will decline (Przeworski 1985; Przeworski and Sprague 1986; Evans et al. 1999). As discussed in Chapter 1, many scholars have previously assumed a deterministic 'bottom up' explanation of the strength of the social bases of voting, in which the transition to a post-industrial society has been accompanied by a blurring of the class structure. This argument holds that class is not a source of political preferences because it is no longer a source of identity and interests. Our detailed analysis of the British case demonstrates that this is simply wrong. It is mainly parties that shape class voting. The political choice approach also explains increasing class differentials in turnout. They also account for positions the preferences of classes are more likely to find expression than when the parties cluster around similar positions. As Labour has changed, working class policy preferences have been left out of the choices presented by parties. A similar omission has occurred in terms of party signals about what sorts of people they stand for. As the working class has become increasingly divorced from Labour, working class people have chosen not to vote. The question that remains is whether this situation is likely to persist.

What Next?

Class Politics Within the Mainstream

The above discussion should not imply that Labour is unique among social democratic parties. As Przeworski and Sprague (1986) observed thirty years ago, the standard Social Democratic dilemma in post-industrial societies is how to retain voters from the shrinking working class while also attracting parts of the expanding educated middle class. As the latter group also forms the recruitment pool for candidates, the tensions inherent in that trade-off for Labour have presented the British media with wry amusement in recent years. As we are writing this, Labour's shadow Europe minister is in the news after complaining that some voters in Derbyshire raised immigration as an issue: 'The very first person I come to is a horrible racist. I'm never coming back to wherever this is' (*Guardian*, 19 May 2016).

Yet parties can change. This particular path has been chosen; it has not been an inevitable consequence of social and economic development. Indeed, the Labour Party changed its policy in many areas quite substantially after the election of Jeremy Corbyn as leader in 2015. If Labour moves to the left then might that reignite mainstream class politics? It might, but Labour under Corbyn is not just more left-wing but also more socially liberal, especially on key issues like immigration. This suggests that Labour will find it difficult to regain its old 'core' voters who tend to be more socially conservative than the average person. Discussion of the strategic difficulty of this combination of policies has recently surfaced in academic journals (Bale 2016; Jackson 2016; Richards 2016), but these tensions are also obvious when we look at current survey evidence on how Corbyn himself is perceived.

Table 9.1 contains data from Waves 5 and 7 of the BES panel survey. This shows how much people in different occupational classes like different party leaders and whether they think Jeremy Corbyn would be a suitable prime minister. Unfortunately, we are not able to separate the middle class into our three standard groups using this data as it is based on the seven NS-SEC categories. Nonetheless, we can still look at the difference between middle class (broadly equivalent to our new and old middle class groups combined) and working class people. Preferences for Corbyn as PM in 2016 are uniformly lower than preferences for David Cameron, but, more interestingly, there are few differences by occupational class in Corbyn's appeal. Equally, although working class people like him a little more than middle class people, this is no different to evaluations of Ed Miliband in 2015. Although the evidence so far

Table 9.1. Judgements of party leaders

Best PM?	Middle class	Working class	All
David Cameron	41%	29%	36%
Jeremy Corbyn	19%	23%	22%
Neither	40%	48%	41%

Leader likeability (0–10)	Middle class	Working class	All
David Cameron (2016)	3.9	3.1	3.7
Jeremy Corbyn (2016)	3.7	4.0	4.0
Ed Miliband (2015)	3.7	4.2	4.0

Note: The table shows responses to questions on 'whether David Cameron or Jeremy Corbyn would make a better Prime Minister' and 'how much they liked' each leader on a 0–10 scale ranging from 'strongly dislike' to 'strongly like'. The distinctions between the middle class groups used elsewhere in the book are not yet available for these data so the classes are constructed from NS-SEC categories: middle class (NS-SEC 1 and 2) and working class (NS-SEC 5, 6, and 7).

Source: British Election Study Panel Wave 5 (2015) and Wave 7 (2016)

is limited, there is little reason to believe that Jeremy Corbyn and what he represents will affect working class non-voters, or change the pattern of class voting.[1]

How long the current Labour leader will even stay in place is not certain given that a large proportion of Labour MPs want to replace him. Perhaps we should therefore ask the question: if Labour wants to maximize its votes, what should it do? It is worth looking at the social composition of party support and how this has changed. Figure 9.1 shows the make-up of the Labour and Conservative electorate since 1964 in terms of occupational class and education. The groupings for both are as we have discussed them in previous chapters with two amendments. For occupation we show an 'other' category which includes personal service workers, foremen, and own account workers, and for education we distinguish between a lowest level (minimum school leaving age) and a low level (above minimum school leaving age, but below A Level).[2]

There have been dramatic changes. Labour used to receive less than a quarter of its votes from the middle class and those with any education beyond minimum school leaving age. Today two thirds of its votes are from those groups. Some of this change is simply demographic; there are more people with degrees, but the comparison with Conservative support is instructive. The class mix for the Conservatives is quite similar over time, and although the average educational level of Conservative voters has clearly increased, changes to the educational composition of the Conservative vote are much smaller than they are for Labour.

This illustrates how the logic of electoral competition has forced Labour to focus on different voters. The new middle class and the highly educated now form large Labour constituencies. Nonetheless, neither of these groups is

a) Labour by occupational class

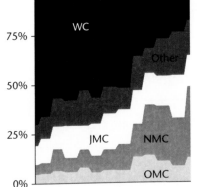

b) Labour by educational group

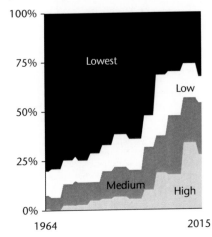

c) Conservative by occupational class

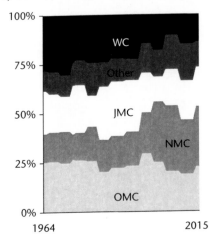

d) Conservative by educational group

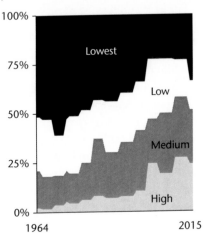

Figure 9.1. Social make-up of Labour and Conservative voters

Note: The figures here show the proportion of voters for Labour and the Conservatives who come from different occupational classes and educational groups. Five occupational class groups are displayed: old middle class (OMC), new middle class (NMC), junior middle class (JMC), other, and the working class (WC). Four educational groups are displayed: people with degree-level education (high), people with A Level equivalent or some higher education (medium), people who left school above the minimum leaving age, but below eighteen (low), and people who left school at the minimum school leaving age for their cohort (lowest).

Source: British Election Study 1964–2015; British Social Attitudes Surveys 2005 and 2010.

electorally 'dominant' in the way that the working class was in the 1960s. The new middle class makes up only a quarter of the population today: this is nothing like the situation fifty years ago when the working class made up over half the population. Similarly, people with degrees are still only a quarter of the population, but in the 1960s nearly 70 per cent of the population had no qualifications whatsoever. We have not seen a replacement of one big class with another big class, but a change to a more heterogeneous mixture of class and educational groups. This is inevitably a more difficult strategic situation for the parties, as there are divisions within the middle classes, to some extent due to educational differences.

Thus, the parties need to bundle together more complex coalitions, which means balancing the preferences of these socially divided classes and education groups. From a top down perspective, it is possible for parties to change the distributions of their class coalitions by concentrating policy appeals and mobilization, but this might not be worthwhile if groups are small. Moreover, while the social composition of Labour voters has changed because of both demographic change and because of Labour's altered policies and image, it is also due to turnout change. Parties need to consider the proportion of actual voters within social groups. We saw in Chapter 8 that our stylized proletariat group is now twice as likely as the intelligentsia to not vote. It is thus difficult to see Labour wanting to compromise its appeal to the latter who vote in large numbers, for the former who are more unlikely to turn out.

It might no longer make sense for the main party of the left to make policy appeals to the working class, but this does not necessarily imply the end of working class-oriented political appeals. Parties could try and reinvigorate the political significance of class identity. As we saw in Chapter 3, with only gentle prompting, 60 per cent of the population think of themselves as working class. Could the widespread extent of working class identity provide an opening for a political strategy of the left? Probably not, because, as Chapter 4 then showed, the middle classes continue to hold different policy preferences to the working class. To try and bind such heterogeneous groups together on the basis of identity is fraught with difficulty, not least when all parties have for many years downplayed class identity politics. Just as importantly, it is not clear that the proportion of people with working class identities will remain high. As Chapter 3 showed, class identity is often a residue of working class origins. Britain experienced a large amount of upward mobility from the working class to the rapidly growing middle classes in the second half of the twentieth century. Since the post-industrial occupational transition has more or less run its course, the proportion of first generation middle class people is already likely to be in decline. As this number falls, so should the number of people with working class identities. They will be replaced by a second generation middle class with a greater degree of consistency between class origins and destinations, and a more consistently middle class social and political outlook (De Graaf et al. 1995; Tolsma and Wolbers 2010).

Class Politics Outside the Mainstream

It seems unlikely that mainstream parties will revive class based appeals. This does not necessarily spell the death of class politics, however. One obvious possibility is that UKIP will become a distinctively working class party. In 2015 UKIP drew only 40 per cent of its support from the three middle class occupational groups. The same figure for the three main parties was between 64 and 72 per cent. This echoes the experience of other countries in which left-wing parties have moved to centrist positions and lost their former working class supporters to radical right parties (Achterberg and Houtman 2006; Kitschelt and McGann 2005; Rennwald and Evans 2014).[3] Indeed, it is now a standard finding that radical right parties are disproportionately supported by the working class (Betz 1994; Kitschelt 1995; Houtman 2003; Ivarsflaten 2005; de Lange 2007; Arzheimer 2008). In that sense, continued working class support for UKIP seems highly likely.

However, there are future obstacles to UKIP providing an effective source of working class representation. Once the party steps away from positions on the EU and immigration, it is less clear that it is in tune with its core voters. UKIP have no clear view on redistributive policies, for example, yet staying within the laager of anti-immigration rhetoric impairs the party's ability to break through more generally in electoral terms.[4] Radical right party success elsewhere has often relied on the avoidance of strong stances on economic left–right policies. But this is more viable in multi-dimensional PR systems where a party can win votes on a single issue. It is more difficult to pull off this trick in Britain's majoritarian system, although the continued success of the Front National in France suggests that it is not impossible.

Moreover, the effects of the referendum are unclear. The outcome may invigorate UKIP. Yet that invigoration may reduce its class appeal if it adopts a raft of consistent economic policies on the right. Equally, an implosion of UKIP would probably reduce class voting, given that there is no obvious contender in the wings waiting to take over its supporters. Indeed, it seems highly likely that its voters, after having once abandoned mainstream politics, would now abandon politics altogether and start to abstain.

Class Non-Politics

If UKIP voters were to stop voting, that would intensify class non-voting. But can we make any predictions about the future of class differences in turnout rates more generally? At one level, since parties seek to win elections, they care less about groups that do not vote. This potentially leads to a spiral of exclusion, in which parties do not represent certain types of people, those people do not vote, and therefore parties become even less likely to represent those non-voting groups. That spiral depends on whether those who have stopped voting can be persuaded to return. The prospects are not promising. Leighley and Nagler (2014) find no increase in working class electoral participation in the US over more than forty years. This is despite the ideological polarization of the parties (Poole and Rosenthal 2011) over the last half of that period, a change which should have increased expressive voting. Once the habit of participation is lost, it appears to be difficult to recover.

This is not that surprising, since voting is often thought of as a habitual act. A substantial body of recent research shows that the act of voting itself increases the likelihood of voting in future elections (Green and Shachar 2000; Gerber et al. 2003; Spahn and Hindman 2014; Denny and Doyle 2009; Plutzer 2002; see Aldrich et al. 2011 for a good overview). This can be due to many factors: lower costs (knowing the location of the polling station), increased benefits (a greater sense of regular voting as part of one's self-image), greater expressive voting (by strengthening a sense of partisanship), and so on. Whatever the exact mechanism, the basic idea is that voting is a habit. Once people are habitual voters they tend to remain voters unless there are individual shocks within someone's life (perhaps moving to a new area) or shocks to the political system that destabilize partisanship (as we describe in Chapter 8).

If voting is a habit, then it seems reasonable that non-voting may be habitual as well. Gerber et al. (2003, p.540) explicitly say that habit works both ways: 'When people abstain from voting, their subsequent proclivity for voting declines; when they vote, they become more likely to vote again.' If that is the case, then it means that shocks that produce decreases in turnout among certain groups will continue to be felt many years later. Class non-voting in Britain will thus continue. Related to this, many have argued that the political context experienced during people's formative years affects the likelihood of entering into the voting habit (Franklin 2004; Gorecki 2013; Plutzer 2002). Most research concentrates on electoral competitiveness, but the wider political context of parties appealing to groups of voters would seem just as important. If this is the case, then it means that working class people who entered the electorate since the late 1990s are rather unlikely to ever start voting.[5] This might mean that class differentials in turnout will not only remain but actually increase as newer generations replace older generations in the electorate.

Conclusions

Modern Britain exemplifies the consequences of a top down influence on cleavage dissolution and formation. When Tony Blair declared that the 'class war is over' in 1999, he did so as an instigator of that ceasefire. Following the changes that Labour underwent in the 1990s, class voting decreased sharply. By 2015 the social composition of Labour's voters was not terribly dissimilar to the Conservatives. Why did Labour change? The reason is a very simple one: the shifting shape of the class structure. The transition from a big working class to a big middle class was the engine of political change. The decisions made by parties then constrained voters' choices.

For the working class, these constraints are not merely about which party to choose but also about no longer having any party to choose. Top down party change has resulted in increasing non-participation in the democratic process by working class and low educated voters. As we have discussed in this chapter, it seems rather unlikely that these processes will be reversed. There is little incentive for mainstream parties to start appealing to the working class, and even if they did, voters who have stopped voting are unlikely to start again easily. Anderson and Davidson (1943) described electoral politics in the 1940s as 'the democratic class struggle'. While that description might have been true of Britain for much of the twentieth century, it is no longer. Politics in Britain today involves middle class parties fighting it out for middle class voters. The working class are bystanders, no longer represented within the political mainstream.

Notes

1. It also seems unlikely that Scottish Labour will quickly recover its appeal to working class voters in Scotland. The transformative effect of the 2014 Referendum has restructured Scottish politics around the independence question (Fieldhouse et al. 2017). This suggests that the Scottish working class will either maintain their recent support for the SNP, or eventually follow the English working class by increasingly abstaining.
2. As in Figure 1.2, we include both people with A Level equivalent education and those with some higher education below a degree in the medium category to maintain continuity over time.
3. For example, Spies's (2013) study of thirteen West European societies from 1980 to 2002 found that, in countries where the economic dimension of party competition decreased, support for radical right parties was considerably higher among the working class.
4. This has been exacerbated by the lack of political professionalism of the party's recently developed organization (Goodwin and Milazzo 2015).
5. This seems to be supported by the BES data. In 2015 the turnout differential between the new middle class and working class was 14 per cent for people under forty but only 3 per cent for people over sixty. Equally, the turnout differential between those with degrees and those with no qualifications was 30 per cent for those under forty, yet only 8 per cent for those over sixty.

10

Postscript: Brexit as an expression of the 'democratic class struggle'

Not long after we finished writing this book a remarkable political event occurred in the UK. The outcome of the referendum on the 23rd June 2016 transformed the landscape of British politics and Britain's relations with the European Union in one fell swoop. It also provides an illustration of our arguments about the suppression of political choice and its impact on class politics.

There has been much post-referendum discussion of Brexit and the social divisions it has exposed. Birch (2016, p.107) refers to 'the new cleavage that has been revealed by the Brexit vote.' Ford (2016), along with Goodwin and Heath (2016), similarly argues that the result was driven by so-called 'left-behind' voters: older, white, economically disadvantaged people who had turned against a political class they regarded as privileged and out-of-touch. Others have focused on divisions produced by globalisation (Curtice 2016), while Bernstein (2016) and Dorling (2016) explicitly attribute the referendum result to recent government austerity measures. Yet it would be wrong to believe that these divisions are in any sense new, even if they have not been so effectively expressed for many years. As we have seen in this book, Britain is no more or less divided by class in 2016 than it was decades earlier. The difference is that the referendum, with a clear choice between two competing visions, allowed voters to give voice to these divisions. In particular, for the first time since the political transformation of the Labour Party in the 1990s, the preferences of the working class could be expressed unambiguously at the ballot box.

It should not surprise us, therefore, to find a pronounced effect of class and education upon people's vote choice in the referendum. This can be seen using data at the council level and at the individual voter level. If we take every council area that reported in the referendum, there is an obvious connection between the social make-up of the area and the percentage of people who voted to remain or leave. Table 10.1 shows how the educational and

Table 10.1. Proportion of people voting Leave in the 2016 EU referendum

% working class (N)	% vote Leave	% with degrees (N)	% vote Leave
<20% (62)	42%	<20% (62)	66%
20–25% (100)	52%	20–25% (90)	59%
25–30% (107)	57%	25–30% (95)	54%
30%+ (77)	63%	30%+ (99)	44%

Note: This table shows the proportions of people who voted to leave the EU by type of council area in England and Wales, excluding the City of London. The proportion of working class people in a council area is derived from the 2011 census and refers to the proportion of people in routine and semi-routine jobs. The proportion of people with degrees is also derived from the 2011 census.

Source: BBC.

occupational character of council areas in England and Wales matches the proportion of people who voted to leave the EU. In the 77 council areas with more than 30 per cent of people in working class jobs, the Leave vote was more than 20 per cent higher than in the 62 council areas with fewer than 20 per cent of the population in working class jobs. Equally, there is more than a 20 per cent gap in the leave vote between the 62 areas with fewer than 20 per cent graduates and the 99 areas with more than 30 per cent graduates.[1] Most of the geographical variation in the Leave vote can be explained by the social make-up of different areas.

These effects of class and education can also be clearly seen at the individual level. We can look at vote choices using data from the British Election Study Referendum Survey carried out directly after the referendum. The differences in vote choice by occupational class and education are enormous. While 72 per cent of people with no qualifications voted to leave, only 35 per cent of people with a degree did. Equally, while 63 per cent of people in working class jobs voted to leave, only 44 per cent of those in new middle class jobs did. These differences persist even when we account for age and regional differences. The first column of Table 10.2 shows vote choices from a model that separates the effects of education and occupational class, and also holds constant other important control variables such as age and region.[2] The effects of education and occupation remain large. There is an almost 10 per cent gap between the new middle class and the working class, and a 30 per cent gap between people with high and low education.

These differences in referendum vote choice are similar to the divisions in attitudes towards the EU and immigration that we saw in Chapter 4. This is unsurprising since there is bound to be a direct link between these policy preferences and vote choice in the referendum. The referendum gave people an opportunity to choose between two distinct outcomes rather than the constrained options offered by the main political parties in recent elections. All of the three main parties[3] were committed to remaining in the EU and were unwilling or unable to reduce immigration. The second column of the table

Table 10.2. Proportion of people voting Leave in the 2016 EU referendum

% vote Leave	Without attitudinal controls	With attitudinal controls
Old middle class	52%	52%
New middle class	47%	50%
Junior middle class	50%	48%
Working class	55%	51%
New middle class – working class	−8%	−2%
High education (degree)	36%	44%
Medium-high education (A Level)	50%	45%
Medium-low education (O Level)	60%	53%
Low education (no qualifications)	66%	58%
High education – low education	−30%	−14%

Note: The numbers here are predicted probabilities from logit regression models to predict a Leave vote. As well as occupational class and education, all models include controls for housing, gender, age, region, religion, and race. The results in the right-hand column are from a model that also includes four attitudinal variables: attitudes towards immigration on a 1–10 scale, attitudes towards the EU on a 1–10 scale, left–right values and liberal–conservative values. The predicted class probabilities are for a white Anglican woman in her 40s who is a homeowner, has middling educational attainment, and lives in the south east of England. The predicted education probabilities are for the same type of person in the junior middle class category. All attitudes are held at their mean.

Source: British Election Study 2016 post-referendum survey.

shows class and educational differences in vote choice once we account for people's attitudes towards the pooling of sovereignty across the EU and attitudes towards immigration.[4] Immigration and the reclamation of powers from EU institutions were the two most frequently cited concerns among those who voted Leave (Prosser et al. 2016), and, as Chapter 4 showed, both these attitudes are strongly linked to class and education. Even though the attitudinal measures we have available are fairly poor (being simply 1–10 scales upon which people place themselves), once we account for them, we see much smaller differences in referendum vote between social groups. Class and education shape attitudes towards immigration and the pooling of sovereignty, and those attitudes were crucial for the decision to vote Remain or Leave. How does this link to the argument that runs through this book? In essence, it shows that when people in different social classes and educational groups are given a choice, they express their different preferences by choosing different outcomes. Removing the top down suppression of social divisions in preferences by parties allows those class divisions to be expressed.

One question that might remain, so to speak, is why did Leave win if the working class is no longer demographically dominant? After all, it is the change to an increasingly highly educated and middle class electorate that we have argued renders a working class focused politics electorally non-viable. There are two answers to this question. The first is to make clear that while divisions on an issue might be class based, the level of general opposition or support is also important. Working class voters are clearly less favourable to immigration than middle class voters, but that does not mean that the middle classes want more immigration. In fact, few people in the British electorate are happy with current rates of immigration. The binary choice of a referendum divides a population into two, regardless of the extremity of people's issue positions.

The second answer requires reflection on the extent to which changes in educational qualifications have actually altered the electoral landscape. As Chapter 4 showed, it is people's education, and not so much their occupational class, which determines their views on social liberalism and EU integration. There is a particularly large effect of higher education. However, the fact that the number of people with degrees has increased does not mean that most people have degrees. As Table 10.1 showed, in only 99 out of 346 councils in England and Wales are more than 30 per cent of the population graduates. Taking the UK electorate as a whole, only slightly over a quarter of people have a degree. As we discussed in Chapter 9, policies that *only* appeal to the university educated, as opposed to the broader middle class, are liable to remain relatively unpopular. EU membership is no exception to that rule.

Reversing the spiral of exclusion?

Chapter 8 focused on the decline in working class representation by the main political parties and the consequent rise in working class non-voting. The question that the referendum poses is, what happens when people's preferences are represented on a level playing field? While turnout was higher at the referendum than it was at the general election a year earlier for all types of people, it seems clear that working class participation increased the most. Again, we can look at both aggregate and individual level data. Table 10.3 shows how turnout changed in the 50 most and least working class areas and the 50 areas with most graduates and 50 areas with fewest graduates.

The differences in levels of turnout between 2015 and 2016 by type of area are not huge, but their direction is interesting. Areas with a large number of middle class graduates saw a smaller increase in turnout than did areas with few middle class graduates. This evidence of a renewal of participation in poorer socio-economic areas is new. As Chapter 8 showed, increases in participation after the nadir of 2001 have been far more pronounced among the middle class and the highly educated than among the working class and less educated. This has partially explained the growing class cleavage in participation. The disproportionate increases in participation between 2015 and 2016 in the working class and less highly educated areas of the country thus mark a partial reversal of this trend.[5]

We can see something similar when we look at survey data as well. Unfortunately the BES post-referendum survey is not suitable for examining

Table 10.3. Proportion of people voting

	2015 election	2016 EU referendum	Difference
50 most working class council areas	61.7%	70.1%	+8.4%
50 least working class council areas	68.9%	75.9%	+7.0%
50 council areas with fewest graduates	62.0%	70.3%	+8.4%
50 council areas with most graduates	68.7%	75.3%	+6.6%

Note: This table shows the proportions of people who voted in the 2015 general election and the EU referendum by type of council area in England and Wales, excluding the City of London. The proportion of working class people in a council area is derived from the 2011 census and refers to the proportion of people in routine and semi-routine jobs. The proportion of people with degrees is also derived from the 2011 census.
Source: BBC.

turnout as it systematically oversamples voters, but we can use a wave of the BSA (the NatCen Panel Pre-Referendum Survey) that happened just before the referendum and that asked people how likely it was that they would vote. If we run similar statistical models to those in Chapter 8 that hold constant age and so forth, then we predict that 87 per cent of the intelligentsia group (highly educated professionals) were likely to vote, compared to 67 per cent of the proletariat (people in working class jobs with low levels of education).[6] There is clearly still a difference, but it is about half the difference (20 per cent compared to 39 per cent) that we saw at the 2015 general election in Chapter 8.

There is good evidence that there was some narrowing of participation differences by class in 2016 compared to the last few general elections. When people are given a choice, and a choice that is not strongly linked with allegiances to political parties, they can re-engage to some extent. The growing habit of non-participation described in earlier chapters can be counteracted, but only under very specific conditions. The referendum produced high turnout and strong class voting because direct democracy did not enable parties to restrict the choices available. In that sense, the Brexit vote clearly confounds sociological, bottom up accounts of political change that assume that the influence of social structure on politics is in terminal decline. Whether the political class will allow voters such expression in the foreseeable future remains to be seen. Yet without such direct democracy, it is difficult to see how the pattern of working class disengagement from party politics shown in Chapter 8 can be reversed. Theresa May's avowal of one-nation Conservatism, complete with references to the working class in her leadership acceptance speech and her first party conference speech as leader, is unlikely to be pursued with sufficient effectiveness to overcome entrenched habits of working class non-voting. Indeed, much like UKIP's appeal to working class voters at the 2015 election, it is more likely to attract soft Labour partisans as the Labour party (and UKIP) stumble through extended leadership crises.

The ongoing convulsions within the Labour Party are between the liberal left and the Blairite right, neither of which provide much likelihood of representing the preferences of the working class, for whom both choices are of mixed appeal. Jeremy Corbyn's resounding victory in the 2016 Labour leadership contest appears to have consolidated an economically left-wing, but also, and more obviously, socially liberal platform. Criticisms of his London-centred cabinet for its lack of connection with the provincial working class have been expressed in the party and the media. Likewise, the party's support for Remain, low-key though it was, will have done little to endear it to its residual working class base.[7] At the same time, the option of choosing UKIP is endangered by its potential redundancy—as a party with a one issue goal that may now have been achieved—and the (current) loss of its high profile, charismatic leader. As with Labour, it too has been beset by internal struggles that threaten to tear it apart, so much so that it is not clear whether UKIP will continue to be an effective electoral party in future elections. These problems are likely to weaken its attraction for disillusioned working class Labour voters, leaving them no viable choice at the ballot box. Thus, despite many working class voters finding themselves on the winning side of the referendum vote, the spiral of working class exclusion from broader electoral politics is likely to continue.

Notes

1. Although both occupational class and education appear to be important when holding the other constant, educational levels seem to matter more. This can be seen when we model the Leave vote share for England and Wales using an OLS regression. The independent variables were the proportion of people in working class jobs, the proportion of people with degrees, the proportion of people over 65, and the proportion of non-whites. This model predicts that a 10 per cent increase in the proportion of people in working class jobs increases the Leave vote share by 3 per cent and a 10 per cent increase in the proportion of people with degrees decreases the Leave vote share by 13 per cent. The adjusted R-square of this model is 0.83 (0.80 with just class and education in the model), showing just how important these characteristics are in explaining the geographical differences in the vote.

2. The model holds constant a number of variables. These are: gender, age (six age groups), region (the eleven standard regions of Britain), religion (eight categories measuring religion and Christian denomination), housing tenure (five categories), and race (five categories). Education is measured by a seven category variable based on qualification and occupational class is based on the full NS-SEC measure.

3. Of course, UKIP arose in part to represent these anti-EU and anti-immigration preferences and, as Chapter 8 showed, UKIP voting is strongly predicted by voter attitudes towards those issues. Yet party politics is by its nature concerned with multiple policy areas; a referendum offers a simple binary choice.

4. We also include measures of economic left–right values and liberal–conservative values. These are batteries of questions that are almost identical to those discussed in Chapter 4. Neither had a very strong effect on vote choice.

5. Again if we model these changes using an OLS regression model predicting turnout change between 2015 and 2016, educational differences by area appear to be most important. A simple model that includes independent variables measuring the proportion of people in working class jobs and the proportion of people with a degree gives a non-statistically significant effect of occupational class on turnout change. Nonetheless education is clearly important: the model predicts that a 10 per cent increase in the proportion of people with degrees would decrease turnout change by 4 points.

6. The turnout question is a 1–10 scale that measures how likely someone is to vote. As is commonly done, we take people who said 9 or 10 as likely voters and the rest as likely non-voters. Taking just 10 as likely voters decreases the gap between the intelligentsia and proletariat further to just 13 per cent. The models include age, housing tenure, region, and sex as control variables, along with education and occupational class. Education is measured by highest qualification and occupational class is based on the NS-SEC schema. The predicted probabilities cited in the text are for a woman in her 40s who lives in the South East and owns her own house. For more details of the data see Cabrera-Alvarez et al. (2016).

7. This seems unlikely to have the extreme consequences that followed from being on the unionist side in the 2014 Scottish independence referendum (Fieldhouse and Prosser 2016) however.

References

Abrams, Mark, and Richard Rose. 1960. *Must Labour Lose?* Harmondsworth: Penguin Books.

Achterberg, Peter, and Dick Houtman. 2006. 'Why do so many people vote "unnaturally"? A cultural explanation for voting behaviour'. *European Journal of Political Research* 45 (1): 75–92.

Adams, James, Jane Green, and Caitlin Milazzo. 2012. 'Has the British public depolarized along with political elites? An American perspective on British public opinion'. *Comparative Political Studies* 45 (4): 507–30.

Adorno, Theodor W, Else Frenkel-Brunswik, Daniel J. Levinson, and Nevitt Sanford. 1950. *The Authoritarian Personality*. New York: Harper and Row.

Alderson, Arthur, Jason Beckfield, and Francois Nielsen. 2005. 'Exactly how has income inequality changed?' *International Journal of Comparative Sociology* 46 (5–6): 405–23.

Aldrich, John H. 1993. 'Rational choice and turnout'. *American Journal of Political Science* 37 (1): 246–78.

Aldrich, John H., Jacob M. Montgomery, and Wendy Wood. 2011. 'Turnout as a habit'. *Political Behavior* 33 (4): 535–63.

Alford, Robert. 1964. *Party and Society: The Anglo-American Democracies*. London: John Murray.

Alt, James, Ivor Crewe, and Bo Särlvik. 1977. 'Angels in plastic: The Liberal surge in 1974'. *Political Studies* 25 (3): 343–68.

Andersen, Robert, and Josh Curtis. 2012. 'The polarizing effect of economic inequality on class identification: Evidence from 44 countries'. *Research in Social Stratification and Mobility* 30 (1): 129–41.

Andersen, Robert, and Tina Fetner. 2008. 'Economic inequality and intolerance: Attitudes towards homosexuality in 35 democracies'. *American Journal of Political Science* 52 (4): 942–58.

Andersen, Robert, James Tilley, and Anthony F. Heath. 2005. 'Political knowledge and enlightened preferences: Party choice through the electoral cycle'. *British Journal of Political Science* 35 (2): 285–302.

Anderson, Christopher J., and M. Shawn Reichert. 1995. 'Economic benefits and support for membership in the EU: A cross-national analysis'. *Journal of Public Policy* 15 (3): 231–50.

Anderson, Dewey, and Percy Davidson. 1943. *Ballots and the Democratic Class Struggle*. Stanford: Stanford University Press.

References

Anderson, Lewis. 2016. 'Inequality in children's mental health and behavioural problems: What are the trends?' *Centre for Social Investigation 19*: briefing note. Available online: http://csi.nuff.ox.ac.uk/?page_id=11.

Ansolabehere, Stephen, and Shanto Iyengar. 1995. *Going Negative: How Political Advertisements Shrink and Polarize the Electorate.* New York: Free Press.

Ansolabehere, Stephen, Jonathan Rodden, and James N. Snyder Jr. 2008. 'The strength of issues: Using multiple measures to gauge preference stability, ideological constraint, and issue voting'. *American Political Science Review* 102 (2): 215–32.

Argyle, Michael. 1994. *The Psychology of Social Class.* Abingdon-on-Thames, UK: Taylor & Francis.

Armstrong, David, and Ryan Bakker. 2006. 'Take that you lousy dimension: A new model for manifesto-based left-right party placement'. *Unpublished working paper.* University of Oxford.

Arzheimer, Kai. 2009. 'Contextual factors and the extreme right vote in Western Europe, 1980–2002'. *American Journal of Political Science* 53 (2): 259–75.

Atherton, Kate, and Chris Power. 2007. 'Health inequalities with the National Statistics Socioeconomic classification: Disease risk factors and health in the 1958 British birth cohort'. *European Journal of Public Health* 17 (5): 486–91.

Autor, David H., and David Dorn. 2013. 'The growth of low-skill service jobs and the polarization of the US labor market'. *American Economic Review* 103 (5): 1553–97.

Bakker, Ryan, and Sara Hobolt. 2013. 'Measuring party positions'. In Geoffrey Evans and Nan Dirk De Graaf (eds.), *Political Choice Matters: Explaining the Strength of Class and Religious Cleavages in Cross-National Perspective.* Oxford: Oxford University Press, 27–45.

Bakker, Ryan, Catherine De Vries, Erica Edwards, Liesbet Hooghe, Seth Jolly, Gary Marks, Jonathan Polk, Jan Rovny, Marco Steenbergen, and Milada Anna Vachudova. 2015. 'Measuring party positions in Europe: The Chapel Hill expert survey trend file, 1999–2010'. *Party Politics* 21 (1): 143–152.

Baldassarri, Delia, and Andrew Gelman. 2008. 'Partisans without constraint: Political polarization and trends in American public opinion'. *American Journal of Sociology* 114 (2): 408–46.

Bale, Tim. 2016. 'The loser takes it all. Labour and Jeremy Corbyn: A response to Steven Richards'. *The Political Quarterly* 87 (1): 18–19.

Balestrini, Pierre P. 2012. 'How citizens' education, occupation, personal economic expectations and national identity interact with one another to sway public opinion on the EU'. *Swiss Political Science Review* 18 (3): 371–84.

Bara, Judith. 2006. 'The 2005 manifestos: A sense of déjà vu?' *Journal of Elections, Public Opinion and Parties* 16 (3): 265–81.

Barry, Brian. 2001. *Culture and Equality: An Egalitarian Critique of Multiculturalism.* Cambridge, UK: Polity Press.

Bartels, Larry M. 2008. *Unequal Democracy: The Political Economy of the New Gilded Age.* Princeton, NJ: Princeton University Press.

Baumberg, Ben, and Nigel Meager. 2015. 'Job quality and the self-employed: Is it still better to work for yourself?' In Alan Felstead, Duncan Gallie, and Francis Green (eds.), *Unequal Britain at Work.* Oxford: Oxford University Press, 105–219.

Beck, Ulrich. 1992. *Risk Society: Towards a New Modernity*. London: Sage.

Beck, Ulrich, and Elisabeth Beck-Gernsheim. 2002. *Individualization: Institutionalized Individualism and its Social and Political Consequences*. London: Sage.

Beckfield, Jason. 2003. 'Inequality in the world polity: The structure of international organization', *American Sociological Review*, 68: 401–24.

Beckfield, Jason. 2006. 'European integration and income inequality'. *American Sociological Review* 71: 964–85.

Bell, Daniel. 1960. *The End of Ideology*. Glencoe, IL: Free Press.

Bell, Wendell, and Robert V. Robinson. 1980. 'Cognitive maps of class and racial inequalities in England and the United States'. *American Journal of Sociology* 86 (2): 320–49.

Bendyna, Mary, and Celinda Lake. 1994. 'Gender and voting in the 1992 Presidential election'. In Elizabeth A. Cook, Sue Thomas, and Clyde Wilcox (eds.), *The Year of the Woman: Myths and Realities*. Boulder, CO: Westview, 237–54.

Bennie, Lynn, Jack Brand, and James Mitchell. 1997. *How Scotland Votes: Scottish Parties and Elections*. Manchester: Manchester University Press.

Benoit, Kenneth, and Michael Laver. 2007. 'Estimating party policy positions: Comparing expert surveys and hand-coded content analysis'. *Electoral Studies* 26 (1): 90–107.

Berelson, Bernard, Paul F. Lazarsfeld, and William N. McPhee. 1954. *Voting: A Study of Opinion Formation in a Presidential Campaign*. Chicago: University of Chicago Press.

Bernstein, J. 2016. 'The Brexit and budget austerity: What's the connection?'. *The Washington Post*, 27 June 2016.

Bernstein, Robert, Anita Chadha, and Robert Montjoy. 2001. 'Overreporting voting: Why it happens and why it matters'. *Public Opinion Quarterly* 65 (1): 22–44.

Best, Henreich, and Maurizio Cotta (eds.). 2000. *Parliamentary Representatives in Europe 1848–2000: Legislative Recruitment and Careers in Eleven European Countries*. Oxford: Oxford University Press.

Betz, Hans-Georg. 1994. *Radical Right-Wing Populism in Western Europe*. New York: St. Martin's Press.

Betz, Hans-Georg, and Susi Meret. 2013. 'Right-wing populist parties and the working-class vote'. In Jens Rydgren (ed.), *Class Politics and the Radical Right*. Abingdon: Routledge, 107–21.

Beynon, Huw. 1973. *Working for Ford*. Harmondsworth, UK: Penguin Books.

Bhatti, Yosef, Kasper M. Hansen, and Hanna Wass. 2012. 'The relationship between age and turnout: A roller-coaster ride'. *Electoral Studies* 31 (3): 588–93.

Birch, Sarah. 2016. 'Our new voters: Brexit, political mobilisation and the emerging electoral cleavage'. *Juncture* 23 (2): 107–10.

Blanden, Jo, and Stephen Machin. 2007. *Recent Changes in Intergenerational Mobility: Report for the Sutton Trust*. London: Sutton Trust.

Bolton, Paul. 2010. 'Higher education and social class'. *House of Commons Library: Research Briefings*. Available online: http://researchbriefings.parliament.uk/ResearchBriefing/Summary/SN00620#fullreport.

Bonham, John. 1954. *The Middle Class Vote*. London: Faber and Faber.

Books, John W., and JoAnn B. Reynolds. 1975. 'A note on class voting in Great Britain and the United States'. *Comparative Political Studies* 8 (3): 360–76.

Bottero, Wendy. 2004. 'Class identities and the identity of class'. *Sociology* 38 (5): 985–1003.

References

Brady, David. 2005. 'The welfare state and relative poverty in rich western democracies, 1967–1997'. *Social Forces* 83 (4): 1329–64.

Brady, David, and Hang Young Lee. 2014. 'The rise and fall of government spending in affluent democracies, 1971–2008.' *Journal of European Social Policy* 24 (1): 56–79.

Brand, Jack, James Mitchell, and Paula Surridge. 1994. 'Social constituency and ideological profile: Scottish nationalism in the 1990s'. *Political Studies* 42 (4): 616–29.

Breen, Richard, and Jan O. Jonsson. 2005. 'Inequality of opportunity in comparative perspective: Recent research on educational and social mobility'. *Annual Review of Sociology* 31: 223–43.

Brennan, Geoffrey, and Alan Hamlin. 1998. 'Expressive voting and electoral equilibrium'. *Public Choice* 95 (1–2): 149–75.

Brooks, Clem, Paul Nieuwbeerta, and Jeff Manza. 2006. 'Cleavage-based voting behavior in cross-national perspective: Evidence from six postwar democracies'. *Social Science Research* 35: 88–128.

Brynin, Malcom, and Kenneth Newton. 2003. 'The national press and voting turnout: British general elections of 1992 and 1997'. *Political Communication* 20 (1): 59–77.

Budge, Ian, Hans-Dieter Klingemann, Andrea Volkens, and Judith Bara. 2001. *Mapping Policy Preferences: Estimates for Parties, Governments and Electors 1945–1998*. Oxford: Oxford University Press.

Bukodi, Erzsebet, Robert Erikson, and John H. Goldthorpe. 2014. 'The effects of social origins and cognitive ability on educational attainment: Evidence from Britain and Sweden'. *Acta Sociologica* 57 (4): 293–310.

Bukodi, Erzsebet, and John H. Goldthorpe. 2016. 'Educational attainment – relative or absolute – as a mediator of intergenerational class mobility in Britain', *Research in Social Stratification and Mobility* 43: 5–15.

Bukodi, Erzsebet, John H. Goldthorpe, Lorraine Waller, and Jouni Kuha.. 2015. 'The mobility problem in Britain: New findings from the analysis of birth cohort data', *The British Journal of Sociology* 66 (1): 93–117.

Bulmer, Martin (ed.). 1975. *Working Class Images of Society*. London: Routledge.

Busch, F. 2015. 'Unemployment and insecurity in the UK labour market'. *Centre for Social Investigation 11*: briefing note. Available online: http://csi.nuff.ox.ac.uk/?page_id=11.

Butler, David, and Gareth Butler. 2000. *Twentieth Century British Political Facts 1900–2000*. London: Macmillan.

Butler, David, and Dennis Kavanagh. 1984. *The British General Election of 1983*. Basingstoke: Macmillan.

Butler, David, and Donald E. Stokes. 1969. *Political Change in Britain: Forces Shaping Electoral Choice*. London: Macmillan.

Butler, David, and Donald E. Stokes. 1974. *Political Change in Britain: The Evolution of Electoral Choice*. 2nd edn. London: Macmillan.

Butler, Tim, and Michael Savage (eds.). 1995. *Social Change and the Middle Classes*. London: UCL Press.

Cabrera-Alvarez, Pablo, Curtis Jessop, and Martin Wood. 2016. 'Public opinion on the EU referendum question: A new approach'. NatCen briefing paper.

Calvert, Peter. 1982. *The Concept of Class: An Historical Introduction*. London: Hutchinson.

Campbell, Angus, Philip E. Converse, Warren E. Miller, and Donald E. Stokes. 1960. *The American Voter*. New York: Wiley.

Campbell, Rosie, and Philip Cowley. 2014. 'What voters want: Reactions to candidate characteristics in a survey experiment'. *Political Studies* 62 (4): 745–65.

Campbell, Rosie, Joni Lovenduski, and Sarah Childs. 2010. 'Do women need women representatives?' *British Journal of Political Science* 40 (1): 171–94.

Cantril, Hadley. 1943. 'Identification with social and economic class'. *The Journal of Abnormal Psychology* 38 (1): 74–80.

Carey, Sean, and Jonathan Burton. 2004. 'Research note: The influence of the press in shaping public opinion towards the European Union in Britain'. *Political Studies* 52 (3): 623–40.

Carnes, Nicholas. 2012. 'Does the numerical underrepresentation of the working class in congress matter?' *Legislative Studies Quarterly* 37 (1): 5–34.

Castles, Frances G., and Peter Mair. 1984. 'Left-right political scales: Some "expert" judgements'. *European Journal of Political Research* 12 (1): 147–57.

Centers, Richard. 1949. *The Psychology of Social Classes. A Study of Class Consciousness*. Princeton, NJ: Princeton University Press.

Chan, Tak W., and John H. Goldthorpe. 2007. 'Class and status: The conceptual distinction and its empirical relevance'. *American Sociological Review* 72 (4): 512–32.

Cheng, Helen, John Brynner, Richard Wiggins, and Ingrid Schoon. 2012. 'The measurement and evaluation of social attitudes in two British cohort studies'. *Social Indicators Research* 107 (2): 351–71.

Childs, Sarah, and Paul Webb. 2010. 'Constituting and substantively representing women: Applying new approaches to a UK case study'. *Politics and Gender* 6 (2): 199–223.

Clark, Alistair. 2012. *Political Parties in the UK*. Basingstoke: Palgrave Macmillan.

Clark, Terry N. 2001a. 'The debate over "are social classes dying?"'. In Terry N. Clark and Seymour M. Lipset (eds.), *The Breakdown of Class Politics. A Debate on Post-Industrial Stratification*. Baltimore, MD: The Johns Hopkins University Press, 273–319.

Clark, Terry N. 2001b. 'What have we learned in a decade on class and party politics?' In Terry N. Clark, and Seymour M. Lipset (eds.), *The Breakdown of Class Politics: A Debate on Post-Industrial Stratification*. Baltimore, MD: The Johns Hopkins University Press, 6–39.

Clark, Terry N., and Seymour M. Lipset. 1991. 'Are social classes dying?' *International Sociology* 6 (4): 397–410.

Clarke, Harold, David Sanders, Marianne Stewart, and Paul Whiteley. 2004. *Political Choice in Britain*. Oxford: Oxford University Press.

Cockerell, Michael. 1988. *Live from Number 10: The Inside Story of Prime Ministers and Television*. London: Faber & Faber.

Coleman, Richard P., and Lee Rainwater. 1979. *Social Standing in America: New Dimensions of Class*. London: Routledge & Kegan Paul.

Conlon, Gavan, and Pietro Patrignani. 2011. 'The returns to higher education qualifications'. *BIS Research Paper Number 45*.

Connelly, Roxanne, Vernon Gayle, and Paul S. Lambert, 2016. 'A review of occupation based social classifications for social survey research.' *Methodological Innovations* 9: 1–14.

References

Converse, Phillip E. 1958. 'The shifting role of class in political attitudes and behaviour'. In Eleanor E. Maccoby, Theodore M. Newcomb, and Eugene L. Hartley (eds.), *Readings in Social Psychology*, 3rd edn. New York: Holt, 388–99.

Cook, Elizabeth. 1994. 'Voter responses to women senate candidates'. In Elizabeth Cook, Sue Thomas, and Clyde Wilcox (eds.), *The Year of the Woman: Myths and Realities*. Boulder, CO: Westview, 217–36.

Corneo, Giacomo, and Hans-Peter Gruner. 2002. 'Individual preferences for political redistribution'. *Journal of Public Economics* 83 (1): 83–107.

Cotta, Maurizio, and Henreich Best (eds.). 2007. *Democratic Representation in Europe: Diversity, Change, and Convergence*. Oxford: Oxford University Press.

Cozzarelli, Catherine, Anna V. Wilkinson, and Michael J. Tagler. 2001. 'Attitudes toward the poor and attributions for poverty'. *Journal of Social Issues* 57 (2): 207–27.

Crawford, Claire. 2014. 'Socio-economic differences in university outcomes in the UK: Drop-out, degree completion and degree class.' *IFS Working Paper W14/31*.

Crewe, Ivor. 1986. 'On the death and resurrection of class voting: Some comments on how Britain votes'. *Political Studies* 34 (4): 620–38.

Crewe, Ivor. 1987. 'A new class of politics?' *The Guardian*, 15 June 1987.

Crewe, Ivor, Tony Fox, and James Alt. 1977a. 'Non-voting in British general elections, 1966–October 1974'. *British Political Sociology Yearbook* 3: 38–109.

Crewe, Ivor, Bo Särlvik, and James Alt. 1977b. 'Partisan dealignment in Britain 1964–1974'. *British Journal of Political Science* 7 (2): 129–90.

Curtice, John. 2016. 'Brexit: Behind the referendum'. *Political Insight*, September 2016: 4–7.

Curtice, John. 1997. 'Is the sun shining on Tony Blair? The electoral influence of British newspapers'. *The Harvard International Journal of Press/Politics* 2 (2): 9–26.

Curtice, John, and Ann Mair. 2008. 'Where have all the readers gone? Popular newspapers and Britain's political health'. In Alison Park, John Curtice, Katrina Thomson, Miranda Phillips, Mark Johnson, and Elizabeth Clery (eds.), *British Social Attitudes: The 24th Report*. London: Sage, 161–72.

Curtice, John, and Holli Semetko. 1994. 'Does it matter what the papers say?' In Anthony Heath, Roger Jowell, and John Curtice (eds.), *Labour's Last Chance?: The 1992 Election and Beyond*. Aldershot: Dartmouth, 43–64.

Curtis, Josh. 2016. 'Social mobility and class identity: The role of economic conditions in 33 societies, 1999–2009'. *European Sociological Review* 32 (1): 108–21.

Cutler, Fred. 2002. 'The simplest shortcut of all: Sociodemographic characteristics and electoral choice'. *Journal of Politics* 64 (2): 466–90.

Cutts, David, Robert Ford, and Matthew J. Goodwin. 2011. 'Anti-immigrant, politically disaffected or still racist after all? Examining the attitudinal drivers of extreme right support in Britain in the 2009 European elections'. *European Journal of Political Research* 50 (3): 418–40.

Dalton, Russell. 2008. *Citizen Politics: Public Opinion and Political Parties in Advanced Industrial Democracies*, 5th edn. Chatham, NJ: Chatham House Publishers.

Davis, James A. 1975. 'Communism, conformity and categories: American tolerance in 1954 and 1972–73'. *American Journal of Sociology* 81 (3): 491–514.

De Graaf, Nan Dirk, Anthony Heath, and Ariana Need. 2001. 'Declining cleavages and political choices: The interplay of social and political factors in the Netherlands.' *Electoral Studies* 20 (1): 1–15.

De Graaf, Nan Dirk, Paul Nieuwbeerta, and Anthony Heath. 1995. 'Class mobility and political preference: Individual and contextual effects.' *American Journal of Sociology* 100 (1): 997–1027.

De Lange, Sarah L. 2007. 'A new winning formula? The programmatic appeal of the radical right'. *Party Politics* 13 (4): 411–35.

Dekker, Paul, and Peter Ester. 1987. 'Working-class authoritarianism: A re-examination of the Lipset thesis'. *European Journal of Political Research* 15 (4): 395–415.

Dennis, Norman, Fernando Henriques, and Clifford Slaughter. 1956. *Coal is Our Life.* London: Eyre and Spottiswoode.

Denny, Kevin, and Orla Doyle. 2009. 'Does voting history matter? Analysing persistence in turnout'. *American Journal of Political Science* 53 (1): 17–35.

Denver, David. 1995. 'Non-voting in Britain'. In Joan Font, and Rosa Virós (eds.), *Electoral Abstention in Europe.* Barcelona: Institut de Ciènces Politiques i Socials.

Dickens, Charles. 1837, 1999. *The Pickwick Papers.* Mark Wormald (ed.), New York: Penguin.

Dolan, Kathleen. 1998. 'Voting for women in the "year of the woman"'. *American Journal of Political Science* 42 (1): 272–93.

Dorling, Danny. 2016. 'Brexit: The decision of a divided country'. *British Medical Journal* 354: i3697.

Dowds, Lizanne, and Ken Young. 1996. 'National Identity'. In Roger Jowell, John Curtice, Alison Park, Lindsay Brook, and Katrina Thomson (eds.), *British Social Attitudes: The 13th Report.* Aldershot: Dartmouth.

Downs, Anthony. 1957. *An Economic Theory of Democracy.* New York: Harper and Row.

Drever, Frances, Tim Doran, and Margaret Whitehead. 2004. 'Exploring the relation between class, gender, and self-rated general health using the new socioeconomic classification. A study using data from the 2001 census'. *Journal of Epidemiology and Community Health.* 58 (7): 590–6.

Dunleavy, Patrick. 1980. 'The political implications of sectoral cleavages and the growth of state employment: Part 1, the analysis of production cleavages'. *Political Studies* 28 (3): 364–83.

Dunleavy, Patrick. 1986. 'The growth of sectoral cleavages and the stabilization of state expenditures'. *Environment and Planning D: Society and Space* 4 (2): 129–44.

Dunleavy, Patrick. 1987. 'Class dealignment in Britain revisited'. *West European Politics* 10 (3): 400–19.

Dunleavy, Patrick, and Christopher T. Husbands. 1985. *British Democracy at the Crossroads.* London: Allen and Unwin.

Eder, Klaus. 1993. *The New Politics of Class.* London: Sage.

Eidlin, Barry. 2014. 'Class formation and class identity: Birth, death, and possibilities for renewal'. *Sociological Compass* 8 (8): 1045–62.

Elff, Martin. 2007. 'Social structure and electoral behavior in comparative perspective: The decline of social cleavages in Western Europe revisited'. *Perspectives on Politics* 5 (2): 277–94.

Elff, Martin. 2009. 'Social divisions, party positions, and electoral behaviour'. *Electoral Studies* 28 (2): 297–308.

Erikson, Robert, and John H. Goldthorpe. 1992. *The Constant Flux: A Study of Class Mobility in Industrial Societies*. Oxford: Clarendon Press.

Erikson, Robert, and John H. Goldthorpe. 2010. 'Has social mobility in Britain decreased? Reconciling divergent findings on income and class mobility'. *The British Journal of Sociology* 61 (2): 211–30.

Erikson, Robert, John H. Goldthorpe, Michelle Jackson, Mair Yaish, and David Cox. 2005. 'On class differentials in educational attainment'. *Proceedings of the National Academy of Sciences of the United States of America* 102 (27): 9730–3.

Ermisch, John, and Cheti Nicoletti. 2007. 'Intergenerational earnings mobility: Changes across cohorts in Britain'. *B.E. Journal of Economic Analysis and Policy* 7 (2): 157–83.

Evans, Geoffrey. 1992. 'Testing the validity of the Goldthorpe class schema'. *European Sociological Review* 8 (4): 211–32.

Evans, Geoffrey. 1993a. 'The decline of class divisions in Britain? Class and ideological preferences in the 1960s and 1980s'. *British Journal of Sociology* 44 (3): 449–71.

Evans, Geoffrey. 1993b. 'Cognitive models of class structure and explanations of social outcomes'. *European Journal of Social Psychology* 23 (5): 445–64.

Evans, Geoffrey. 1993c. 'Class conflict and inequality'. In Roger Jowell, Lindsay Brook, Lizanne Dowds, and Daphne Ahrendt (eds.), *International Social Attitudes: The 10th BSA Report*. Aldershot: Dartmouth.

Evans, Geoffrey. 1996. 'Putting men and women into classes: An assessment of the cross-sex validity of the Goldthorpe class schema'. *Sociology* 30 (2): 209–34.

Evans, Geoffrey. 1997. 'Political ideology and popular beliefs about class and opportunity: Evidence from a survey experiment'. *British Journal of Sociology* 48 (3): 450–70.

Evans, Geoffrey (ed.). 1999. *The End of Class Politics? Class Voting in Comparative Context*. Oxford: Oxford University Press.

Evans, Geoffrey, and Nan Dirk de Graaf (eds.). 2013. *Political Choice Matters: Explaining the Strength of Class and Religious Cleavages in Cross-National Perspective*. Oxford: Oxford University Press.

Evans, Geoffrey, and Anthony Heath. 1995. 'The measurement of left-right and libertarian-authoritarian values: A comparison of balanced and unbalanced scales'. *Quality and Quantity* 29 (2): 191–206.

Evans, Geoffrey, Anthony Heath, and Mansur Lalljee. 1996. 'Measuring left-right and libertarian-authoritarian values in the British electorate'. *British Journal of Sociology* 47 (1): 93–112.

Evans, Geoffrey, Anthony Heath, and Clive Payne. 1999. 'Class: Labour as a catch-all party?' In Geoffrey Evans and Pippa Norris (eds.), *Critical Elections: British Parties and Voters in Long-term Perspective*. London: Sage, 87–101.

Evans, Geoffrey, and Jonathan Mellon. 2016a. 'Working class votes and Conservative losses: Solving the UKIP puzzle'. *Parliamentary Affairs* 69 (2): 464–79.

Evans, Geoffrey, and Jonathan Mellon. 2016b. 'Identity, awareness and political attitudes: Why are we still working class?' *British Social Attitudes: The 33rd Report*. London: Sage.

Evans, Geoffrey, and Colin Mills. 1998. 'Identifying class structure: A latent class analysis of the criterion-related and construct validity of the Goldthorpe class schema'. *European Sociological Review* 14 (1): 87–106.

Evans, Geoffrey, and Colin Mills. 2000. 'In search of the wage-labour/service contract: New evidence on the validity of the Goldthorpe class schema'. *British Journal of Sociology* 51 (4): 641–61.

Evans, Geoffrey, and James Tilley. 2011. 'Private schools and public divisions: The influence of fee-paying education on social attitudes'. *British Social Attitudes: The 28th Report*. London: Sage, 37–52.

Evans, Geoffrey, and James Tilley. 2012a. 'How parties shape class politics: Explaining the decline of class party support'. *British Journal of Political Science* 42 (1): 137–61.

Evans, Geoffrey, and James Tilley. 2012b. 'The depoliticization of inequality and redistribution: Explaining the decline of class voting'. *Journal of Politics* 74 (4): 963–76.

Evans, Geoffrey, and James Tilley. 2013. 'Ideological convergence and the decline of class voting in Britain'. In Geoffrey Evans and Nan Dirk de Graaf (eds.), *Political Choice Matters: Explaining the Strength of Class and Religious Cleavages in Cross-National Perspective*. Oxford: Oxford University Press, 87–113.

Evans, Geoffrey, and Stephen Whitefield. 2006. 'Explaining the rise and persistence of class voting in postcommunist Russia, 1993–2001'. *Political Research Quarterly* 59: 23–34.

Evans, Mariah D. R., and Jonathan Kelley. 2004. 'Subjective social location: Data from 21 nations'. *International Journal of Public Opinion Research* 16 (1): 3–38.

Feagin, Joseph. R. 1975. *Subordinating the Poor: Welfare and American Beliefs*. Englewood Cliffs, NJ: Prentice-Hall.

Felstead, Alan, Duncan Gallie, and Francis Green (eds.). 2015. *Unequal Britain at Work*. Oxford: Oxford University Press.

Fieldhouse, Edward, and Christopher Prosser. 2016. 'When attitudes and behaviour collide: How the Scottish independence referendum cost Labour'. Working paper.

Fielding, Steven. 2003. *The Labour Party: Continuity and Change in the Making of 'New' Labour*. Basingstoke: Palgrave Macmillan.

Finkel, Steven E. 1993. 'Re-examining the "minimal effects" model in recent presidential campaigns'. *The Journal of Politics* 55 (1): 1–21.

Finlayson, Alan, and Judi Atkins. 2015. 'British Political Speech Archive'. Available online: http://www.britishpoliticalspeech.org/speech-archive.htm.

Fischer, Claude S., and Michael Hout. 2006. *Century of Difference: How America Changed in the Last One Hundred Years*. New York: Russell Sage Foundation.

Flanagan, Scott C. 1987. 'Value change in industrial societies'. *American Political Science Review* 81 (4): 1289–319.

Fleishman, John. 1988. 'Attitude organization in the general public: Evidence for a bi-dimensional structure'. *Social Forces* 67 (1): 159–84.

Ford, Robert. 2016. 'Older 'left-behind' voters turned against a political class with values opposed to theirs'. *The Guardian*, 25 June 2016.

Ford, Robert, and Matthew J. Goodwin. 2010. 'Angry white men: Individual and contextual predictors of support for the British National Party'. *Political Studies* 58 (1): 1–25.

Ford, Robert, and Matthew J. Goodwin. 2014. *Revolt on the Right: Explaining Support for the Radical Right in Britain*. London: Routledge.

References

Ford, Robert, Matthew J. Goodwin, and David Cutts. 2012. 'Strategic eurosceptics and polite xenophobes: Support for the United Kingdom Independence Party (UKIP) in the 2009 European Parliament elections'. *European Journal of Political Research* 51 (2): 204–34.

Franklin, Mark. 1992. 'The decline of cleavage politics'. In Mark Franklin, Thomas Mackie, Henry Valen, et al. (eds.), *Electoral Change: Responses to Evolving Social and Attitudinal Structures in Western Countries*. Cambridge: Cambridge University Press, 383–405.

Franklin, Mark, Thomas Mackie, Henri Valen, et al. (eds.). 1992. *Electoral Change: Responses to Evolving Social and Attitudinal Structures in Western Countries*. Cambridge: Cambridge University Press.

Franklin, Mark N. 1984. 'How the decline in class voting opened the way to radical change to British politics'. *British Journal of Political Science* 14 (4): 483–508.

Franklin, Mark N. 1985. *The Decline of Class Voting in Britain: Changes in the Basis of Electoral Choice, 1964–1983*. Oxford: Clarendon Press.

Franklin, Mark N. 2004. *Voter Turnout and the Dynamics of Electoral Competition in Established Democracies since 1945*. Cambridge: Cambridge University Press.

Fraser, Ronald. 1968/9. *Work* (2 vols.). Harmondsworth, UK: Penguin Books.

Furnham, Adrian. 1982. 'Why are the poor always with us? Explanations for poverty in Britain'. *British Journal of Social Psychology* 21 (4): 311–22.

Furnham, Adrian. 1988. *Lay Theories: Everyday Understanding of Problems in the Social Science*. Oxford: Pergamon.

Gabel, Matthew. 1998a. 'Public support for European integration: An empirical test of five theories'. *Journal of Politics* 60 (2): 333–54.

Gabel, Matthew. 1998b. *Interests and Integration: Market Liberalization, Public Opinion and the European Union*. Ann Arbor: University of Michigan Press.

Gabel, Matthew, and Harvey D. Palmer. 1995. 'Understanding variation in public support for European Integration'. *European Journal of Political Research* 27 (1): 3–19.

Gallie, Duncan. 2015. 'Class inequality at work: Trends to polarization?' In Alan Felstead, Duncan Gallie, and Francis Green (eds.), *Unequal Britain at Work*. Oxford: Oxford University Press, 22–41.

Garry, John, and James Tilley. 2009. 'The macro economic factors conditioning the impact of identity on attitudes towards the EU'. *European Union Politics* 10 (3): 361–79.

Gavin, Neil T. 1996. 'Class voting and the Labour Party in Britain: The analysis of qualitative data on voting preference in the 1987 General Election'. *Electoral Studies* 15 (3): 311–26.

Gelman, Andrew, and Gary King. 1993. 'Why are American presidential election campaign polls so variable when votes are so predictable?' *British Journal of Political Science* 23 (4): 409–51.

Gerber, Alan, Donald Green, and Ron Shachar. 2003. 'Voting may be habit forming: Evidence from a randomized field experiment'. *American Journal of Political Science* 47 (3): 540–50.

Glenn, Norval D., and Michael Grimes. 1968. 'Aging, voting, and political interest'. *American Sociological Review* 33 (4): 563–75.

Golder, Matt. 2003. 'Explaining variation in the success of extreme right parties in Western Europe'. *Comparative Political Studies* 36 (4): 432–66.

Goldstein, Kenneth, and Travis N. Ridout. 2004. 'Measuring the effects of televised political advertising in the United States'. *Annual Review of Political Science* 7: 205–26.

Goldthorpe, John H. 1995. 'The service class revisited'. In Tim Butler and Michael Savage (eds.). *Social Change and the Middle Classes*. London: UCL Press, 313–29.

Goldthorpe, John H. 2004. *The Economic Basis of Social Class*. LSE STICERD Research Paper No. CASE080. London: London School of Economics and Political Science.

Goldthorpe, John H. 2007. 'Social class and the differentiation of employment contracts'. In *On Sociology*, vol. 2. Stanford: Stanford University Press, 101–24.

Goldthorpe, John H. 2016. 'Social class mobility in modern Britain: Changing structure, constant process'. *Centre for Social Investigation 21*: briefing note. Available online: http://csi.nuff.ox.ac.uk/?page_id=11.

Goldthorpe, John H., David Lockwood, Frank Bechhofer, and Jennifer Platt. 1969. *The Affluent Worker in the Class Structure*. Cambridge: Cambridge University Press.

Goldthorpe, John H., and Abigail McKnight. 2006. 'The economic basis of social class'. In Stephen L. Morgan, David B. Grusky, and Gary S. Fields (eds.). *Mobility and Inequality: Frontiers of Research in Sociology and Economics*. Stanford: Stanford University Press.

Goldthorpe, John H., and Colin Mills. 2008. 'Trends in intergenerational class mobility in modern Britain: Evidence from national surveys, 1972–2005'. *National Institute Economic Review* 205 (1): 83–100.

Goodhart, David. 2013. *The British Dream: Successes and Failures of Post-War Immigration*. London: Atlantic Books.

Goodwin, Matthew, and Oliver Heath. 2016. 'The 2016 referendum, Brexit and the left behind: An aggregate-level analysis of the result'. *The Political Quarterly* 87 (3): 323–32.

Goodwin, Matthew, and Caitlin Milazzo. 2015. *UKIP: Inside the Campaign to Redraw the Map of British Politics*. Oxford: Oxford University Press.

Gorecki, Maciej A. 2013. 'Electoral context, habit-formation and voter turnout: A new analysis'. *Electoral Studies* 32 (1): 140–52.

Green, Donald P., and Ron Shachar. 2000. 'Habit formation and political behaviour: Evidence of consuetude in voter turnout'. *British Journal of Political Science* 30 (4): 561–73.

Grunberg, Gerard, and Etienne Schweisguth. 1993. 'Social libertarianism and economic liberalism'. In Daniel Boy and Nonna Mayer (eds.), *The French Voter Decides*. Ann Arbor: University of Michigan Press, 45–64.

Güveli, Ayse, Ariana Need, and Nan Dirk De Graaf. 2007a. 'Socio-political, cultural and economic preferences and behaviour of the social and cultural specialists versus the technocrats. Social class or education?' *Social Indicators Research* 81 (3): 597–631.

Güveli, Ayse, Ariana Need, and Nan Dirk De Graaf. 2007b. 'The rise of "new" social classes within the service class in the Netherlands: Political orientation of social and cultural specialists and technocrats between 1970 and 2003'. *Acta Sociologica* 50 (2): 129–46.

Hamlin, Alan, and Colin Jennings. 2011. 'Expressive political behaviour: Foundations, scope and implications'. *British Journal of Political Science* 41 (3): 645–70.

Harrison, Eric, and David Rose. 2006. *The European Socio-economic Classification User Guide*. Colchester, UK: Institute for Social and Economic Research (ISER), University of Essex.

Harrop, Martin, Judith England, and Christopher T. Husbands. 1980. 'The bases of National Front support'. *Political Studies* 28 (2): 271–83.

References

Hayes, Bernadette. 1995. 'The impact of class on political attitudes: A comparative study of Great Britain, West Germany, Australia and the United States'. *European Journal of Political Research* 27 (1): 69–91.

Heath, Anthony, John Curtice, and Gabriella Elgenius. 2009. 'Individualization and the decline of class identity'. In Margaret Wetherell (ed.), *Identity in the 21st Century: New Trends in Changing Times*. Basingstoke: Palgrave, 21–40.

Heath, Anthony, Geoffrey Evans, and Jean Martin. 1994. 'The measurement of core beliefs and values: The development of balanced socialist/laissez-faire and libertarian/authoritarian scales'. *British Journal of Political Science* 24 (1): 115–32.

Heath, Anthony, Roger Jowell, and John Curtice. 1985. *How Britain Votes*. Oxford: Pergamon Press.

Heath, Anthony, Roger Jowell, and John Curtice. 1987. 'Trendless fluctuation: A reply to Crewe.' *Political Studies* 35 (2): 259–77.

Heath, Anthony, Roger Jowell, John Curtice, Geoffrey Evans, Julia Field, and Sharon Witherspoon. 1991. *Understanding Political Change: The British Voter 1964–1987*. Oxford: Pergamon.

Heath, Anthony, and Bridget Taylor. 1999. 'New sources of abstention?' In Geoffrey Evans and Pippa Norris (eds.), *Critical Elections: British Parties and Voters in Long-Term Perspective*. London: Sage, 164–79.

Heath, Anthony F., Nan Dirk De Graaf, and Yu Li. 2010. 'How fair is the route to the top? Perceptions of social mobility'. *British Social Attitudes: The 27th Report: Exploring Labour's Legacy*. London: Sage.

Heath, Anthony F., Roger M. Jowell, and John K. Curtice. 2001. *The Rise of New Labour: Party Policies and Voter Choices: Party Policies and Voter Choices*. Oxford: Oxford University Press.

Heath, Oliver. 2007. 'Explaining turnout decline in Britain, 1964–2005: Party identification and the political context'. *Political Behavior* 29 (4): 493–516.

Heath, Oliver. 2015. 'Policy representation, social representation and class voting in Britain'. *British Journal of Political Science* 45 (1): 173–93.

Heath, Oliver. 2016. 'Policy alienation, social alienation and working class abstention in Britain, 1964–2010'. *British Journal of Political Science*. Available online: http://dx.doi.org/10.1017/S0007123416000272.

Hill, Kim Q., and Jan E. Leighley. 1996. 'Political parties and class mobilization in contemporary United States elections'. *American Journal of Political Science* 40 (3): 787–804.

Hobolt, Sara B. 2014. 'Ever closer or ever wider? Public attitudes towards further enlargement and integration in the European Union'. *Journal of European Public Policy* 21 (5): 664–80.

Hodge, Robert W., and Donald J. Treiman. 1968. 'Class identification in the United States'. *American Journal of Sociology* 73 (5): 535–47.

Hoggart, Richard. 1957. *The Uses of Literacy*. London: Chatto and Windus.

Hoggart, Richard. 1989. 'Foreword'. In George Orwell, *Road to Wigan Pier*. New York: Penguin Random House.

Hooghe, Liesbet, Ryan Bakker, Anna Brigevich, Catherine De Vries, Erica Edwards, Gary Marks, Jan Rovny, Marco Steenbergen, and Milada Vachudova. 2010. 'Reliability and validity of the 2002 and 2006 Chapel Hill expert surveys on party positioning'. *European Journal of Political Research* 49 (5): 687–703.

Hooghe, Liesbet, and Gary Marks. 2004. 'Does identity or economic rationality drive public opinion on European integration?' *PS: Political Science and Politics* 37 (3): 415–20.

Hooghe, Liesbet, and Gary Marks. 2005. 'Calculation, community, and cues: Public opinion on European integration'. *European Union Politics* 6 (4): 419–43.

House of Commons Information Office. 2009. *Ministerial Salaries*. Factsheet M6, Members Services. Appendix A.

Hout, Michael. 2008. 'How class works: Objective and subjective aspects of class since the 1970s'. In Annette Lareau, and Dalton Conley (eds.), *Social Class: How Does it Work?* New York: Russell Sage Foundation, 25–64.

Hout, Michael, Clem Brooks, and Jeff Manza. 1993. 'The persistence of classes in post-industrial societies'. *International Sociology* 8 (3): 259–77.

Hout, Michael, Clem Brooks, and Jeff Manza. 1995. 'The democratic class struggle in U.S. presidential elections, 1948–1992'. *American Sociological Review* 60 (6): 805–28.

Houtman, Dick. 2003. 'Lipset and "working-class" authoritarianism'. *The American Sociologist* 34 (1): 85–103.

Houtman, Dick, Peter Achterberg, and Anton Derks. 2008. *Farewell to the Leftist Working Class*. New Brunswick: Transaction Publishers.

Huber, Joan, and William H. Form. 1973. *Income and Ideology*. New York: The Free Press.

Huddy, Leonie. 1994. 'The political significance of voters' gender stereotypes'. In Michael X.D. Carpini, Leonie Huddy, and Robert Y. Shapiro (eds.), *Research in Micropolitics: New Directions in Political Sociology*. Greenwich, CT: JAI Press, 169–93.

Huddy, Leonie, and Nayda Terkildsen. 1993. 'Gender stereotypes and the perception of male and female candidates'. *American Journal of Political Science* 37 (1): 119–47.

Ichheiser, Gustav. 1949. 'Misunderstandings in human relations: A study in false social perception'. *American Journal of Sociology* 55 (2): 1–70.

Inglehart, Ronald. 1997. *Modernization and Postmodernization: Cultural, Economic and Political Change in 43 Societies*. Princeton, NJ: Princeton University Press.

Inglehart, Ronald, and Jacques-René Rabier. 1986. 'Political realignment in advanced industrial society: From class-based politics to quality-of-life politics'. *Government and Opposition* 21 (4): 457–79.

Irwin, Sarah. 2015. 'Class and comparison: Subjective social location and lay experiences of constraint and mobility'. *British Journal of Sociology* 66 (2): 259–81.

Ivarsflaten, Elisabeth. 2005. 'The vulnerable populist right parties: No economic realignment fueling their electoral success'. *European Journal of Political Research* 44 (3): 465–92.

Ivarsflaten, Elisabeth. 2006. 'Reputational shields: Why most anti-immigrant parties failed in Western Europe, 1980–2005'. *Annual Meeting of the American Political Science Association*, Philadelphia.

Ivarsflaten, Elisabeth. 2008. 'What unites right-wing populists in Western Europe? Re-examining grievance mobilization models in seven successful cases'. *Comparative Political Studies* 41 (1): 3–23.

Iversen, Torben, and David Soskice. 2001. 'An asset theory of social policy preferences'. *American Political Science Review* 95 (4): 875–93.

Iyengar, Shanto, and Donald Kinder. 1987. *News That Matters: Television and Public Opinion*. Chicago: University of Chicago Press.

Iyengar, Shanto, and Adam F. Simon. 2000. 'New perspectives and evidence on political communication and campaign effects.' *Annual Review of Psychology* 51: 149–69.

Jackman, Mary R., and Robert W. Jackman. 1983. *Class Awareness in the United States.* Berkeley: University of California Press.

Jackson, Ben. 2016. 'Commentary: Hard Labour.' *The Political Quarterly* 87 (1): 4–5.

Jackson, Brian, and Dennis Marsden. 1966. *Education and the Working Class.* Harmondsworth, UK: Penguin Books.

Jacobsen, Dag I. 2001. 'Higher education as an arena for political socialization: Myth or reality?' *Scandinavian Political Studies* 24 (4): 351–68.

Janssen, Giedo, Geoffrey Evans, and Nan Dirk De Graaf. 2013. 'Class voting and left-right party positions: A comparative study of 15 western democracies, 1960–2005'. *Social Science Research* 42: 376–400.

Johns, Robert, David Denver, James Mitchell, and Charles Pattie. 2010. *Voting for a Scottish Government: The Scottish Parliament Elections of 2007.* Manchester: Manchester University Press.

Johnson, Brian, and Alaa Al-Hamad. 2011. 'Trends in socio-economic inequalities in female mortality, 2001–08. Intercensal estimates for England and Wales'. *Health Statistics Quarterly* 52 (1): 3–32.

Johnston, Ron, and Charles Pattie. 2003. 'The growing problem of electoral turnout in Britain? Voters and non-voters at the British 2001 General Election'. *Representation* 40 (1): 30–43.

Jones, Owen. 2011. *Chavs: The Demonization of the Working Class.* London: Verso Books.

Kalmijn, Matthijs, and Gerbert Kraaykamp. 2007. 'Social stratification and attitudes: A comparative analysis of the effects of class and education in Europe'. *British Journal of Sociology* 58 (4): 547–76.

Kantomaa, Marko T., Tuija H. Tammelin, Panayotes Demakakos, Hannah E. Ebeling, and Anja M. Taanila. 2010. 'Physical activity, emotional and behavioural problems, maternal education and self-reported educational performance of adolescents'. *Health Education Research* 25 (2): 368–79.

Katz, Michael B. 1989. *The Undeserving Poor: From the War on Poverty to the War on Welfare.* New York: Pantheon Books.

Kavanagh, Dennis, and Peter Morris. 1994. *Consensus Politics from Attlee to Major.* Oxford: Blackwell.

Kellas, James G. 1968. *Modern Scotland: The Nation since 1870.* New York: Praeger.

Kelley, Jonathan, and Maria D. R. Evans. 1993. 'The Legitimation of Inequality: Occupational earnings in nine nations'. *American Journal of Sociology,* 99 (1): 75–125.

Kelley, Jonathan, and Maria D. R. Evans. 1995. 'Class and class conflict in six Western nations'. *American Sociological Review* 60 (2): 157–78.

Key, Valdimer O. 1966. *The Responsible Electorate: Rationality in Presidential Voting, 1936–1960.* Cambridge, MA: Belknap Press.

King, Anthony. 1997. 'Why Labour won – at last'. In Anthony King (ed.), *New Labour Triumphs: Britain at the Polls.* Chatham, NJ: Chatham House Publishers.

Kirby, Simon, and Rebecca Riley. 2008. 'The external returns to education: UK evidence using repeated cross-sections'. *Labour Economics* 15 (4): 619–30.

Kitschelt, Herbert. 1994. *The Transformation of European Social Democracy*. Cambridge: Cambridge University Press.

Kitschelt, Herbert. 1995. *The Radical Right in Western Europe: A Comparative Analysis*. Ann Arbor: University of Michigan Press.

Kitschelt, Herbert, and Anthony J. McGann. 2005. 'The radical right in the Alps: Evolution of support for the Swiss SVP and Austrian FPO'. *Party Politics* 11 (2): 147–71.

Klapper, Joseph T. 1960. *The Effects of Mass Communication*. Glencoe, IL Illinois: The Free Press.

Klingemann, Hans-Dieter, Andrea Volkens, Judith Bara, Ian Budge, and Michael D. McDonald. 2006. *Mapping Policy Preferences II: Estimates for Parties, Governments and Electors in the OECD, EU and Central and Eastern Europe 1990–2003*. Oxford: Oxford University Press.

Klingeren, Marijn V., Hajo G. Boomgaarden, and Claes H. De Vreese. 2013. 'Going soft or staying soft: Have identity factors become more important than economic rationale when explaining Euroscepticism?' *Journal of European Integration* 35 (6): 689–704.

Kluegel, James R., and Eliot R. Smith. 1986. *Beliefs about Inequality: Americans' Views of What Is and What Ought To Be*. New York: Aldine de Gruyter.

Kriesi, Hanspeter. 1989. 'New social movements and the new class in the Netherlands'. *American Journal of Sociology* 94 (5): 1078–116.

Ladd, Jonathan M., and Gabriel S. Lenz. 2009. 'Exploiting a rare communication shift to document the persuasive power of the news media'. *American Journal of Political Science* 53 (2): 394–410.

Lancee, Bram, and Oriane Sarrasin. 2015. 'Educated preferences or selection effects? A longitudinal analysis of the impact of educational attainment on attitudes towards immigrants'. *European Sociological Review* 31 (4): 490–501.

Langford, Ann, and Brian Johnson. 2010. 'Trends in social inequalities in male mortality, 2001–08. Intercensal estimates for England and Wales'. *Health Statistics Quarterly* 47: 1–28.

Laver, Michael, and Ian Budge (eds.). 1992. *Party Policy and Government Coalitions*. London: Macmillan.

Laver, Michael, and John Garry. 2000. 'Estimating policy positions from political texts'. *American Journal of Political Science* 44 (3): 619–34.

Laver, Michael, and W. Ben Hunt. 1992. *Policy and Party Competition*. New York and London: Routledge.

Lawler, S. (ed). 2005. Class, Culture and Identity. *Special Issue, Sociology* 39 (5).

Lazarsfeld, Paul F., Bernard Berelson, and Hazel Gaudet. 1948. *The People's Choice: How the Voter Makes Up His Mind in a Presidential Campaign*. New York: University of Columbia Press.

Leighley, Jan E., and Jonathan Nagler. 1992a. 'Socioeconomic class bias in turnout, 1964–1988: The voters remain the same'. *American Political Science Review* 86 (3): 725–36.

Leighley, Jan E., and Jonathan Nagler. 1992b. 'Individual and systemic influences on turnout: Who votes? 1984'. *The Journal of Politics* 54 (3): 718–40.

Leighley, Jan E., and Jonathan Nagler. 2014. *Who Votes Now?: Demographics, Issues, Inequality, and Turnout in the United States*. Princeton: Princeton University Press.

Lemieux, Anthony F., and Felicia Pratto. 2003. 'Poverty and Prejudice'. In Stuart C. Carr and Todd S. Sloan (eds.), *Poverty and Psychology: From Global Perspective to Local*. New York: Kluwer Academic/Plenum.

Linos, Katerina, and Martin West. 2002. 'Self-interest, social beliefs, and attitudes to redistribution. Re-addressing the issue of cross-national variation'. *European Sociological Review* 19 (4): 393–409.

Lipset, Seymour M. 1959. *Political Man: The Social Bases of Politics*. Garden City, NY: Doubleday.

Lipset, Seymour M. 1981. *Political Man*. 2nd edn. Garden City, NY: Doubleday.

Lipset, Seymour M. 1991. 'No third way: A comparative perspective on the left'. In Daniel Chirot (ed.), *The Crisis of Leninism and the Decline of the Left*. Seattle: University of Washington Press, 183–232.

Lottes, Ilsa, and Peter Kuriloff. 1994. 'The impact of college experience on political and social attitudes'. *Sex Roles* 31 (1): 31–54.

Lowe, Will, Kenneth Benoit, Slava Mikhaylov, and Michael Laver. 2011. 'Scaling policy preferences from coded political texts'. *Legislative Studies Quarterly* 36 (1): 123–55.

Lucassen, Geertje, and Marcel Lubbers. 2012. 'Who fears what? Explaining far-right-wing preference in Europe by distinguishing perceived cultural and economic ethnic threats'. *Comparative Political Studies* 45 (5): 547–74.

Lynch, Peter. 2002. *SNP: The History of the Scottish National Party*. Cardiff: Welsh Academic Press.

Marshall, Gordon, David Rose, Howard Newby, and Carolyn Vogler. 1988. *Social Class in Modern Britain*. London: Hutchinson.

Marwick, Arthur. 1980. *Class: Image and Reality*. London: Collins.

McCutcheon, Allan. 1985. 'A latent class analysis of tolerance for nonconformity in the American public'. *Public Opinion Quarterly* 49 (4): 474–88.

McDonald, Michael D., and Ian Budge. 2014. 'Getting it (approximately) right (and centre and left)'. *Electoral Studies* 35 (1): 67–77.

McKenzie, Robert, and Allan Silver. 1968. *Angels in Marble: Working Class Conservatives in Urban England*. Chicago: University of Chicago Press.

McLaren, Lauren. 2002. 'Public support for the European Union: Cost/benefit analysis or perceived cultural threat?' *Journal of Politics* 64 (12): 551–66.

McLaren, Lauren. 2004. 'Opposition to European integration and fear of loss of national identity: Debunking a basic assumption regarding hostility to the integration project'. *European Journal of Political Research* 43 (6): 895–912.

McLaren, Lauren. 2006. *Identity, Interests and Attitudes to European Integration*. Basingstoke: Palgrave Macmillan.

McLaren, Lauren. 2007. 'Explaining mass-level Euroscepticism: identity, interests, and institutional distrust'. *Acta Politica* 42 (2): 233–51.

McLaren, Lauren. 2015. *Immigration and Perceptions of National Political Systems in Europe*. Oxford: Oxford University Press.

McLaren, Lauren, and Mark Johnson. 2007. 'Resources, group conflict and symbols: Explaining anti-immigration hostility in Britain'. *Political Studies* 55 (4): 709–32.

McLean, Iain. 1970. 'The rise and fall of the Scottish National Party'. *Political Studies* 18 (3): 357–72.

McLeod, Jane D., and Karen Kaiser. 2004. 'Childhood Emotional and Behavioral Problems and Educational Attainment'. *American Sociological Review* 69 (5): 636–58.

Meguid, Bonnie M. 2005. 'Competition between unequals: The role of mainstream party strategy in niche party success'. *American Political Science Review* 99 (3): 347–59.

Merton, Robert K. 1957. *Social Theory and Social Structure*. London: MacMillan.

Michaels, Walter B. 2006. *The Trouble with Diversity: How We Learned to Love Identity and Ignore Inequality*. Basingstoke: Palgrave Macmillan.

Middendorp, Cees, Hans J. W. Luyten, and R. Dooms. 1993. 'Issue voting in the Netherlands: Two-dimensional issue-distances between own position and perceived party position as determinants of the vote'. *Acta Politica* 28 (1): 39–59.

Mills, Colin. 2015a. 'The Great British Class Survey: Requiescat in pace'. *Sociological Review* 63 (2): 393–9.

Mills, Colin. 2015b. 'Is class inequality at KS4 decreasing?' *Centre for Social Investigation 11*: briefing note. Available online: http://csi.nuff.ox.ac.uk/?page_id=11.

Mitchell, James, Lynn Bennie, and Robert Johns. 2012. *The Scottish National Party: Transition to Power*. Oxford: Oxford University Press.

Moene, Karl Ove, and Michael Wallerstein. 2001. 'Inequality, social insurance, and redistribution'. *American Political Science Review* 95 (4): 859–74.

Moller, Stephanie, Arthur S. Alderson, and Francois Nielsen. 2009. 'Changing patterns of income inequality in U.S. counties, 1970–2000'. *American Journal of Sociology* 114 (4): 1037–101.

Moorhouse, H. F. 1976. 'Attitudes to class and class relationships in Britain'. *Sociology* 10 (3): 469–96.

Mount, Ferdinand. 2004. *Mind the Gap: Class in Britain Now*. London: Short Books.

Mudde, Cas. 2007. *Populist Radical Right Parties in Europe*. Cambridge: Cambridge University Press.

Napier, Jaime L., and John T. Jost. 2008. 'The "anti-democratic personality" revisited: A cross-national investigation of working class authoritarianism'. *Journal of Social Issues* 64 (3): 595–617.

National Equality Panel. 2010. *An Anatomy of Economic Inequality in the UK: Report of the National Equality Panel*. London: Government Equalities Office.

Neckerman, Kathryn M., and Florencia Torche. 2007. 'Inequality: Causes and consequences'. *Annual Review of Sociology* 33: 335–57.

Newman, Saul. 1992. 'The rise and decline of the Scottish National Party: Ethnic politics in a post-industrial environment'. *Ethnic and Racial Studies* 15 (1): 1–35.

Newton, Kenneth. 1991. 'Do people read everything they believe in the papers? Newspapers and voters in the 1983 and 1987 elections'. *British Elections & Parties Yearbook* 1 (1): 49–74.

Newton, Kenneth. 2006. 'May the weak force be with you: The power of the mass media in modern politics'. *European Journal of Political Research* 45 (2): 209–34.

Newton, Kenneth, and Malcom Brynin. 2001. 'The national press and party voting in the UK'. *Political Studies* 49 (2): 262–85.

NHS Information Centre for Health and Social Care. 2009. 'GP Earnings and Expenses Enquiry 2006/7: Final Report'. Available online: http://digital.nhs.uk/catalogue/PUB02373/gp-earn-expe-enqu-2006-07-fina-rep.pdf.

References

Nieuwbeerta, Paul. 1995. *The Democratic Class Struggle in Twenty Countries, 1945–1990*. Amsterdam: Thesis Publishers.

Nieuwbeerta, Paul. 1996. 'The democratic class struggle in post-war societies: Class voting in twenty countries, 1945–1990'. *Acta sociologica* 39 (4): 345–83.

Nisbet, Robert, A. 1959. 'The decline and fall of social class'. *Pacific Sociological Review* 2 (1): 11–17.

Nordlinger, Eric A. 1967. *The Working-Class Tories: Authority, Deference and Stable Democracy*. London: MacGibbon & Kee.

Norris, Pippa. 2005. *Radical Right: Voters and Parties in the Electoral Market*. New York: Cambridge University Press.

Norris, Pippa, John Curtice, David Sanders, Margaret Scammell, and Holli E. Semetko. 1999. *On Message: Communicating the Campaign*. London: Sage.

Norris, Pippa, and Joni Lovenduski. 1995. *Political Recruitment: Gender, Race and Class in the British Parliament*. Cambridge: Cambridge University Press.

Norton, Philip. 1994. 'The growth of the constituency role of the MP'. *Parliamentary Affairs* 47 (4): 705–21.

Oddsson, Gudmundur A. 2010. 'Class awareness in Iceland'. *International Journal of Sociology and Social Policy* 30 (5/6): 292–312.

Oesch, Daniel. 2006. *Redrawing the Class Map. Stratification and Institutions in Britain, Germany, Sweden and Switzerland*. Basingstoke: Palgrave Macmillan.

Oesch, Daniel. 2008. 'Explaining workers' support for right-wing populist parties in Western Europe: Evidence from Austria, Belgium, France, Norway, and Switzerland', *International Political Science Review* 29 (3): 349–73.

Oesch, Daniel. 2013. *Occupational Change in Europe: How Technology and Education Transform the Job Structure*. Oxford: Oxford University Press.

O'Leary, Nigel C., and Peter J. Sloane. 2005. 'The return to university education in Great Britain'. *National Institute Economic Review* 193 (1): 75–89.

Oskarson, Maria. 2005. 'Social structure and party choice'. In Jacques Thomassen (ed.), *The European Voter. A Comparative Study of Modern Democracies*. Oxford: Oxford University Press, 84–105.

Ossowski, Stanisław. 1963. *Class Structure in the Social Consciousness*. New York: Free Press.

Pahl, Ray, David Rose, and Liz Spencer. 2007. '*Inequality and Quiescence: A Continuing Conundrum*', *ISER Working Paper 2007–22*. Colchester: University of Essex.

Pakulski, Jan, and Malcolm Waters. 1996a. *The Death of Class*. London: Sage.

Pakulski, Jan, and Malcolm Waters. 1996b. 'The reshaping and dissolution of class'. *Theory and Society* 25 (5): 667–91.

Parkin, Frank. 1968. *Middle Class Radicalism*. Manchester: Manchester University Press.

Parry, Geraint, George Moyser, and Neil Day. 1992. *Political Participation and Democracy in Britain*. Cambridge: Cambridge University Press.

Pattie, Charles, and Ron Johnston. 1998. 'Voter turnout at the British general election of 1992: Rational choice, social standing or political efficacy?' *European Journal of Political Research* 33 (2): 263–83.

Pattie, Charles, and Ron Johnston. 2001. 'A low turnout landslide: Abstention at the British General Election of 1997'. *Political Studies* 49: 286–305.

Pérez-Ahumada, Pablo. 2014. 'Class consciousness in a mature neoliberal society: Evidence from Chile'. *Research in Social Stratification and Mobility* 38: 57–75.

Pierson, Paul. 2001. *The New Politics of the Welfare State*. Oxford: Oxford University Press.

Piketty, Thomas. 2014. *Capital in the Twenty-First Century*. Harvard: Harvard University Press.

Pimlott, Ben. 1992. *Harold Wilson*. London: Harper & Collins.

Pitkin, Hanna. 1967. *The Concept of Representation*. Berkeley: University of California Press.

Plutzer, Eric. 2002. 'Becoming a habitual voter: Inertia, resources, and growth in young adulthood'. *American Political Science Review* 96 (1): 41–56.

Plutzer, Eric, and John F. Zipp. 1996. 'Identity politics and voting for women candidates'. *Public Opinion Quarterly* 60 (1): 30–57.

Poole, Keith T., and Howard L. Rosenthal. 2011. *Ideology and Congress*. Piscataway, NJ: Transaction Publishers.

Popkin, Samuel L. 1991. *The Reasoning Voter*. Chicago: University of Chicago Press.

Price, Robert, and George Sayers Bain. 1988. 'The labour force'. In A. H. Halsey (ed.), *British Social Trends Since 1900: A Guide to the Changing Social Structure of Britain*. Palgrave Macmillan UK, 162–201.

Prosser, Christopher. 2014. 'Building policy scales from manifesto data: A referential content validity approach'. *Electoral Studies* 35: 88–101.

Prosser, Christopher, Jon Mellon, and Jane Green. 2016. 'What mattered most to you when deciding how to vote in the EU referendum?'. *British Election Study*, 11 July 2016.

Przeworski, Adam. 1985. *Capitalism and Social Democracy*. Cambridge: Cambridge University Press.

Przeworski, Adam, and John Sprague. 1986. *Paper Stones: A History of Electoral Socialism*. Chicago: University of Chicago Press.

PWC. 2005. 'The economic benefits of higher education qualifications'. *Price Waterhouse Cooper:* report for the Royal Society of Chemistry and the Institute of Physics.

PWC. 2007. 'The economic benefits of a degree'. *Price Waterhouse Cooper:* report for Universities UK.

Ragnarsdóttir, Berglind Hólm, Jón Gunnar Bernburg, and Sigrún Ólafsdóttir. 2013. 'The global financial crisis and individual distress: The role of subjective comparisons after the collapse of the Icelandic economy'. *Sociology* 47 (4): 755–75.

Ray, John J. 1982. 'Authoritarianism/libertarianism as the second dimension of social attitudes'. *The Journal of Social Psychology* 117 (1): 33–44.

Ray, John J. 1983. 'The workers are not authoritarian: Attitude and personality data from six countries'. *Sociology and Social Research* 67 (2): 166–89.

Reardon, Sean F., and Kendra Bischoff. 2011. 'Income inequality and segregation'. *American Journal of Sociology* 116 (4): 1092–153.

Rehm, Philipp, and Tim Reilly. 2010. 'United we stand: Constituency homogeneity and comparative party polarization'. *Electoral Studies* 29 (1): 40–53.

Richards, Steve. 2016. 'Leadership, loyalty and the rise of Jeremy Corbyn'. *The Political Quarterly* 87 (1): 12–17.

Rennwald, Line, and Geoffrey Evans. 2014. 'When supply creates demand: Social-democratic parties' electoral strategies and the evolution of class voting'. *West European Politics* 37 (5): 1108–35.

References

Roberts, Elizabeth. 1984. *A Woman's Place: An Oral History of Working-Class Women.* Oxford: Blackwell.

Roberts, Kath, Nick Cavill, Caroline Hancock, and Harry Rutter. 2013. *Social and Economic Inequalities in Diet and Physical Activity.* London: Public Health England.

Roberts, Robert. 1971. *The Classic Slum.* Harmondsworth, UK: Penguin Books.

Robertson, David. 1984. *Class and the British Electorate.* Oxford: Blackwell.

Robinson, Robert V., and Jonathan Kelley. 1979. 'Class as conceived by Marx and Dahrendorf: Effects on income inequality and politics in the United States and Great Britain'. *American Sociological Review* 44 (1): 38–58.

Rose, David, and Eric Harrison (eds.). 2010. *Social Class in Europe: An Introduction to the European Socio-Economic Classification.* London: Routledge.

Rose, David, and David Pevalin. 2003. *A Researcher's Guide to the National Statistics Socio-economic Classification.* London: Sage.

Rose, Richard, and Ian McAllister. 1986. *Voters Begin to Choose: From Closed Class to Open Elections in Britain.* London: Sage.

Rosenstone, Steven, and John M. Hansen. 1993. *Mobilization, Participation, and Democracy in America.* New York: Macmillan.

Ross, Lee. 1977. 'The intuitive psychologist and his shortcomings: Distortions in the attribution process'. In L. Berkowitz, *Advances in Experimental Social Psychology*, vol. 10. New York: Academic Press, 173–220.

Runciman, Walter Gary. 1966. *Relative Deprivation and Social Justice: A Study of Attitudes to Social Inequality in Twentieth-Century England.* London: Routledge & Kegan Paul.

Russell, Andrew, and Edward Fieldhouse. 2005. *Neither Left Nor Right: The Liberal Democrats and the Electorate.* Manchester: Manchester University Press.

Rydgren, Jens. 2008. 'Immigration sceptics, xenophobes or racists? Radical right-wing voting in six West European countries'. *European Journal of Political Research* 47 (6): 737–65.

Sandbrook, Dominic. 2006. *Never Had It So Good: A History of Britain from Suez to the Beatles, 1956–1963.* London: Abacus.

Sandbrook, Dominic. 2012. *Seasons in the Sun: The Battle for Britain, 1974–1979.* London: Penguin.

Särlvik, Bo, and Ivor Crewe. 1983. *Decade of Dealignment: The Conservative Victory of 1979 and Electoral Trends in the 1970s.* Cambridge: Cambridge University Press.

Sartori, Giovanni. 1969. 'From the sociology of politics to political sociology'. In Seymour M. Lipset (ed.), *Politics and the Social Sciences.* Oxford: Oxford University Press, 65–100.

Savage, Mike. 2000. *Class Analysis and Social Transformation.* Milton Keynes: Open University Press.

Savage, Mike, Gaynor Bagnall, and Brian J. Longhurst. 2001. 'Ordinary, ambivalent and defensive: Class identities in the Northwest of England'. *Sociology* 35 (4): 874–92.

Savage, Mike, Fiona Devine, Niall Cunningham, Mark Taylor, Yaojun Li, Johs Hjellbrekke, Brigitte Le Roux, Sam Friedman, and Andrew Miles. 2013. 'A new model of social class? Findings from the Great British class experiment'. *Sociology* 47 (2): 219–50.

Savage, Mike, Elizabeth Silva, and Alan Warde. 2010. 'Dis-identification and class identity'. In Elizabeth Silva and Alan Warde (eds.), *Cultural Analysis and Bourdieu's Legacy: Settling Accounts and Developing Alternatives.* London: Routledge, 60–74.

Schneider, Silke. 2008. 'Anti-immigrant attitudes in Europe: Outgroup size and perceived ethnic threat'. *European Sociological Review* 24 (1): 53–67.

Scott, Janny, and Leonhardt, David. 2005. 'Shadowy lines that still divide'. *The New York Times,* 15 May: p.11.

Sears, David O. 1975. 'Political socialization'. In Fred I. Greenstein and Nelson W. Polsby (ed.), *Handbook of Political Science: Micropolitical Theory.* Reading: Addison-Wesley.

Sears, David O. 1983. 'The persistence of early political pre-dispositions: The roles of attitude objects and life-stage'. In Lad Wheeler and Phillip Shaver (ed.), *Review of Personality and Social Psychology No. 4.* Beverly Hills: Sage.

Sears, David O. 1993. 'Symbolic politics: A socio-psychological theory'. In Shanto Iyengar and William J. McGuire (ed.), *Explorations in Political Psychology.* Durham, NC: Duke University Press.

Sears, David O., Richard R. Lau, Tom R. Tyler, and Harris M. Allen. 1980. 'Self-interest versus symbolic politics in policy attitudes and presidential voting'. *American Political Science Review* 74 (3): 670–84.

Seawright, David. 2000. 'A confessional cleavage resurrected? The denominational vote in Britain'. In David Broughton and Hans-Martien ten Napel (eds.), *Religion and Mass Electoral Behaviour in Europe.* London: Routledge, 44–60.

Seawright, David, and John Curtice. 1995. 'The decline of the Scottish Conservative and Unionist Party 1950–92: Religion, ideology or economics?' *Contemporary Record* 9 (2): 319–42.

Seldon, Anthony (ed.). 2007. *Blair's Britain, 1997–2007.* Cambridge: Cambridge University Press.

Seldon, Anthony. 2008. Speech given to the Head Teachers conference at Wellington College.

Seyd, Patrick. 1997. 'Tony Blair and New Labour'. In Anthony King (ed.), *New Labour Triumphs: Britain at the Polls.* Chatham, NJ: Chatham House.

Shibutani, Tamotsu. 1955. 'Reference groups as perspectives'. *American Journal of Sociology* 60 (6): 562–9.

Shirazi, Rez, and Anders Biel. 2005. 'Internal-external causal attributions and perceived government responsibility for need provision: A 14-culture study'. *Journal of Cross-Cultural Psychology* 36 (1): 96–116.

Sides, John, and Jack Citrin. 2007. 'European opinion about immigration: The role of identities, interests and information'. *British Journal of Political Science* 37 (3): 477–504.

Siegel, Alberta E., and Sidney Siegel. 1957. 'Reference groups, membership groups, and attitude change'. *Journal of Abnormal and Social Psychology* 55 (3): 360–4.

Sigelman, Carol, Lee Sigelman, Barbara Walkosz, and Michael Nitz. 1995. 'Black candidates, white voters: Understanding racial bias in political perceptions'. *American Journal of Political Science* 39 (1): 243–65.

Sillitoe, Alan. 1958, 2008. *Saturday Night and Sunday Morning.* London: Harper Perennial.

Silver, Brian D., Barbara A. Anderson, and Paul R. Abramson. 1996. 'Who overreports voting?' *American Political Science Review* 80 (2): 613–24.

Skeggs, Beverley. 1997. *Formations of Class and Gender.* London: Sage.

Skeggs, Beverley. 2004. *Class, Self, Culture.* London: Routledge.

References

Spahn, Bradley, and Matthew Hindman. 2014. 'Eccentric circles and non-habitual voting: Turnout patterns in a 2-million-voter national panel dataset'. *Midwest Political Science Association Meeting*: April 4–7, Chicago, IL.

Spies, Dennis. 2013. 'Explaining working-class support for extreme right parties: A party competition approach'. *Acta Politica* 48 (3): 296–325.

Steenbergen, Marco, and Gary Marks. 2007. 'Evaluating expert surveys'. *European Journal of Political Research* 46 (3): 347–66.

Stuart, Graham, Neil Carmichael, Alex Cunningham, Bill Esterson, Pat Glass, Siobahn McDonagh, Ian Mearns, Caroline Nokes, Dominic Raab, David Ward, and Craig Whittaker. 2014. 'Underachievement in education by white working class children'. *House of Commons Education Committee: Report*. Available online: http://www.publica tions.parliament.uk/pa/cm201415/cmselect/cmeduc/142/142.pdf.

Stubager, Rune. 2008. 'Education effects on authoritarian-libertarian values: A question of socialisation'. *British Journal of Sociology* 59 (2): 327–50.

Stubager, Rune. 2009. 'Education-based group identity and consciousness in the authoritarian-libertarian value conflict'. *European Journal of Political Research* 48 (2): 204–33.

Stubager, Rune. 2010. 'The development of the education cleavage: Denmark as a critical case'. *West European Politics* 33 (3): 505–33.

Stubager, Rune, James Tilley, Geoffrey Evans, and Joshua Robinson. 2016. 'In the eye of the beholder: What determines how people sort others into social classes?' Paper presented at the MPSA annual conference, Chicago, 7–10 April.

Sturgis, Patrick. 2002. 'Attitudes and measurement error revisited: A reply to Johnston and Pattie'. *British Journal of Political Science* 32 (4): 691–8.

Surridge, Paula. 2007. 'Class belonging: A quantitative exploration of identity and consciousness'. *The British Journal of Sociology* 58 (2): 207–26.

Surridge, Paula. 2016. 'Education and liberalism: Pursuing the link'. *Oxford Review of Education* 42 (2): 146–64.

Sutton Trust. 2009. 'The educational backgrounds of leading lawyers, journalists, vice chancellors, politicians, medics and chief executives'. *The Sutton Trust Submission to the Milburn Commission on Access to the Professions*. Available online: http://www. suttontrust.com/wp-content/uploads/2009/04/ST_MilburnSubmission.pdf.

Sveinsson, Kjartan P. (ed.). 2009. *Who Cares about the White Working Class?* London: Runnymede.

Swaddle, Kevin, and Anthony Heath. 1989. 'Official and reported turnout in the British general election of 1987'. *British Journal of Political Science* 19 (4): 537–51.

Tate, Katherine. 1993. *From Protest to Politics: The New Black Voters in American Elections*. Cambridge, MA: Harvard University Press.

Terkildsen, Nayda. 1993. 'When white voters evaluate black candidates: The processing implications of candidate skin color, prejudice, and self-monitoring'. *American Journal of Political Science* 37 (4): 1032–53.

Thau, Mads. 2016. 'The changing role of social groups in party competition: From cleavage to consensus in Britain'. Paper presented at the Midwest Political Science Association annual meeting, Chicago, 7–10 April.

Thomas, James. 1998. 'Labour, the tabloids, and the 1992 general election'. *Contemporary British History* 12 (2): 80–104.

Tilley, James. 2005. 'Libertarian-authoritarian value change in Britain, 1974–2001'. *Political Studies* 53 (2): 442–53.

Tilley, James. 2015. 'We don't do God? Religion and party choice in Britain'. *British Journal of Political Science* 45 (4): 907–27.

Tilley, James, and Anthony Heath. 2007. 'The decline of British national pride'. *British Journal of Sociology* 58 (4): 661–78.

Tolleson Rinehart, Sue. 1992. *Gender Consciousness and Politics*. New York: Routledge.

Tolsma, Jochem, and Maarten H. J. Wolbers. 2010. 'Onderwijs als nieuwe sociale scheidslijn? De gevolgen van onderwijsexpansie voor sociale mobiliteit, de waarde van diploma's en het relatieve belang van opleiding in Nederland'. *Tijdsschrift Voor Sociologie* 31 (3): 239–59.

Turner, Alwyn. 2015. *A Classless Society: Britain in the 1990s*. London: Aurum Press.

Universities UK. 2006. *Patterns of Higher Education Institutions in the UK: 6th Report*. Available online: http://www.universitiesuk.ac.uk/policy-and-analysis/reports/Documents/2006/patterns-and-trends-uk-higher-education-06.pdf.

Van de Werfhorst, Herman G., and Nan Dirk De Graaf. 2004. 'The sources of political orientations in post-industrial society: Social class and education revisited'. *British Journal of Sociology* 55 (2): 211–35.

Van de Werfhorst, Herman G., and Gerbert Kraaykamp. 2001. 'Four field-related educational resources and their impact on labor, consumption and sociopolitical orientation'. *Sociology of Education* 74 (4): 296–317.

Van Heerde-Hudson, Jennifer, and Rosie Campbell. 2015. *Parliamentary Candidates UK Dataset* (v. 1).

Vanneman, Reeve, and Lynn W. Cannon. 1987. *The American Perception of Class*. Philadelphia, PA: Temple University Press.

Verba, Sidney, and Norman H. Nie. 1972. *Participation in America*. New York: Harper and Row.

Verba, Sidney, Norman H. Nie, and Jae-On Kim. 1978. *Participation and Political Equality: A Seven-Nation Study*. Cambridge: Cambridge University Press.

Verba, Sidney, Kay Lehman Schlozman, and Henry E. Brady. 1995. *Voice and Equality: Civic Voluntarism in American Politics*. Cambridge, MA: Harvard University Press.

Volkens, Andrea, Pola Lehmann, Theres Matthieß, Nicolas Merz, Sven Regel, and Annika Werner. 2015. *The Manifesto Data Collection. Manifesto Project (MRG/CMP/MARPOR)*. *Version 2015a*. Berlin: Wissenschaftszentrum Berlin für Sozialforschung (WZB).

Weakliem, David. 1989. 'Class and party in Britain, 1964–83'. *Sociology* 23 (2): 285–97.

Weakliem, David. 2001. 'Social class and voting: The case against decline'. In Terry N. Clark and Seymour M. Lipset (eds.), *The Breakdown of Class Politics: A Debate on Post-Industrial Stratification*. Baltimore, MD: The Johns Hopkins University Press, 197–223.

Weakliem, David. 2002. 'The effects of education on political opinions: An international study'. *International Journal of Public Opinion Research* 13 (2): 141–57.

Weakliem, David, and Anthony Heath. 1994. 'Rational choice and class voting'. *Rationality and Society* 6 (2): 243–70.

References

Weakliem, David, and Anthony F. Heath. 1999. 'The secret life of class voting: Britain, France, and the United States since the 1930s'. In Geoffrey Evans (ed.), *The End of Class Politics? Class Voting in Comparative Context*. Oxford: Oxford University Press, 97–126.

Webb, Paul. 2004. 'Party responses to the changing electoral markets in Britain'. In Peter Mair, Wolfgang Muller, and Fritz Plasser (eds.), *Political Parties and Electoral Change*. London: Sage.

Weeden, Kim, Young-mi Kim, Matthew Di Carlow, and David B. Grusky. 2007. 'Social class and earnings inequality'. *American Behavioral Scientist* 50 (5): 702–36.

Westergaard, John. 1995. *Who Gets What? The Hardening of Class Inequality in the Late Twentieth Century*. Cambridge, UK: Polity Press.

White, Chris, Folkert van Galen, and Yuan Huang Chow. 2003. 'Trends in social class differences in mortality by cause, 1986 to 2000'. *Health Statistics Quarterly* 20: 25–37.

Whiteley, Paul, Harold Clarke, David Sanders, and Marianne Stewart. 2001. 'Turnout'. *Parliamentary Affairs* 54 (4): 775–88.

Willmott, Peter, and Michael Young. 1960. *Family and Class in a London Suburb*. London: Mentor.

Williams, Raymond. 1961. *The Long Revolution*. Harmondsworth, UK: Penguin Books.

Willis, Paul. 1977. *Learning to Labour*. Farnborough, UK: Saxon House.

Wolfinger, Raymond E., and Steven J. Rosenstone. 1980. *Who Votes?* New Haven, CT: Yale University Press.

Wring, Dominic, and David Deacon. 2010. 'Patterns of press partisanship in the 2010 General Election'. *British Politics* 5 (4): 436–54.

Young, Michael. 1958. *The Rise of the Meritocracy, 1870–2023: An Essay on Education and Equality*. London: Thames and Hudson.

Zucker, Gail S., and Bernard Weiner. 1993. 'Conservatism and perceptions of poverty: An attributional analysis'. *Journal of Applied Social Psychology* 23 (4): 925–44.

Zweig, Ferdynand. 1952. *The British Worker*. Harmondsworth, UK: Penguin Books.

Index